GW00357196

MIAMI
THE EVERGLADES &
FLORIDA KEYS

Part of the Langenscheidt Publishing Group

ABOUT THIS BOOK

Editorial

Editor
Freddy Hamilton
Editorial Director
Brian Bell

Distribution

UK & Ireland
GeoCenter International Ltd
The Viables Centre, Harrow Way
Basingstoke, Hants RG22 4BJ
Fax: (44) 1256-817988

United States
Langenscheidt Publishers, Inc.
46–35 54th Road, Maspeth, NY 11378
Fax: (718) 784-0640

Canada
Prologue Inc.
1650 Lionel Bertrand Blvd., Boisbriand
Québec, Canada J7H 1N7
Tel: (450) 434-0306. Fax: (450) 434-2627

Worldwide
Apa Publications GmbH & Co.
Verlag KG (Singapore branch)
38 Joo Koon Road, Singapore 628990
Tel: (65) 865-1600. Fax: (65) 861-6438

Printing

Insight Print Services (Pte) Ltd
38 Joo Koon Road, Singapore 628990
Tel: (65) 865-1600. Fax: (65) 861-6438

©2000 Apa Publications GmbH & Co.
Verlag KG (Singapore branch)
All Rights Reserved
First Edition 1991
Fourth Edition 2000

CONTACTING THE EDITORS
Although every effort is made to provide accurate information, we live in a fast-changing world and would appreciate it if readers would call our attention to any errors or outdated information that may occur by writing to:
Insight Guides, P.O. Box 7910, London SE1 1WE, England. Fax: (44 20) 7403-0290. e-mail: insight@apaguide.demon.co.uk

www.insightguides.com

This guidebook combines the interests and enthusiasms of two of the world's best-known information providers: Insight Guides, whose titles have set the standard for visual travel guides since 1970, and Discovery Channel, the world's premier source of nonfiction television programming.

The editors of Insight Guides provide both practical advice and general understanding about a destination's history, culture, institutions and people. Discovery Channel and its popular website, www.discovery.com, help millions of viewers explore their world from the comfort of their own home and encourage them to explore it first hand.

How to use this book

This updated edition of *Insight Guide: Miami* is structured to convey an understanding of the city and its culture as well as to guide readers through its sights and activities:

♦ The **Features** section, indicated by a yellow bar at the top of each page, covers the history and culture of the city in a series of essays.

♦ The main **Places** section, indicated by a blue bar, is a complete guide to all the sights and the areas worth visiting. Places of

special interest are coordinated by number with the maps.

◆ The **Travel Tips** listings section, with an orange bar, provides a handy point of reference for information on travel, hotels, shops, restaurants and more.

The contributors

This fully revised edition of *Insight Guide: Miami* was masterminded in the series' editorial headquarters in London by **Freddy Hamilton**. It is Insight Guides' policy to use local contributors whenever possible, and playing a key role in this edition were two Miami-based writers, **Yves Colon** and **Melissa Moonves**, both reporters at the *Miami Herald* and both residents of the city for nearly two decades. They updated and reworked most of the book and contributed new features on recent history, sport, Miami in fiction, and the city's nightlife, as well as the picture stories on shopping and Vizcaya.

Many of the bold and beautiful photographs in the book were taken by Florida-based photographer **Tony Arruza**, who has produced top-class images for several other Insight Guides, including Florida, Barbados, Portugal and Lisbon.

Other invaluable contributions to the new edition came from writers **Fred Mawer**, **Cindy Rose Stiff** and **Fred Wright Jr**, and from commissioning editor **Emily Hatchwell**.

This book builds on the success of previous editions, which were overseen by **Martha Ellen Zenfell**. She worked closely on the first edition with project editor **Joann Biondi**, who is also a major contributor to *Insight Guide: Florida*.

Contributors to the earlier editions – and much of their work still appears in this edition – included the late **Isaac Bashevis Singer** (My Love Affair with Miami Beach), **Arva Moore Parks** (History), **Lisandro Perez** (Many Faces of Miami), **Alex Stepick** (Northern Miami), **Geoffrey Tomb** (Taste of Miami, Heading South), **Patrick May** (Body Culture, Vice as Virtue, Downtown Miami), **Sandra Dibble** (Little Havana), **Ian Glass** (Coral Gables, Coconut Grove), **Alice Klement** (Festivals, Key Biscayne), **Henry Green** (Many Faces of Miami), **Christina Cheakalos** (Miami Beach), **Ivan A. Rodriguez** (Northern Miami) and **Herb Hiller** (Excursions).

Thanks go also to **Sylvia Suddes**, who proofread this edition, and to **Elizabeth Cook**, who indexed it.

Map Legend

—··—	International Boundary
————	State Boundary
—•—	National Park/Reserve
————	Ferry Route
●	Metrorail
●	Metromover
✈ ✈	Airport: International/Regional
🚌	Bus Station
❶	Tourist Information
✉	Post Office
🏛 † ✝	Church/Ruins
†	Monastery
☾	Mosque
✡	Synagogue
🏰 🏯	Castle/Ruins
∴	Archeological Site
⋒	Cave
𝟏	Statue/Monument
★	Place of Interest

The main places of interest in the Places section are coordinated by number with a full-colour map (e.g. ❶), and a symbol at the top of every right-hand page tells you where to find the map.

CONTENTS

Introduction

History

Features

Art Deco facades on Ocean Drive

Insight on ...

Information panels

Travel Tips

Places

THE MIAMI MYSTIQUE

*Sweltering summers, tropical colors and Hispanic faces give
Miami a Latin-Caribbean flavor unique among American cities*

Grab a table at a sidewalk cafe on Ocean Drive, order a rum punch and sit back. Watch muscled hunks and tall, slim models in skimpy dresses as they sashay along. The brilliant blue sea is just on the other side of the street, teasing you with its gentle breezes rustling the palm fronds.

Nearby, pricey boutiques and restaurants line Lincoln Road and part of Collins Avenue, tantalizing with trendy decadence. As night falls, the sensual rhythms of salsa, rumba and *compas* music start to spill out from the clubs on Washington Avenue, as they gear up for the parties that go on until dawn.

There's another Miami too, just across the MacArthur Causeway from South Beach. With its growing skyline boasting vibrant and experimental architecture, this one moves to a different rhythm. It is where the deals are made. It is the working capital of Latin America and the Caribbean. Money is flowing in from all over the world to finance new hotels, condominiums and restaurants. It is a city that has come of age enough to demand its own ballet, symphony, opera, art museums and professional sports – not just sand, sea and sun.

"Greater Miami," as it is often called, sits inside Miami-Dade County and consists of 30 different municipalities. Its population is about 2 million – around half of whom speak Spanish as their native tongue. It sprawls over 500 sq. miles (1,300 sq. km), including a 15-mile (24-km) stretch of soft, sandy beaches where, despite nudity being limited to one stretch, rear-end revealing tongas and topless sun-bathers often decorate the landscape. Topographically, it is a one-dimensional experience; there are no hills. But the lush foliage – orchids, bougainvillea, hibiscus, palms – more than makes up for it.

The average yearly temperature is a mild 75°F (24°C). But, although the National Weather Service insists the mercury has never hit 100°F (38°C) in Miami "proper," the summers can sometimes get so steamy that the entire city feels on fire. Hurricane season – the most easily identifiable "season" of the year except for the tourist months – brings an occasional threat. But more than likely it means a bathtub filled with beer, candles just in case, and a *cause célèbre* for a party.

Punctuated with pink houses and aquamarine waters, Miami is casual and clean, cosmopolitan and chic. If it were an automobile, Miami would be a sleek, white convertible cruising to catch a sunrise at the beach after a night on the town. Travelers, who swarm to the city by the millions each year, often become addicted to its ways.

PRECEDING PAGES: umbrella in the sun; Deco lines and tropical pastels; wheels of choice for cruising on Ocean Drive; retro-kitsch is cool.
LEFT: getting from A to B, Miami Beach-style.

Elsewhere in Florida they call it "Sin City." This town is too volatile, too Latin, pretentious, flamboyant and fast for the good-old-boys to the north or the Waspy snowbirds to the west.

For the rest of the country, Miami means more than just a bustling Sun Belt baby; it is the new Ellis Island, an immigrant's dream. It hosts a ragtag collection of characters – Cubans, Haitians, Brazilians, Jamaicans, Colombians, Nicaraguans, Venezuelans, Bahamians, Dominicans and Russians. Young Turks and old Jews. It's the city of the future, where those who revel in the energy of its diversity are those who prosper.

The "newest" of immigrants hawk bags of limes to motorists in traffic and in a few months can "move up" to selling carnations from a push-cart. It is a wide-open land of endless possibilities where a Cuban who rafted to its shores can, within 10 years, own a cafeteria, car lot and Cadillac. In Miami, "old money" means a mere generation.

It has become the most "foreign" of US cities, full of dark eyes and heavy accents. It feels like a first cousin to the Caribbean, a total stranger to the state of Montana. It sounds like merengue, conga, reggae and calypso. Salsa seems an integral part of the collective local subconscious.

Billboards address passers-by in Spanish, as do radio stations, newspapers and many restaurant menus. Across America, Hispanics represent about 12 percent of the total population; here, the figure is close to 50. After years of immigration from Haiti, Creole is now Miami's third language. The city's multi-cultural identity is evident in everyday life. When an invitation to a party says dinner at 8pm, it always prompts the question: Latin time (2 hours later) or American time (exactly 8 o'clock)?

While in recent years Miami has undergone a renaissance that has included a generous sprinkling of big-city sophistication, some of its old tourist-town mentality still remains. Not far from the chi-chi fashion boutiques, tawdry souvenir shops sell rubber alligators, canned sunshine and orange perfume.

Throughout the city, this contrast is constant. Inside pastel-painted apartments, the *beau monde* indulge on stone crabs and champagne while on the streets, bag ladies scrounge for food as down-and-out young men do a window-washing dance begging for a dollar. A juxtaposition of affluence and survival, hedonism and hardships – the stuff the city is made of.

Welcome to the Miami mystique. ❏

RIGHT: Haitian carnival night at Tap Tap restaurant in Miami Beach.

Decisive Dates

circa 8000 BC Nomadic tribes reach Florida, probably having migrated from the North American northwest. The Tequesta people settle the verdant areas surrounding present-day Miami.

AD 1400s About 10,000 Native Americans are living on the peninsula by the time the Spanish arrive.

CONQUEST AND SETTLEMENT

1492 Christopher Columbus arrives in the New World, landing first on Hispaniola.

1513 Spanish conquistador Juan Ponce de León

"discovers" Florida and sails into Biscayne Bay.

1562 The French arrive in Florida to challenge the Spanish, who then strengthen their hold.

1566 Pedro Menéndez de Avilés, the first Spanish governor of Florida, visits the Tequesta people of the Miami area to set up trade links.

1580s–1760s Florida is disputed between Britain, France and Spain.

1763 The French and Indian War ends, with Florida becoming a British colony.

1784 Britain swaps with Spain, trading Florida for the Bahamas. Spain begins a new settlement program. Miami's first residents Pedro Fornells and John Egan are granted land.

1817–18 First Seminole War.

1821 The US gains control of Florida and hundreds of runaway slaves settle in the area.

1825 Cape Florida Lighthouse, the first permanent structure in South Florida, begins operating.

1835 Seminole Indians attack settlers and the bloody "Dade Massacre" occurs. This sparks off the Second Seminole War, which lasts for seven years. Many Seminoles are deported to Oklahoma.

1838 Fort Dallas is built to defend against Seminole attack.

1843 William English settles in Miami area. He is the first to use the name "Miami."

1845 Florida becomes the 27th state in the Union.

1850 Miami's first post office is in operation.

1855–8 The Third Seminole War makes the area unstable once more.

1861–5 As a major slave-holding state, Florida joins forces with the South in the American Civil War. However, the Miami area is barely affected.

1870s Developer William Brickell arrives in Miami and establishes a trading post.

MIAMI STARTS TO GROW

1896 Julia Tuttle convinces Henry Flagler to bring his railroad to Miami. City status is conferred on Miami. The city's first newspaper, the *Miami Metropolis*, hits the streets.

1898 Miami's growth accelerates after being chosen as a military training base for the Spanish-American War.

1905–12 The final section of the East Coast Railway, from Miami to Key West, is built.

1906 Governor Broward begins to drain parts of the Everglades to open up the area around Miami to farming.

1914 Chicago millionaire James Deering starts work on Vizcaya, his grand Miami retreat.

1915 Collins Bridge, now the Venetian Causeway, is built to link Miami with present-day Miami Beach. The latter becomes a city, as casinos, cabanas and cafes blossom.

1917 World War I transforms Miami's Dinner Key into a US Navy air base.

1920 The city's population nears 30,000.

1920s The Roaring Twenties bring a real estate boom, population growth and modernization to Miami. Prohibition fails to take hold in the city, and it becomes a haven for "rumrunners."

1921 George Merrick begins work on the new suburb of Coral Gables.

1926 The University of Miami is founded. A brutal hurricane batters the city, leaving over 200 dead.

1928 The Tamiami Trail opens – the first major

road across the Everglades, linking Miami with Tampa. Gangster Al Capone moves to Miami.

1930s Miami Beach's Art Deco hotels are built and tourism thrives in South Florida.

1933 An attempt is made on the life of Franklin D. Roosevelt at Bayfront Park.

1935 A huge hurricane hits the Keys, killing over 400 people.

1936 Miami hosts the Orange Festival, beginning the tradition of the annual Orange Bowl Parade.

1942 Hotels are transformed into barracks and hospitals during World War II.

1947 Everglades National Park is created.

1950s The tourism boom brings grand-scale hotels to Miami Beach, and the government cracks down on Miami's mobsters and illegal gambling halls.

THE CUBAN FACTOR

1959 Fidel Castro leads a revolution in Cuba, and later embraces communism.

1960s In the years following the Cuban Revolution, thousands of Cubans flee the island and settle in the Miami area. More emigrés from Central and South America follow.

1961 Cuban exiles unite with US agents in the foiled Bay of Pigs invasion of Cuba. Almost 100 people die.

1962 The Cuban Missile Crisis threatens war, and exiles realize that Miami is no longer just a temporary home. The city's population reaches 1 million.

1970s US economic recession badly hurts Miami. President Nixon vacations on Key Biscayne as four Miamians break into a Washington DC office, triggering the Watergate scandal. Conditions on the island of Haiti worsen considerably, and thousands of Haitians sail rickety boats to Miami.

1973 The Miami Dolphins win the Superbowl and finish the first-ever unbeaten, no-tie season in the history of the NFL.

1980 A race riot erupts in the neighborhood of Liberty City over the acquittal of a white police officer accused of murdering a black man. In the so-called Mariel Boatlift, President Castro allows 125,000 Cubans, many of them convicted criminals, to leave the island and come to Miami.

1980s The city becomes known as the principal east coast entry point for drug runners. The campaign to restore the Art Deco district of Miami

---

PRECEDING PAGES: the Spanish landing at Tequesta (Miami). **LEFT:** Juan Ponce de León. **RIGHT:** Gianni Versace's brother and sister carrying the ashes at the designer's funeral.

Beach gathers pace and launches the area's renaissance as a resort.

1984 The glitzy television series *Miami Vice* premiers, vastly changing the public image of Miami.

1985 The city elects Xavier Suárez, its first Cuban mayor.

1990 Manuel Noriega, former chief of state of Panama, is tried in Miami on drugs charges.

1992 "Andrew," the biggest hurricane for decades, makes a direct hit on South Miami. The damage is estimated at $25 billion.

1994 Economic collapse in Cuba brings another wave of refugees, scores of whom are plucked from the water by the US Coast Guard.

1995 Two American planes flown by members of the Miami-based Cuban group Brothers to the Rescue are shot down by the Cuban Air Force.

1997 Fashion designer Gianni Versace is murdered outside his Miami Beach mansion. The Florida Marlins win the baseball World Series, and become the youngest ever champions. Jorge Mas Canosa, unofficial leader of Miami's Cubans, dies aged 58.

1999–2000 Six-year-old Cuban boy Elián González is plucked from the sea after his mother dies fleeing the island with him. Emotions run high in the Cuban-American community when the Cuban government insists that Elián should be returned to his father on the island. After extended legal wranglings, he is flown back to Cuba. ❑

BEGINNINGS

The first inhabitants arrived as early as 8,000 BC, but the Miami area remained a remote outpost until Flagler's railroad reached town in 1896

For 10,000 years people have been coming to South Florida. The early Indians, who may have migrated from Alaska and Siberia seeking the sun, lived along the river banks in a tropical Garden of Eden. Lacking metal, they fashioned their tools from sea shells. A Spanish adventurer was the first to intrude on their simple way of life.

Juan Ponce de León traveled the world in search of glory. What he hoped to discover, as he sailed north from Puerto Rico on March 3, 1513, was an island called Bimini and its fabled spring that gave eternal youth. What he found instead was the tip of a huge new continent, which he named "Pascua Florida" (Feast of Flowers, or Easter). Three months after he landed somewhere between today's St Augustine and Jacksonville, Ponce de León sailed into Biscayne Bay, noting in his journal that he had reached Tequesta (present-day Miami).

For the next half-century, Spaniards tried unsuccessfully to conquer this unruly peninsula. They were no match for the native people – or for a worse enemy, the ubiquitous mosquito. Challenged by the French, who in 1562 established an outpost near present-day Jacksonville named Fort Caroline, Spain's King Philip II sent Pedro Menéndez de Avilés as governor to secure Florida. By 1565, Menéndez had routed the French and founded St Augustine, the first permanent settlement in what is now the United States.

A Jesuit mission at Tequesta flourished briefly, then failed. It was reopened, and failed again. However, the Spaniards and the native Indians had formed an alliance that, over the years, resulted in friendly treatment for Spanish ships and shipwrecked sailors who landed on the Tequesta coast.

Slowly, Spain began to cede to England its claim to supremacy in the New World. As the English took over Creek Indian land, renegade Creeks crossed over the border into Spanish

Florida, plundering and burning as they came. The native Indians, who were now Spanish allies, fled before them. The Spanish, unhappy about the possibility of a Florida populated by hostile Creeks, decided to make another attempt to settle in South Florida, sending Father Joseph María Mónaco and Father Joseph Xavier de

Alana to Tequesta in the summer of 1743. They established a settlement, which consisted of a triangular fort with mortared corners, and called it "Pueblo de Santa María de Loreto" – Miami's second name. By this time the Indians had grown unfriendly, however, and the settlement did not flourish; the king ultimately ordered the mission to be abandoned.

A British colony

In 1763 the Treaty of Paris, which ended the Seven Years' War (the "French and Indian War" to Americans), made Florida a British colony after two centuries of Spanish rule. When the Spanish left South Florida, the remaining Indians

---

LEFT: Indian woman with body decoration.
RIGHT: Seminole man in traditional garb.

followed them to Cuba. Britain thus became the proud owner of a new land with very few inhabitants. The British were quick to map the area (the entire east coast of Florida was surveyed between 1765 and 1771) and to change the Spanish names to English ones. With the stroke of a pen, Biscayne Bay became "Sandwich Gulf."

During the 20 years of the British period there were several grand plans to settle South Florida, "the most precious jewel of His Majesty's American dominion," but none of them succeeded.

A DIM LIGHT

A lighthouse at Cape Florida, built by Bostonian Samuel Lincoln, began operating in 1825. Its light was so ineffective that sailors said they'd "go ashore looking for it."

lization" in South Florida the "Cape Florida Settlement." Although it was officially Spanish, South Florida was in reality almost part of the Bahama Islands, linked through trade and sentiment.

Florida became a haven for runaway slaves – just one point of contention between the US and Spain. By 1819, the Spanish were ready to cut their losses on their unsuccessful Florida adventure. By 1821, a deal had been struck, and the Stars and Stripes fluttered over the US's most tropical territory.

Britain shocked the Tories, who had poured into Florida during the American Revolution, with the announcement that it would exchange Florida for the Bahamas, which Spain had captured during the war. Many Loyalists fled again, this time to the Bahamas, as Spain took control and the second Spanish period (1784–1821) began.

Miami's first two landowners date from this time, when Pedro Fornells was granted 175 acres (70 hectares) on "Cayo Biscaino" (today's Key Biscayne) and John Egan received 100 acres (40 hectares) on the north bank of the "*Rio nombrado de aqua dulze*" (now the Miami River). People called the small oasis of "civi-

The US confirmed the Egan family's land claim, with additional grants, plus land for Polly and Jonathan Lewis along the banks of the bay and the river that from this time on was called the "Miami." Mary Ann Davis received title to land on Key Biscayne that she had bought from Pedro Fornells. In all, just a little over 3,000 acres (1,200 hectares) in the whole of South Florida was privately owned.

In the 1830s, Richard Fitzpatrick, who dreamed of recreating his South Carolina plantation here, bought all the land grants on the mainland. Fitzpatrick was the first to campaign for the development of the Miami area. But Indian troubles interfered.

Seminole wars

In Florida, as in the rest of the country, the history of settlers and Indians was one of shattered promises and broken treaties. Land-hungry whites wanted to send the Indians west, to reservations, but a steadfast group of Seminoles refused to go.

What began with the "Dade Massacre" in December 1835, when Major Francis Langhorne Dade (for whom the newly formed Dade County was named) and 109 of his men died during a bloody Seminole attack, did not end until 1857.

SCORES TO SETTLE

The Seminole people are still officially at war with the US. They say that a valid peace treaty has never been signed.

village of Miami on the river's south bank. He was the first to call the area "Miami."

The US Coastal Survey made the first map of the new town in 1849. But continuing Indian problems took their toll, and by 1860 Miami, with its handful of inhabitants, had disappeared from public records.

The Civil War that tore the nation apart barely touched Miami. Florida joined the Confederacy, but Key West remained in Federal control. The monthly mailboat, Miami's link with the outside world, was

The US responded by sending in the troops, who erected Fort Dallas as a defensive outpost on the north bank of the Miami River. Among the many who died during the years of the three Seminole Wars was the New York horticulturalist Henry Perrine, who managed to save his wife and children before he was killed by Seminoles attacking Indian Key in August, 1840.

Richard Fitzpatrick sold his land for $16,000 to his nephew, William English. Within a year of his arrival in 1842, English had settled the

suspended and South Florida sat out the war in complete isolation.

William Gleason was a carpetbagger who came to Miami in 1866, liked what he saw, and decided to keep it for himself. He was responsible for foiling a plan to settle former slaves in South Florida under the 1862 Homestead Act, which granted 160 acres (65 hectares) of land free to any citizen who would live on it for five years and improve it. Gleason maintained almost total control of the area for many years, to the point that when a land dispute forced him to leave the Miami River area he took Miami with him – that is, the Miami post office, whose name he changed to "Biscayne."

LEFT: Fort Dallas, built near the Miami River as a defense against Seminole attack. **ABOVE:** early settlers pose on the steps of Kirk Munroe's home.

Early snowbirds

Settlers were beginning to come into the area. Long-time resident Edmund Beasley filed a claim for land in what is now Coconut Grove in 1868. Two years later William B. Brickell and Ephraim T. Sturtevant arrived from Cleveland, Ohio. Brickell bought land and built a home and trading post on the bank of the Miami River. Sturtevant acquired land in Biscayne, where his daughter, Julia Tuttle, visited him as early as 1875.

In 1873 settlers opened a post office in the bayfront community called Cocoanut Grove (as it was spelled then). Government engineers

completed Fowey Rock lighthouse in 1878, and the old Cape Florida Light was darkened.

As would be the case for years to come, Miami's mild winters attracted northern visitors, the first of the tourists. Among them was Ralph M. Munroe of Staten Island, who stayed with his friends Charles and Isabella Peacock at the Bay View House (which overlooked the bay from the bluff in what is today Peacock Park), the first lodging place in the area.

Club for women

Coconut Grove became a community of "firsts" as civilized institutions began to pop up on the Florida frontier. Ralph and Kirk

Munroe (no relation) founded the Biscayne Bay Yacht Club in 1887. A school was opened the next year, and in 1891 Ralph Munroe donated a parcel of his land so that the Union Chapel (later to become Plymouth Congregational Church) could be built. That same year schoolteacher Flora McFarlane, the area's first woman homesteader, organized the Housekeepers Club for women, out of which the Pine Needles Club for young girls would come, and the area's first library on the second floor of Charles Peacock's store.

The future city of Miami, however, was still only an idea – an idea in the mind of a recently widowed Cleveland matron named Julia Sturtevant Tuttle. She decided to start a new life for herself in Florida, not on her late father's homestead, but on the "best" piece of property available, on the north bank of the Miami River. She arrived with her 23-year-old daughter and 21-year-old son on November 13, 1891, and immediately began to plan her city.

She had hoped that Henry Plant, the railroad magnate whose line had reached as far south as Tampa in 1893, would extend his train to tiny Miami. In this she was disappointed. But another railroad man, Henry M. Flagler, who made his first millions in Standard Oil with John D. Rockefeller, had recently begun to fall in love with Florida. His railroad inched southward from St Augustine, reaching Palm Beach by 1893. Still, he proclaimed that he wasn't interested in bringing it the last 66 miles (106 km) to Mrs Tuttle's doorstep. That, however, was before the winter of 1894–95.

A killer freeze hit Florida that winter, destroying most of the area's valuable citrus crops. But in semi-tropical Miami, orange blossoms still bloomed. Mrs Tuttle invited James Ingraham, Flagler's lieutenant, to come and see for himself. He did, and was impressed. When Mrs Tuttle offered Flagler half of her land, plus some of Brickell's, the deal was made. The railroad was coming.

The new era, pulled by a locomotive and greeted wildly by the whole populace (all 300 of them), arrived on April 15, 1896. The clanging of the engine's bell decisively marked the end of Miami's days as a sleepy frontier town.   ❏

LEFT: Julia Sturtevant Tuttle, one of Miami's most aggressive pioneers. **RIGHT:** Flagler's famous railroad finally chugs into town.

BIRTH OF A CITY

*In the early 1900s, Miami went from strength to strength, but then the property
boom peaked and crashed, and the city was hit by a devastating hurricane*

Important events followed each other with dizzying speed after Flagler's famous railroad came to town. Within a month the first newspaper, the *Miami Metropolis,* rolled off the press. Local citizens voted to incorporate the city (which was never, officially, a town) on July 28 and elected Flagler's man, John B. Reilly, as mayor. The city fathers laid out streets (rather badly) and founded churches and schools. Then, on Christmas morning, a fire started in Brady's grocery store at what is today Miami Avenue and SW Second Street and destroyed 28 buildings, wiping out almost the entire business district.

Miami citizens, undaunted by this first crisis, set about the task of rebuilding their downtown district. Just three weeks later they had a reason to celebrate when Flagler's enormous, elegant Royal Palm Hotel opened with a gala dinner.

The city, which had already begun to proclaim itself as "America's sun porch" to potential tourists, hosted some very different visitors during the scorching summer of 1898. They were American troops on their way to Cuba to fight the Spanish after the sinking of the battleship *Maine* in Havana harbor. But 7,000 bored soldiers plus humidity plus swarms of mosquitoes do not equal peace, quiet and happiness. As one frustrated soldier put it: "If I owned both Miami and Hell, I'd rent out Miami and live in Hell." Fortunately, the war was brief and the troops were soon on their way.

Early growth

In the early years of the 20th century Miami began a modest boom. The Tatum brothers built a toll bridge across the river at Flagler Street and began developing the Riverside subdivision. A new business district, which was growing rapidly, included Seybold's ice-cream parlor, two rival Burdines department stores,

LEFT: an early promotional poster sings the city's praises. **RIGHT:** a Miami postcard showing the seaside look of the 1920s.

banks, saloons, moving picture theaters and a new newspaper, the *Miami Evening Record,* edited by Frank M. Stoneman.

Until 1909 what there was of Miami's downtown area and outlying communities such as Coconut Grove and Larkins (today's South Miami) was built on the narrow, 4-mile (6-km)

wide coastal ridge sandwiched between the Atlantic Ocean to the east and the Everglades to the west, which began at today's NW 27th Avenue. The governor, Napoleon Bonaparte Broward, campaigned on a promise of draining Florida's vast wetlands to create an "Empire of the swampy Everglades." As part of the plan, government engineers dug the Miami Canal to facilitate drainage in the Everglades.

They also dug "Government Cut," which would later become the Port of Miami, across the lower end of the future Miami Beach, improving the access to Miami's harbor and in the process creating Fisher Island. Florida began its infamous tradition of selling wetlands and, as developers dreamed of profits from land where there was none before, dredges began to hum in the wilderness west of Miami. (It was not until 1916 that the Florida Federation of Women's Clubs, concerned about preserving the Everglades, acquired a large tract of land, which they called Royal Palm State Park. It would become the nucleus of the wildlife-rich Everglades National Park.)

Miami had a way of attracting visionaries. One was John Collins, a New Jersey Quaker who became sole owner of Ocean Beach in 1909. He borrowed money and began building a bridge that would connect Miami with the beach. But halfway through, his money ran out. Fortunately, this man with land and a grand dream met up with a man with hard cash: Carl Graham Fisher, who had made his mint with Prest-O-Lite, the first really bright automobile headlight. Fisher loaned Collins $50,000 to finish his bridge; in return, Collins gave Fisher a piece of his land on the island that would become Miami Beach.

On June 12, 1913, a long line of motor cars rattled over the wooden planks of Collins' bridge. When they got to Bull Island (now Belle Isle), where the bridge temporarily ended, the drivers hopped out, lifted their lightweight

FLAGLER'S FOLLY

Flagler's goal of extending his railroad along the 100-mile (160-km) string of islands to Key West became known as "Flagler's Folly." Three years after work began in 1905, the construction crews embarked on their greatest challenge yet: the famous 7-mile (11-km) bridge.

William Krome, Flagler's chief of construction, aimed for the impossible: to complete the railroad a year ahead of schedule, in time for his boss's 82nd birthday. He succeeded. The *Extension Special* train, filled with VIPs, arrived in Key West on January 22, 1912. The old man, greeted by 10,000 cheering people, declared: "We did it. Now I can die in peace." Sixteen months later he did just that.

automobiles, turned them around, and headed back to the mainland. That same summer workmen leveled the beach's native mangroves which allowed Fisher's dredge to go to work, throwing up sand and shells from the bay bottom night and day to create his island.

Miami Beach

In 1915 the citizens of Miami Beach voted to incorporate and elected J.N. Lummus their first mayor. Ocean Beach, on the south end of the island, became a "people's playground." It boasted several casinos, swimming pools and cabana complexes, as well as a restaurant that Joe and Jennie Weiss ran out of their home, which would later become Joe's Stone Crab. Farther north, Fisher envisioned an exclusive playground for the wealthy, complete with golf, tennis and polo.

Back in Miami, Ev Sewell, a pioneer merchant, had become the city's first great promoter. His nationwide advertising campaign lured thousands, including the rich and famous, many of whom built homes on Brickell Avenue or Coconut Grove's "Millionaires' Row." The most lavish of these was Vizcaya, a European-style palace surrounded by formal gardens

BOOM TOWN

From 1910 to 1920, migrants in search of the good life swelled the city's population from 5,500 to 30,000, a 440-percent rise.

Naval Air Station. By the end of the war, 128 seaplanes were based there, filling Miami's once peaceful skies with noise.

Roaring Twenties

Nowhere did the 1920s roar louder than in Miami. The war was barely over when developers began to carve up orange groves and tomato patches into subdivisions. The city, faced with a nightmarish jumble of street names and numbers, adopted a new naming system, the Chaille Plan, in 1921. Avenue D became Miami Avenue, 12th Street

constructed by James Deering of International Harvester, which was finished in 1916.

Sewell had convinced Glenn Curtiss, a pioneer in the aviation industry and a pilot himself, to open a flying school in Miami. After Congress declared war on Germany in April 1917, Sewell began promoting the idea of a naval aviation school. In October 1917 the American government purchased land in Coconut Grove and began building Dinner Key

LEFT: instructors cutting a dash beside their biplane at the Miami flying school.
ABOVE: another postcard from paradise, showing women fishing on the edge of Biscayne Bay.

turned into Flagler Street, and streets and avenues were then renumbered outward from the intersection of these two thoroughfares. The post office was temporarily happy.

Between 1920 and 1923 the population doubled. City fathers moved forward with a grand plan for "modernization," which included a large new bayfront park and a skyscraper courthouse. Downtown parking became a disaster; downtown land became a gold mine.

But the real boom was yet to come. By 1925 the frenzy, fueled by Miami's superb climate and huge amount of available land, was well out of control. The list of new subdivisions grew long: Hialeah, Biltmore, Melrose Gardens,

Flagler Manor, Miami Shores, Miami Beach, plus Central Miami and dozens of others.

One stands out: George Merrick's "Coral Gables, Miami's Master Sub-urb," a totally planned community of Mediterranean homes, graceful plazas and wide boulevards. Unlike many developers, Merrick delivered on his promises. He made enormous profits and poured them back into his suburb. He spent millions on advertising, increasing the nation's interest in booming Miami. He hired silver-tongued orator William

AN ADMAN'S DREAM

Between 1925 and 1926, at the peak of the city's boom, the *Miami Herald* ran more pages of advertising copy than any other newspaper in the world.

With three replicas of Spain's Giralda Tower under construction (the Biltmore Hotel, the *Miami News* Tower and Miami Beach's Roney Plaza Hotel) and the University of Miami on the drawing board, the bottom began to fall out of the boom. In August 1925 the Florida East Coast Railway announced an embargo on all but essential freight so that it could repair its tracks, cutting off the supply of building materials via land. So developers turned to the sea, using anything that would float to transport their lumber and supplies. The flotilla was interrupted in January 1926 when the *Prinz Valdemar* overturned in the middle of Miami's shipping canal, closing the port for more than three weeks.

Anti-Florida campaigns in northern states hurt, too. Still, the Biltmore Hotel opened on January 16, 1926, and in February workmen began construction of the University of Miami. But the boom was clearly over. By mid-summer even Coral Gables' previously excellent sales were slipping.

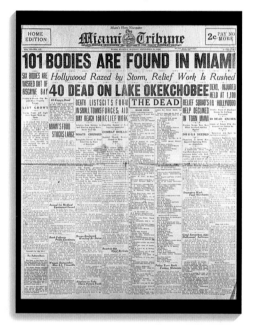

The big one

Few people paid much attention to the newspaper headlines on September 17, 1926, that warned of an impending tropical storm. They should have. They awoke in the middle of the night in a city without electricity and with storm gusts screaming past their windows. The winds were measured at 128 miles (206 km) per hour before the wind gauge blew away. At dawn the torrents of rain and tidal surge seemed to have stopped, and many people ran from their homes to survey the terrible destruction, not realizing that they were in the eye of the storm. The hurricane resumed, this time from the opposite direction, stranding thousands. More than 200 people lost their lives.

Jennings Bryan for $100,000 to make promotional speeches at Coral Gables' Venetian Pool on DeSoto Boulevard. Few structures exemplified the flamboyance of the period better than this architectural bit of whimsy. Once a rock pit, the pool featured extravagant waterfalls, caves made of coral and landscaping on a grand scale.

The talk of the town – in fact, all over Florida – was real estate. It seemed like everyone was making a bundle as land changed hands once, twice, many times a day at spiraling prices. "Binder boys," real estate salesmen who sold "binders" (10 percent deposits) on land, then resold them, flocked to the state. But most of the profits were on paper.

By the afternoon of September 18, when the brutal storm had at last blown itself away, Miami was in chaos. The hurricane left houses smashed to pieces and businesses destroyed. Boats had been lifted out of the water and thrown on to dry land. Miami had been reeling before the hurricane. Afterwards, it was ruined. ❑

LEFT: newspaper headlines tell the deadly story.
RIGHT: the city wiped out by a hurricane tries to recover amid the floods, destruction and debris.

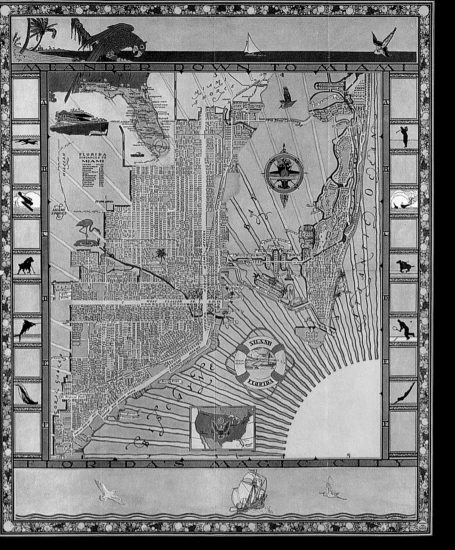

FLORIDA'S MAGIC CITY

GROWING PAINS

Following the disasters of the late 1920s, Miami benefited from Roosevelt's New Deal and saw prosperity again with the influx of troops and post-war tourists

The national headlines that proclaimed "Miami is Wiped Out!" were correct – but only temporarily. The damage was great, but so was the spirit of the stricken city. Within a week Mayor Ed Romfh was already talking about Miami's comeback. University of Miami officials gave South Florida hope for the future when they opened their "cardboard college" on October 15, 1926. They had converted a bankrupt apartment hotel into classrooms with thin cardboard partitions. It was a start.

The next couple of years brought a few bright spots, such as the opening of the Everglades and Robert Clay hotels and the completion of the Tamiami Trail (the first major road across the Everglades) in 1928. But for the first time the majority of traffic was flowing north, out of Miami, away from the abandoned skeletons of buildings rising stark against the sky – ruined by the winds of the storm.

With the passage of the 18th Amendment in 1920, the US had become officially dry. Miami hardly noticed. Rumrunners loved the canals and coves of South Florida and soon the area had acquired yet another nickname: "the leakiest spot in America." Miami's reputation for winking at both the liquor and the gambling laws attracted some new, far-from-desirable residents, including the infamous gangster Al "Scarface" Capone, who bought a mansion on Palm Island in 1928.

Aviation history

Most of the local leaders, including the Sewell brothers and George Merrick, were bankrupt. Much-needed cash flowed into Miami from outsiders like Joseph Widner, who purchased Hialeah racetrack in 1932, and the Phipps family, who completed Biscayne Boulevard in 1927. At this time Miami's aviation industry was born. What began as Florida Airways Corporation, founded by the air ace Eddie Ricken-

backer in 1926, became Eastern Airlines by 1930; Pan Am began its Key West–Havana service in 1927. Airports were built, and in 1929 Miami hosted both Charles Lindbergh and Amelia Earhart at the "Olympics of Aviation."

In 1932 America elected Franklin D. Roosevelt as president, with hopes that he would lead

Nesting at Hialeah Race Course, Miami, Fla.

ROOSEVELT'S CLOSE SHAVE

Franklin D. Roosevelt, who had been vacationing in South Florida, agreed to make an appearance in Bayfront Park on February 15, 1933. Miami's voters had supported him in the previous year's election and he came to thank them. It nearly cost him his life. Among the 18,000 people there that night was an unemployed bricklayer named Guiseppe Zangara. Zangara, who resented people with wealth and authority, fired an $8 pawn-shop pistol five times. He wounded four people before hitting Chicago Mayor Anton Cermak, who was standing only inches from Roosevelt. Cermak died on March 6; Zangara went to the electric chair soon afterwards.

LEFT: a map of Greater Miami in its youth.
RIGHT: early postcard from Hialeah racetrack, showing one of the famous flamingos on its nest.

the country out of the Depression. Once Roosevelt was in office, his New Deal programs launched an "alphabet soup" of agencies. Among them was the CCC (Civilian Conservation Corps), which employed young men to work in the nation's parks. In Miami they worked on Matheson Hammock and built Greynolds Park. The PWA (Public Works Administration) constructed many new buildings, including the Coral Gables Fire Station, Miami Shores Golf Club and Liberty Square, which was Florida's first public housing project.

The government also hired unemployed World War I veterans to work on an overseas of the future Orange Bowl. The newly named "Orange Festival" held its first New Year's Eve parade in 1936. A Miami tradition was born.

The economy was looking up in Miami Beach, too. New "modern" hotels and apartments sprang up along Collins Avenue. Unhappily, anti-Semitism also began to flourish. Carl Fisher and John Collins had originally developed the north part of the beach as a "restricted" area, and now "Gentiles Only" signs began to appear in hotels and apartments. Across the ocean, an Austrian paperhanger named Adolf Hitler came to power in Germany. A second world war was on the horizon.

highway to Key West. Many of them met a tragic fate when a monster hurricane struck on Labor Day in 1935, killing more than 400 people and wrecking both the uncompleted highway (which in the end did not open until 1938) and Flagler's Overseas Railroad.

Tourists, including many from Latin America, were starting to flock to Miami. In 1933 the Palm Fete, which had been sporadically celebrated in the past, put on a New Year's Day football game between the University of Miami and Manhattan College. Against all predictions, the local team won, and the success of the event prompted the organisers to schedule a game for the following year, which was played at the site

World War II

Tourism, already the mainstay of Miami's economy, dropped dramatically after the Japanese bombed Pearl Harbor and the US declared war. German submarines torpedoing a tanker in full view of Florida's coast in February 1942 didn't help. Suddenly the city's hotels were empty – but not for long.

The solution was American soldiers – lots of them. The city's fathers convinced the government that warm and deserted South Florida would make a good place to train soldiers. By the end of 1942, the military had turned 147 Miami hotels into barracks. GIs drilled on golf courses and exercised on wide sandy beaches.

Miami became a war camp. Even the country's ultimate matinée idol, Clark Gable, came to Miami Beach in uniform. Before the war was over, one-fourth of the officers and one-fifth of the enlisted men in the US Army Air Corps had trained in Miami Beach.

The Navy took command of Miami's only post-boom sky-scraper, the Alfred I duPont Building, which was promptly nicknamed the "USS Neversink." Still, since most US ships were in the Pacific Ocean, German submarines roamed the Florida Straits

BERMUDA TRIANGLE

On December 5, 1945, five Navy bombers vanished without trace off the coast of South Florida, thus instigating the popular myth of the Bermuda Triangle.

War-born prosperity prompted tourists to return to Miami and hoteliers to clamor to get their facilities back from the government for civilian use. People sensed that a major change was in the air. As early as 1942 the *Miami Herald* confidently predicted that "political, economic and geographical factors slowly are swinging Miami into a position that will make the Indian wars, the coming of the railroad, the land boom and even the present military cauldron look like a quiet Sunday afternoon on a Swiss alp."

practically at will. Germans torpedoed four tankers in full view of Miami, and 25 between Key West and Cape Canaveral during 1942.

Many hotels were turned into temporary hospitals for wounded soldiers. (After the war the Biltmore Hotel continued to be an Army hospital until 1968.) The government held German prisoners of war at camps in Kendall and Homestead. Rationing, blackouts, dimouts, thousands of servicemen around town, and, above all, the ever-present submarine threat just offshore, made Miami feel very close to the war.

LEFT: soldiers in gas masks training on Miami Beach.
ABOVE: one of the first Orange Bowl parades.

The talk across America that started back in 1896 about Miami being the "coming metropolis" was coming true. After the war, thousands of soldiers returned to the place where they'd gotten "sand in their shoes." Rows of pastel-painted boxy GI houses sprang up in isolated, outlying areas. GIs swarmed to the University of Miami, breathing new life into a moribund institution. By 1947 the main campus, so long vacant, was the site of the Memorial Classroom Building. The skeleton of the university's planned administration building, abandoned after the boom, became the Merrick Building in 1949.

A record eight hurricanes hit Miami between 1945 and 1950. The two that hit a month apart in the fall of 1947 were minimal but very wet. After the storm on October 11, 1947, more than four-fifths of Dade and Broward counties was under water. The flooding in the Orange Bowl stadium was knee-deep, and areas west of Red Road resembled lakes full of houseboats instead of subdivisions. People clamored for action that would prevent future floods. The government obliged, sending the Army Corps of Engineers to build new canals, locks and levees that would dry up much of the eastern Everglades. The legacy of these projects,

> ### LIBERAL LEADER
>
> In 1954 Florida's Leroy Collins became the first southern state governor to declare that racial segregation was "morally wrong."

in addition to large tracts of new land for development, was an ongoing threat to the Everglades and to South Florida's water supply.

Crime again became a problem in the late 1940s, as gangsters took over casinos and public officials looked the other way. Influential citizens formed the "Secret Six," a group dedicated to stopping illegal gambling. Their efforts exposed corruption in high places (including the governor's office) and culminated in 1950 in an investigation by Senate crime fighter Estes Kefauver. Miami's door was no longer wide open to criminals.

A new era arrived in 1949 when WTVJ, Florida's first television station, began to broadcast.

Although at first few homes boasted TVs, it wouldn't be long before tuning in to watch Miami newsman Ralph Renick would become a nightly ritual. Arthur Godfrey, whose show was one of the most popular on television, broadcast from the Kennilworth Hotel in Bal Harbour for many years. To express the city's appreciation for this wonderful coast-to-coast publicity, Miami Beach renamed 41st Street "Arthur Godfrey Road."

Florida had its share of unpleasantness during the communist scares of the early 1950s. The 1950 Senate campaign between Miamian George Smathers and incumbent Senator Claude Pepper turned nasty when Smathers said his opponent was soft on communism and called him "Red Pepper." (Smathers won that election. Pepper, who had moved to Miami, ran for the House of Representatives in 1962 and served there until his death in 1989.)

In 1951 racial violence erupted in Carver Village, a black housing project. The first Dade County Council for Human Relations was organized in response and by the late 1950s several area schools had been desegregated. In 1952 the contralto Marian Anderson sang to an integrated audience in the Dade County auditorium.

Tourism grows

Newcomers continued to arrive in the Miami area in record numbers. Farmland became suburbs as the town turned into a metropolis. The voters approved a metropolitan government for Dade County in a highly debated decision in 1957. By the end of the decade the population was nearing 1 million people.

Air-conditioning and glamorous grand-scale hotels like the Fontainebleau, which boasted 1,206 rooms, crystal chandeliers and marble staircases, encouraged tourism. Movie stars and business moguls arrived in droves, eager to be seen in such lavish surroundings. The "Gentiles Only" and "Whites Only" signs that had haunted hotel entrances for years disappeared. The future looked upbeat and promising.

But fate had a surprise waiting for Miami. His name was Fidel Castro. ❑

LEFT: mobster Al Capone called Miami home.
RIGHT: tourism takes hold as new, glamorous hotels spring up in Miami Beach.

THE CUBAN REVOLUTION

Fidel Castro's 1959 revolution and the resultant mass emigration of disaffected Cubans to Miami's shores changed the face of the city forever

The celebration of the new year in 1959 continued well beyond the traditional "morning after." Crowds were cheering about events in Cuba, where a 32-year-old rebel named Fidel Castro had deposed dictator Fulgencio Batista. But most Miamians paid little attention. It seemed like just another upheaval

in the nearby island's rickety power structure.

It proved to be more than that, as today's Miamians will readily attest. As disillusionment with the "conquering hero" set in, and Castro revealed his communist leanings, more and more Cubans fled their homeland. By the summer of 1960, six planes a day departed Havana carrying destitute exiles, most of whom left with $5 and the clothes they stood up in.

Initially, Miamians welcomed these refugees, taking pity on their plight and admiring their hard-working ways and strong family structure. Some resentment and hostility followed, however, as almost overnight schools and neighborhoods filled with people speaking only Spanish.

The Bay of Pigs

The Cubans weren't happy either; most of them wanted to go home. Until 1961 they believed they would – and soon. The CIA organized and trained a small exile brigade of 1,300 to invade Cuba and depose Castro. On April 17, 1961, "Brigada 2506," as it was called, landed on Playa Giron, a beach on Cuba's southern coast near the Bay of Pigs. The men were counting on US air support. It was not forthcoming, and the mission was doomed from the start. Almost 100 men died and about 1,000 were taken prisoner. Exile leaders in Miami believed their valiant fighters had been betrayed by the United States.

In the fall of 1962, US planes discovered signs of a military build-up in Cuba. Once more soldiers swarmed into Miami. President John F. Kennedy addressed the nation on October 22 to explain what became known as the Cuban Missile Crisis. War loomed. In the end, Soviet leader Nikita Khrushchev backed down and agreed to remove the Russian missiles from Cuba. In return, the US promised not to invade the island – or allow anyone else to. The exile community, now standing at about 100,000, had to face the realization that Miami was to be more than just a temporary home.

Kennedy honored the Bay of Pigs prisoners (freed in late 1962 in exchange for $62 million) at a ceremony in the Orange Bowl. The young president visited Miami once more, in November 1963, en route to his fatal stop in Dallas.

Beginning in 1965, twice-daily flights took off from Havana to bring refugees to Miami. By the end of the 1960s, a Cuban refugee was arriving every seven minutes. Miami's Cuban population doubled, reaching 300,000 by the time the so-called Freedom Flights ended in 1973. In order to process this wave of immigrants, the government took over the old *Miami News* tower. It was renamed the "Freedom Tower."

Illegal drugs

As the era of "Camelot" faded into the Vietnam protest years, Coconut Grove attracted flower children and hippies, who congregated in Peacock Park and made long-time residents feel as if their town was under siege. The hard-to-patrol coastline that made South Florida so inviting to rumrunners in the 1920s proved equally attractive to smugglers eager to supply America's growing appetite for illegal drugs. Huge amounts of drugs, and drug-tainted money, poured into Miami.

"Great Society" urban renewal brought bulldozers to Overtown as new housing projects and expressways took shape. Displaced residents poured into Liberty City, once a model black

Island. A professional football team called the Dolphins came to town and Jackie Gleason broadcast weekly television shows from Miami Beach. A long-haired singing group, the Beatles, crossed the Atlantic in 1964. When they arrived in Miami to appear on the *Ed Sullivan Show* (broadcast live from Miami Beach), thousands of teenage girls went wild. It was the shape of things to come.

While the city continued to grow (the population reached 1 million in February 1962), people began to express concern about the

community. Substandard housing became horribly overcrowded. A time bomb began to tick.

Liberty City exploded in August 1968, just as Richard Nixon, who had vacationed for years on Key Biscayne, was giving his acceptance speech to the Republican National Convention in Miami Beach. It was Miami's first race riot.

The 1960s had their good moments, too. Miami-Dade Junior (later Community) College opened, as well as a new seaport at Dodge

PRECEDING PAGES: the first wave of Cuban refugees arrives in Miami. **LEFT:** President Kennedy honors veterans of the ill-fated Bay of Pigs operation. **ABOVE:** the Beatles pay a visit.

environment. Their efforts led to the saving of the old Cape Florida Lighthouse and the establishment of John Pennekamp State Park (which contains Florida's last living coral reef) and Biscayne National Park in the upper Keys.

The Seventies

At the beginning of the 1970s Miami seemed poised on the brink of a new boom. Community pride ran high as President Nixon's "vacation White House" on Key Biscayne and the Dolphins' perfect 1973 season and Super Bowl victories kept Miami in the news. Florida International University, Miami's long-awaited state college, opened in 1972. Cubans, no longer refugees, were running successful businesses; "Calle Ocho" (SW Eighth Street in Little Havana) was thriving. Then a recession hit – the worst since the 1930s. Construction projects were abandoned and once again half-finished buildings marred the skyline. Unemployment was as high as 13 percent by 1975.

In spite of hard times and Watergate, the nation paused to celebrate its Bicentennial. During the celebration in Miami, one of the official Bicentennial cities, 7,300 people, mainly Cuban refugees,

LOCAL HEROES

Of the five men caught breaking into the Watergate building in Washington DC, thus sparking off the scandal that led to Nixon's resignation, four were Miamians.

other areas erupted in riots. The city despaired. Meanwhile, "Haitian boat people" were landing on the beaches daily, fleeing dictatorship but putting extra pressure on the Miami infrastructure.

The Mariel boatlift

Also in 1980, events in Cuba once again rewrote Miami's history. Fidel Castro announced that anyone who wished to leave the island could do so, and thousands did. Miami Cubans sailed to Mariel harbor to help their countrymen escape. Castro's government

became American citizens in a huge ceremony.

City leaders formed the Downtown Action Committee and began to revitalize downtown Miami and make big plans for the future. The city became an international banking center; it seemed like a bank was going up on practically every corner. By the late 1970s a rapid transit system was under construction and new government and cultural centers were growing up.

But the new decade got off to a bad start. The popular black Superintendant of Schools was charged (and later convicted) of theft of school property. In May 1980, after a Tampa jury acquitted a white policeman of the slaying of a black man, Arthur McDuffie, Liberty City and

forced them to bring back to Miami unwanted passengers as well: the refuse from Cuba's jails and mental institutions. Miami struggled under the weight of 125,000 "Marielitos," many of them criminals. Tent cities sprang up to house them and the prison population swelled.

Things looked bleak as Miami moved into the 1980s. Residents who were tired of crime and upheaval and of listening to Spanish and Creole and "Spanglish" moved to quieter, calmer places. Cars sported bumper stickers that read: "Will the last American leaving Miami please bring the flag?" ❏

ABOVE: Mariel refugees on their way to Miami.

Fidel Castro

He is the most hated man in Miami. Spanish radio commentators refer to him as "the tyrant." Others curl their lips and spit his name in disdain. Even his sister Juanita, owner of a Little Havana pharmacy, despises her brother.

The longest reigning military leader in Latin America, Fidel Castro is still the controversial and charismatic leader he was when he first captured Cuba in 1959. But, in the political arena, his hardline, purist stance has earned him the title "Fossil Communist."

While much of the communist world has crumbled away, Castro remains faithful to his "socialism or death" philosophy and continues to condemn Yankee imperialism. And his miraculous perseverance has given him an undeniable mystique.

Soon after the Revolution, American mobster Meyer Lansky, who lost a fortune in the communist take-over, offered a million-dollar bounty to anyone who could bring him Castro's head. No-one did. Later, several CIA plots, including an invasion, exploding cigars and drops of poison, were also thwarted. And amid it all, in a country severely short of food, clothing and medicine, Castro has kept a chokehold on his island's own dissidents.

Ironically, Castro has had as great an influence on Miami as any individual in the city's history, and many say much of what is good about modern Miami could not have happened were it not for the impetus of Fidel Castro.

But for the more than 700,000 Cubans in Miami-Dade County, this influence has reared its head in the form of a powerful anti-Castro feeling that is as much a personal vendetta against the man as it is a political statement against communism. For exiles who still pine for the "good life" of their homeland, and for their children who feel deprived of their roots, Castro-bashing is one of Miami's most passionate pastimes. Sometimes, the city seems awash in the Honk-If-You-Hate-Fidel sentiment. Bumper stickers shout "No Castro, No Problem."

Several exile groups in the city constantly dream of toppling him. During the 1970s and early 1980s, the anti-Castro crusade took a violent course. Local "freedom fighters" turned into bomb-tossing terrorists who targeted Miami businesses and individuals whom they thought were "soft on Fidel" because they advocated peaceful dialogue with Cuba. Many Miamians were injured and several killed.

RIGHT: Fidel in full oratorical flow.

The city has also been the center for the heated airwave wars that caught the nation's attention. Radio Marti and TV Marti – two US broadcasts designed to transmit American programs and anti-communist propaganda to Cuba – have had the support of much of the Cuban community. Both programs have brought pleasure to Miami's Cubans, who see them making the "dirty little worm squirm."

When Panamanian General Manuel Noriega was captured by the US government, a billboard was set up with the slogan: "Now Manuel, Next Fidel." Motorists honked in approval. When the communist governments in East Germany and Nicaragua were given their last rites, Miami's anti-Castro enthusi-

asm turned into euphoria – so much so that police began to plan for the possibility of Castro's fall and the inevitable wild street party.

But Miami's Cuban community is still waiting. In 1996, when Cuban MIG fighters shot down two planes, killing four Cuban-Americans, Castro said he was defending his air space. Three years later he found renewed energy – but was the object of sustained local hatred – in the eight-month custody battle over 6-year-old refugee Elián González.

More than four decades of dictatorial rule on the isolated tropical island have left their mark. When Fidel Castro finally fades into history, it will take Miami many years to recover from the most passionate hate affair it has ever had. ❏

THE MAGIC CITY

Since the early 1980s Miami has grown in stature and sophistication. South Beach is seriously hip and the city's Cubans are playing an ever-bigger role

Miami had had a bumpy year in 1980. But the city had been down before and it never lasted long. This time was no exception. It soon began to make headlines for reasons other than the frequent drug stories. In 1982 the *Wall Street Journal* referred to its business as "bustling." The next year *House and Garden* magazine called Miami "magical." A $3 billion building boom was underway downtown. But none of this captured the nation's imagination as much as the TV debut of *Miami Vice*, on September 16, 1984. The hit show's slick style glamorized Miami life and people flocked to the city to experience it for themselves.

Miami passed a political milestone in 1985 when its citizens elected Xavier Suarez as its first Cuban-born mayor. The new open-air Bayside Marketplace attracted tourists and shoppers. Metrorail and Metromover facilitated transportation to, from and around downtown. Even the Pope came to town, visiting for two days in September 1987 as part of his US tour.

Miami became a sports fan's paradise, as the new Miami Arena welcomed a professional basketball team, the "Miami Heat," with sell-out crowds. Key Biscayne hosted tennis luminaries at the Lipton Tournament, and every spring downtown reverberated with noise and excitement as Grand Prix race cars roared through the streets. The University of Miami basked in the limelight as its football team took the national championship three times in the decade: 1983, 1987 and 1989. Joe Robbie Stadium (now called Pro Player Stadium) opened in the fall of 1987 and hosted the Super Bowl in January 1989.

Future promise

Miami entered the 1990s with a new sense of self. The skyline had suddenly become beautiful. South Beach's Art Deco district was experiencing a comeback. People were even coming back to downtown – for sports, culture and fun.

But most of all, for the first time in years – possibly the first time ever – Miami had a feeling that it was coming into its own.

No longer just sun and fun, Miami was beginning to be taken seriously. As the world became smaller and political changes that were unthinkable a short time earlier unfolded daily, Miami's

rather rapid transformation into a diverse, international metropolis gave the rest of the nation a preview of what to expect in the 21st century.

The city thrived thanks to an influx of Europeans, South Americans, Canadians, Japanese and others, who saw South Florida as one big investment opportunity. In addition to winter homes, they invested in hotels, restaurants and businesses. Tourism continued to grow.

Then, on August 24, 1992, Hurricane Andrew paid a visit and left its mark, destroying thousands of homes and causing billions of dollars in property damage. It was the costliest natural disaster ever in American history. The disaster, though, brought Miamians together. It peeled

LEFT: Miami Dolphins fans show their appreciation at Pro Player Stadium. **RIGHT:** Gloria Estefan in concert.

away many layers of differences and placed everyone in the same boat, with no water, no electricity and no air conditioning.

In 1994 another wave of Cuban rafters and Haitian refugees headed for Miami, and the city struggled to cope with the influx as it faced financial trouble. Many of Miami's wealthier and non-Spanish speaking residents decided enough was enough and headed north. But Miami still hung on.

South Beach continued its renaissance and was making big waves in the tourism industry. Fashion models, photographers, and trendsetters elbowed each other for space at Ocean Drive cafes and bars. Limousines and convertibles competed for parking spaces. Gianni Versace bought a choice property on the drive, and lived here until he was gunned down on the street in 1997. Other celebrities, from Madonna and Gloria Estefan to Jack Nicholson and Cameron Diaz, hung out in South Beach.

The music industry discovered the appeal of the local Latin sound and hometown diva Gloria Estefan and her Miami Sound Machine made it big. Her marriage to Emilio Estefan created a Latin music giant that can now make or break new stars in the business. The word was out that Miami was a great place to be.

1990s DECO

Art Deco hotels such as the Colony and the Leslie, built in the 1930s and '40s, were the first stars of South Beach. In the 1990s, though, movie stars brought their own luster to the district, making it the hippest tropical playground for the rich and famous. In their wake, developers have rushed to renovate the Deco hotels. Many of them, purists say, have sacrificed historical integrity for designer fancy.

The Delano, originally built in 1947, was controversially renovated in 1995 by glam hotelier Ian Schrager and badboy Parisian designer Phillipe Starck. While Schrager and Starck preserved the exterior, they radically changed the interior, covering the lobby's terrazo with planks of cherry, enclosing the mezzanine, ripping out the skywalk and demolishing more than half of the ballroom.

Others, like the 1939 Albion and the 1936 Tides, have retained the original architecture, while the 1939 National compromises, with an original chandelier in the dining room and a new glass tile reproduction of Woman in the White Gloves, a famous painting of the era, on the lobby ceiling.

In 1998, Todd Oldham redesigned the 1939 Tiffany and changed its name to The Hotel when the famous jeweler threatened to sue. The lobby features a fawn-colored terrazo floor, velvet-dressed windows and a huge mosaic mirror. Atop the hotel, Oldham put in a gem-shaped pool.

Cuban-American traumas

What Gloria and Emilio were doing in the arts, other Cuban-Americans were accomplishing in politics and business. Cuba, though, and what it represents, were still kept at arms length. The wounds were still too raw after 40 years of exile, and performers from the island only 90 miles (145 km) south of Key West were still not welcome in the city. Miami's Cubans lived by the words "never forget." Thus, they were ready to declare war when Castro's MIG fighters shot down four Cuban-American flyers in 1995. The young Miamians belonged to *Hermanos al Rescate* (Brothers to the Rescue), a group of pilots who scanned the Florida Straits searching for rafters fleeing Cuba's hardships. The incident forced President Clinton to put the brakes on efforts to loosen the four-decade-old trade embargo.

> **CUBAN NOTABLES**
>
> In 1999, the president of Miami's largest bank, the owner of the top real estate developer, the head of the biggest law firm and two of Florida's six members of Congress were all of Cuban descent.

Jorge Mas Canosa, a prominent Miami businessman whom many predicted would try to make Cuba into a capitalist paradise after Castro's demise, never got to see that dream come true. In 1997 he died aged 58, following an "American-dream" rise from refugee to power broker. His funeral was a major event, attracting thousands. His legacy is the powerful Cuban American National Foundation, which lobbies Congress for democratic changes in Cuba. The success of his telecommunications company symbolized the progress many first-generation Cubans were making in the booming city.

In 1999, the CANF occupied a prominent spot when a six-year-old Cuban boy named Elián González was found at sea and quickly captured the spotlight. Mas Canosa's son, Jorge Mas Santos, who inherited the mantle of exile leadership from his father, could be seen directing Elián's Miami relatives as they bid to keep the boy from returning to his father in Cuba. It was another opportunity to stick a finger in Castro's eye. Once again, Miami's Cubans lost that fight against their arch nemesis, as federal agents stormed the Little Havana home where Elián had lived for five months and seized the boy. He was eventually returned to Cuba in June 2000.

LEFT: the late Gianni Versace's villa on Ocean Drive in Miami Beach. **RIGHT:** a Cuban-American mourner at Jorge Mas Canosa's funeral in 1997.

In the meantime, the fallout from the Elián affair was as destructive as a bomb. Cubans, feeling betrayed by Washington, protested at the federal government's action by taking to the streets waving hundreds of Cuban flags. Whites and blacks organized their own protest, flying the Stars and Stripes. Ethnic differences that had been simmering were suddenly being brought to the surface. Thousands wrote letters to the newspaper, both for and against the seizure. It was a community catharsis, an exercise in true

democracy. Cuban-Americans began publicly to voice their roles in Miami. In later protests, American flags were more prevalent than Cuban flags. In just a few weeks, the community took a step from exile to immigrant.

The city was reinventing itself, once again. And again, it would blossom from the ashes of another painful episode. The outlook is bright. Lavish development projects continue, cruise ships fill the port and tourists fill the shops and restaurants. In 2000, South Beach was named best urban beach in the US. At night the downtown skyline, its colors reflected in Biscayne Bay and the Miami River, shows a city that has come a long way in a short time. ❏

THE MANY FACES OF MIAMI

Miami's geographical position has made it a haven for Caribbean and Latin American immigrants. Ethnic diversity is what makes the city buzz

What is perhaps most distinctive about Miami among American cities is the peculiar role ethnicity has played in shaping, and even dominating, the social, economic and political landscape of the city. Delving into Miami's ethnic dynamics is not an excursion into the world of quaint foreign customs and interesting immigrant subcultures at the margins of the city. Rather, it is to reach into what has become the soul of Miami. Ethnicity is at the core of Miami's uniqueness.

For those familiar with the long history of immigration and ethnicity in the United States, a visit to Miami may well prove unsettling, or at least puzzling. Many of the expected patterns do not materialize. The rules of the game appear – and indeed are – different. What is supposed to be a marginal and struggling minority is a dominant and successful majority. What is "foreign" is commonplace, what is "native" is hard to find. The newcomer feels at home, while the established resident feels alienated. Miami's actors do not play their expected roles. Some regard it as the world of immigrant America turned upside down. Others view it as a preview of what the rest of the United States will soon become. It might be both.

Cuban presence

There are few who would argue with the premise that it is the Cubans who are primarily responsible for Miami's unique ethnic character. The "Cubanness" of contemporary Miami is evident not only in demonstrable terms, such as economic activities and cultural events, but also in a more intangible manner, an "ambience." David Rieff, a New Yorker who has written on Miami, observed that Cubans have largely taken control of the "atmosphere" of the city.

There is a demographic basis for the role of the exiles from Castro's Cuba. Persons born in

Cuba or of Cuban descent represent Miami's largest ethnic group by far, larger than the white native-born English-speaking population. Those born in Cuba account for 60 percent of metropolitan Miami's foreign-born population, and persons of Cuban origin constitute the bulk – nearly 70 percent – of all Latin Americans in

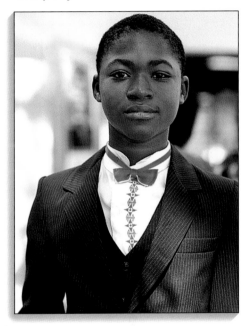

the area. More than a third of the population of Greater Miami is of Cuban birth or descent. The Cuban community of South Florida exceeds 800,000.

Its growth has been fueled not only by migration from the island, but also by the increasing concentration of Cubans from other parts of the United States. Miami is the capital and mecca for US Cubans, to the point now where more than half of the Cuban immigrant population lives in South Florida.

But the importance of the Cuban community for Miami is not just a question of numbers. It also has to do with the very nature of that community. At the heart of Cuban Miami is entre-

PRECEDING PAGES: lounging in the Florida sun; a family returns from a day at the beach.
LEFT: Bahamian beauty at the Goombay Festival in Coconut Grove. **RIGHT:** Haitian boy in Sunday finery.

preneurship, plenty of it and of many different types. Of all US cities, Miami has by far the largest number, per capita, of Hispanic-owned businesses. Many of those businesses are small family-run operations while others are large corporations. They range from the typical ethnic businesses – such as restaurants and grocery stores – to professional and financial services. The basis of such a community was established largely by the wave of Cuban exiles that arrived in the early 1960s, those who were among the first to feel alienated by the island's rapid transformation from a capitalist to a socialist system. First in the exodus were the

But business ownership among Cubans is not confined to retail. It also extends to wholesale trade, financial and professional services, manufacturing, construction and commerce. Cubans are very present in the public sector, too. For example, Miami-Dade's mayor and the heads of several county departments are all Cuban-Americans, as are the leaders of many of the municipalities within the county.

The wide variety of self-employment that flourishes in the ethnic community has led to the creation of a true enclave, an institutionally complete ethnic community. Such a community makes it possible for the immigrant to live

entrepreneurial, managerial and professional sectors; those who possessed skills and attitudes that would ease their entry into self-employment in the United States. To put it simply, as one sociologist once did, they had experience in the "art of buying and selling."

The importance of entrepreneurship among Cubans in Miami is evident driving along SW Eighth Street, Flagler Street, or some of the main roads in Hialeah. Countless small businesses line the streets, many concentrated within small shopping centers. Restaurants and cafeterias, grocery stores and fruit stalls, flower shops, drugstores, boutiques, barbershops and beauty salons, and even jewelry stores abound.

out his or her entire life, if desired, entirely with like-minded people. Unlike most ethnic neighborhoods whose residents must go outside of it to satisfy many of their needs, Miami's Cubans can literally go from cradle to grave existing entirely within the confines of their community. There is no shortage in Miami of Cuban pediatricians and funeral directors, and everything in between.

Along with this goes a unique set of implications for Miami's social climate. A strong ethnic enclave is largely responsible for the "Cubanization" of Miami's "atmosphere." It also has a number of consequences for the relationship between Cubans and other ethnic groups.

Bilingual blues

The characteristics of the Cuban enclave largely shape what is the most evident ethnic issue – or perhaps battlefield – in Miami: language. Because of the institutional completeness of the Cuban community, Spanish is a very public language. It is heard everywhere, and is literally in Miami's air – on radio and television waves. There are myriad Spanish-language radio stations on both the AM and FM dials, and two television networks transmit exclusively in Spanish.

> ### CARNIVAL TIME
>
> The biggest Cuban festival in Florida is a gigantic party along Calle Ocho through Little Havana in March – a mixture of cultural and religious celebration and old-fashioned Cuban-style carnival.

vokes as much controversy – and acrimony – in Miami. It is no coincidence that the movement to make English the official language in the United States was born in Miami. In 1980, after the Miami-Dade County Commission passed an ordinance officially declaring the county bilingual, a grassroots citizens' movement succeeded in passing a referendum to abrogate the ordinance and require that the county's public documents and publicly supported events be in English. Years later, in

In most immigrant communities, the language of the country of origin is the language of intimacy, spoken only among family and friends. But in Miami one can conduct the entire spectrum of one's affairs in Spanish, from shopping, banking, working and recreational activities to obtaining specialized professional services.

It is precisely this widespread and public use of Spanish that has raised the issue of bilingualism. No other issue related to ethnicity pro-

1988, Florida voters overwhelmingly approved a constitutional initiative to declare English the official language of the state.

For most Cubans in Miami, the anti-bilingualism movement is of little consequence or relevance. The enclave is built on self-employment and private enterprise. It is a community that works primarily in the private sector, beyond the reach of the ambiguous language requirements imposed on government business. The tendency of the immigrants to speak Spanish, the *lingua franca* of the enclave, has not been affected. Consequently, the use of Spanish in public has not been officially curtailed and continues to be a major irritant to many English

LEFT: the white faces of Miami Beach, shooting the breeze at Ocean Drive's News Cafe.
ABOVE: sisters in Little Haiti.

speakers in the city. Complaints are frequently aired by those who do not speak Spanish that they cannot understand what is being said in stores, offices and crowded elevators. Those complaints transcend linguistics and have more to do with the broader question of feeling at home in one's city and one's country. Those who are supposed to be the natives, the established residents, feel as if they are outsiders, while the newcomers feel at home. And so one common response has been "Anglo flight." The white non-Latin population of Miami-Dade County has declined dramatically in the past two decades.

But the Cubans do feel at home. With the exception of the elderly and the new arrivals from the island, many Cubans in Miami are fully bilingual. There is a sense that this is "their city." There are, as one would expect, dramatic inter-generational differences within the Cuban community in the use of language. The younger generation shows a marked preference for English, a phenomenon that parents have largely encouraged because it remains the language that must be mastered if one is ambitious and planning to enter the professional and managerial worlds. But the retention of Spanish, even as a second language, is also useful in

THE ELIAN CONTROVERSY

Miami hasn't been the same since November 1999, when a six-year-old boy, Elián González, was plucked from the sea and handed to relatives in Miami's Little Havana. He and his mother had fled Cuba on a raft, but she had drowned.

To Cuban-Americans, he represented their quest for freedom and they refused to let him return to Cuba, where his father and the rest of the island wanted him back.

When the US government seized Elián from his Miami relatives five months later, the city was left deeply divided. On one side were Cuban-Americans who saw this as freedom against communism, good versus evil. To them, sending Elián back was handing him over to a ruthless

dictator. On the other side were whites, called Anglos, and African-Americans. To them, a son belongs with his father.

After the raid, Miami's Cubans took to the streets. They waved Cuban flags and tried to burn the US flag. Anglos and blacks mounted their own protests supporting the government. They called the Cubans, who are automatically granted asylum once they touch land, ungrateful.

The city's multi-ethnic fabric was tearing apart. The mayor, a Cuban-American who opposed Elián's siezure, fired the Anglo city manager. The police chief resigned. Anglos began to call Miami a banana republic. Eventually Elián was returned to Cuba, but anger continued to bubble in the city.

getting ahead in Miami. Its retention is based not so much on immigrant nostalgia as it is on the economic realities of a bilingual Miami. This is different from the experience of other immigrants in the United States, for whom their native language was expendable in the process of adjustment.

Hispanic advantage

In Miami, there is an economic advantage to being Cuban and speaking Spanish. Within the community, an ethnic network helps in the search for employment, the establishment of business and professional contacts and the creation of opportunities for self-employment.

It has been argued that the enclave is as much a cause as it is a consequence of the much-touted "Cuban success story." The economic vitality of the community was a major factor in the eventual economic integration of the large influx that arrived from Cuba in 1980 during the famous Mariel boatlift. Many of the new arrivals were able to get their first jobs in the US largely through the ethnic network and within a familiar language and culture.

To a large extent, the economic benefits of the enclave extend to those immigrants who are not Cuban but speak Spanish. The community established by the Cubans has served as the entry into the US labor market for many Central and South Americans who represent a growing segment of Miami's Hispanic population. Although there continues to be small-scale migration from Cuba, many of the entry-level jobs in the enclave are now largely being filled by non-Cuban Latins. It is typical, for example, to find that the waitresses in a Cuban restaurant are Nicaraguan, Salvadoran or Colombian.

The increasing mixture in the national origins of Miami's Latin American community is becoming more and more evident in the proliferation of retail businesses that cater to specific national clienteles: restaurants, cafeterias, bakery shops, and so on. Entrepreneurship is no longer limited to the Cubans. The Colombian pastry shops and the Nicaraguan restaurants are

COLOMBIAN TUNES

In contrast to ten years earlier, the most popular radio station in Miami at the end of the 20th century played predominantly Colombian, not Cuban, music.

found primarily in Little Havana, Sweetwater, West Miami-Dade and Hialeah, the same areas where Cubans are concentrated.

The black community

If it can be said that Cubans and other Latin Americans are fairly well integrated, economically and spatially, with each other, the same cannot be said about the relationship between Miami's Latin Americans (including Cubans) and African-Americans. Accounting for about 18 percent of the population of Greater Miami,

African-Americans live in one of the most racially segregated cities in the US. Miami's black neighborhoods are not "predominantly black"; they are black. And there is considerable physical distance between them and almost every other ethnic group.

The physical segregation is compounded by an undeniable social distance. In many US cities, especially in the Northeast and the Midwest, there is an evident solidarity between Latins and African-Americans. They usually share a political agenda and have been successful in combining their strengths at the polls to elect sympathetic candidates.

This is not the case in Miami. There is little

LEFT: a Puerto Rican woman at a street-food counter in Little Havana. **RIGHT:** practicing for the catwalk in North Miami Beach.

political and social integration between Latins and African-Americans, no shared sense that they have overlapping concerns. The explanation probably rests on the immigrant character of Miami's Latins. In other US cities, where Mexican-Americans and/or Puerto Ricans comprise the bulk of the Latin population, there is an emphasis on issues that are typical of a "minority" agenda: public housing, access to education and public services, employment, etc.

The "minority" worldview predominates – that is, the view that the dominant society discriminates against members of the minority and that there are entrenched barriers to the advance-

African-Americans and to make even more acute their sense of powerlessness. (This ethnic tension became deadly in 1980 when riots broke out in the African-American neighborhood of Liberty City over the acquittal of Hispanic police officers who were accused of killing black insurance agent Arthur McDuffie.)

Haitians in Miami

An immigrant orientation is one of the factors that differentiates foreign-born blacks in Miami from native African-Americans. The Haitians are the most numerous of the foreign black community, numbering in excess of 200,000.

ment of racial and ethnic groups. These are concerns and views shared with African-Americans and are an expected response to many decades and generations of discrimination.

Miami's Latins, however, are recent immigrants. They have not accumulated the experiences that would lead them to think like members of minority groups. They came here because they believe this place is a better place than where they came from. Their view of US society is a positive one: a land of opportunity and political freedoms. There is little basis for embracing a minority agenda and identifying with the plight of African-Americans. This, of course, serves to further isolate Miami's

WHAT MIGHT HAVE BEEN

The whole of South Florida might have been a black community had a plan of the post-Civil War's Freedmen's Bureau worked out.

The bureau, which was responsible for helping black people adjust to emancipation, devised several plans for deeding land to people who had been enslaved. One suggested that the bottom half of Florida, then virtually uninhabited, be set aside for homesteaders. The plan called for 50,000 former slaves from Virginia to be relocated on 500,000 acres (200,000 hectares) of federal land in South Florida. The scheme never materialized, but a limited homesteading program was approved.

Little Haiti is perched on the southeastern territorial limits of Liberty City.

Although Haitians, as blacks, have been subjected to much prejudice and discrimination, especially in negative treatment by the US Immigration and Naturalization Service, they still share many patterns with immigrants in Miami that are distinct from African-Americans. The most evident is the importance given to self-employment and entrepreneurship. The business district of Little Haiti exemplifies this. During the 1970s the area became predominantly black and during the 1980s those blacks were increasingly Haitian. The neighborhood began to appear

men are energetic and optimistic. They envision Little Haiti becoming another Little Havana or San Francisco-style Chinatown. It is hoped that the only Little Haiti in the US will become a cultural and tourist attraction based on the Haitians' drive and enthusiasm and their unique cultural attributes – world-renowned painting, wood crafts, music, French-inspired cuisine, architecture and numerous skilled trades.

While Little Haiti is far from reaching this goal, the modest accomplishments of Miami's Haitian entrepreneurs remain a notable development even in an area that is well accustomed to rapid and spectacular growth. Most signifi-

neglected. Previously crowded stores were empty and streets littered. Tumbledown houses with absentee owners showed the wear of years without care. In the last half of the 1980s, however, change unfolded. Little Haiti began to take shape as an enclave of Caribbean culture. The area's vivid tropical colors and community pride are now most evident in the folk murals seen throughout Little Haiti, especially along NE Second Avenue and NE 54th Street.

The Haitian community leaders are both businessmen and political organizers. The business-

cantly, these achievements have come in spite of profound obstacles. Miami's Haitians are one of the most persecuted and suffering of immigrant groups in the US. While Cubans have always been encouraged to come to Miami and have received substantial government assistance, Haitians have always been rejected. The government has labeled them as economic refugees, in contrast to the Cuban political refugees.

In reality, the conditions and motivations impelling both the Haitian and Cuban flows are similar: underdevelopment, desires to improve oneself and political repression. For reasons of US foreign policy and racism, Haitians have not been welcomed into Miami.

LEFT: Hispanic girls having fun at Bayside Marketplace. **ABOVE:** corn-row coiffure.

But Haitians have resisted US governmental efforts to send them back to their island, and with the assistance of organizations and lawyers they have achieved partial victories. Few have been deported, and a community has gradually emerged. For a while they were identified as one of the main sources of Aids. Subsequent research revealed that Haitians were not a primary at-risk group and that Aids was probably first imported to Haiti from the US by so-called "sex-tourists". Haitian refugees are also commonly perceived as desperately poor, illiterate and unskilled.

The facts are that recent Haitian immigrants to Miami are much like any other immigrant

Exile politics

The absence of a minority-group orientation is, of course, especially acute among Cubans who perceive themselves as political exiles and who disproportionately represent Cuba's pre-revolutionary elite. Their agenda has been characterized by a concern with affairs of the homeland, with only secondary interest in "immigrant" issues, and much less in "minority" issues.

There is little basis for the perception of a common ground between Cubans and African-Americans. This was painfully evident when the results came in for a special election to

group: better off, more educated and more skilled than their typical countrymen back home. Moreover, there's a significant middle and even upper-class group of Haitians in Miami. Some came directly from Haiti, but most are secondary migrants, coming to Miami after living often 20 years or more in New York, Boston, Montreal or some other northern city. They are usually fluent in English, college educated and the business owners and political leaders of the community.

The black Jamaican community, another sizable group in the city, also shows more similarities to Latins than to African-Americans, being highly educated and financially successful.

select a successor to the late US Congressman Claude Pepper, a longtime Miami Democrat. More than 90 percent of the Cubans voted for one of their own, a conservative Republican who won the election, while more than 90 percent of the Black voting precincts went for the Democratic candidate.

The distinctly "exile" political culture of the Cubans is yet another wrinkle in the ethnic fabric of Miami. The staunchly anti-Castro and anti-communist views of Miami's Cubans represent their most visible trademark. It is this political militancy that frequently attracts national attention to the Cuban community. It is regarded as a conservative and right-wing community with deeply felt opinions about the political status of the homeland and an intolerance of opposing viewpoints.

Jewish presence

The decidedly conservative bent of the political culture of Cuban Miami is frequently a source of distancing and tension with another, older, ethnic group in the area. The elderly and predominantly Jewish community that has long settled in South Florida after retirement in the Northeast has usually been characterized by strong liberal and civil libertarian traditions that contrast with the conservatism of the Cubans.

the horrors that were about to strike in Europe.

Others came to salvage the wreckage left over from the 1926 real estate bust and the hurricanes that followed. And still others were galvanized by the idealism and romanticism of being a part of something new.

Many of Miami's early Jewish institutions still stand: Beth David, Miami's first synagogue (originally B'nai Zion), founded in 1912; Temple Israel, one of the most beautifully designed Reform temples in America, erected in 1927; and Beth Jacob, Miami Beach's first synagogue, which opened in 1929. The birth of these synagogues helped mold the Jewish com-

The handful of early Jewish settlers tended to be Key Westers in pursuit of employment and Northerners in search of better health. One such pioneer family was that of Joe and Jennie Weiss who moved to Miami Beach in 1913 and would soon after open the landmark Joe's Stone Crab restaurant. But it was not until the inter-war years that Miami's Jewish community developed a prominent profile. The promise of land booms, natural beauty and employment drew many to the city. Some came in order to escape

LEFT: Jewish retirees tell stories of days gone by.
ABOVE: herb and grocery vendors, entrepreneurs in Little Haiti.

munity and spawn the growth of other Jewish organizations, as well as periodicals such as the *Jewish Floridian*, which served the Jewish community from 1928 to 1990. In addition to these historic temples, the old Miami City Cemetery has a Jewish section full of ornate tombstones that date back to the early 1900s.

Community acceptance

Just as World War II changed the contours of Europe, so it changed the map of Miami. With the US Supreme Court outlawing covenants that discriminated against Jews and promulgating a series of rulings promoting the rights of minorities, Miami Beach began to attract

Jewish property developers. The building of the Fontainebleau Hotel in 1954 by Ben Novak and his architect Morris Lapidus appeared to many to crown Miami Beach's reputation as the winter playground for American Jews. Soon after, Yiddish became a Beach staple along with Kosher butchers and Hebrew classes.

In the late 1950s Jews began to move out of Miami Beach and into other areas of the city and further up the Florida coast. More comfortable with themselves and with their inte-

> **SNOWBIRDS**
>
> Senior citizens who come to Florida from northern states every winter are called "snowbirds," because they follow fowl that fly southward for the winter months and return north in the spring.

gration in Miami, a new generation emerged. Communities were formed and leaders weaned. Shepard Broad was a leader of this generation. Broad, a migrant from New York, built Bay Harbor Islands and at the same time was instrumental in the purchasing of ships locally that would eventually be donated to the state of Israel when it was in need of a navy. He also helped build a synagogue on the former site of the Nautilus Club's polo grounds from which Jews had been excluded in earlier years.

The 1960s brought more of the same. Meyer Lansky, reputedly the Mafia's Jewish *consigliere*, walked his dog along Collins Avenue unrecognized. Miami's Jewish population exploded with Jews from the Northeast seeking vacations in the South and Cuban Jews fleeing Fidel Castro's take-over. Miami's 10,000-strong Jewish Cubans remain an enigma. Locked in a subculture that exhibits their most recent experience, they remain loyal Cubans to the point of voting Cuban over Jewish in local elections. Although they have built several congregations, they remain apart from the Miami Jewish community.

Today, in the winter season, Miami is the capital for Jewish-American as well as Israeli events. Comedians regularly fly down from the North to visit their moms. Teenagers come to visit their grandparents. After their much ado in Washington, Israeli politicians relax and gather support in Miami. Local radio stations offer Israeli/Hebrew programs featuring Yiddish music, and cable television stations broadcast a choice of Jewish cultural shows.

A city still in the making

Miami is a new city, one that developed entirely in the 20th century. Appropriately, its immigrant groups are also new. The Cubans, who largely set the tone for the ethnic character of the city, started arriving, in massive numbers, only within the past four decades, and the same can be said of virtually every other ethnic group. Yet, for a young city that was once a winter resort for wealthy transients, four decades is a long time. Cubans and other immigrants have come to form part of the city's "establishment" and to define the core of what Miami has become as it begins the 21st century.

While Miami's multi-ethnic character is at times conflictive and gives the appearance of a city divided along racial and ethnic lines, it also imbues the city with a unique and varied dynamism. Miami's ethnic groups have yet to demonstrate that they have been mixed into a salad, and much less a stew. Rather, Miami offers a wide selection of separate and distinct dishes. To visit Miami and its distinctive neighborhoods without becoming aware of its ethnic diversity is virtually impossible. Ethnicity permeates Miami. ❑

LEFT: Cuban grandmother.
RIGHT: Jewish man on his way to temple.

BODY CULTURE

More so than almost any other city in America, Miami aspires to the body beautiful. Here, if you've got it, flaunt it; if you haven't, buy it

Miami has always been a city in love with itself. It rests not on bedrock, but on a shallow sand spit of fantasy and flamboyance. Like the convertibles whisking tourists from Miami International Airport to the closest beach, this is a top-down, look-at-me, full-tilt metropolis. Look at the ice-blue glass towers along Brickell Avenue, each bank with its own sky-high logo as corporate ego. Look at the "Longest Conga Line In The World" bumping 23 blocks up and down Little Havana's Calle Ocho. It's spelled out right there in the tan lines: Miami is stalled in a perpetual Me Generation.

"It's Miami," went one recent, catchy booster jingle. "It's my Miami. And Miami's for me."

It figures. Like the great seasonal storms that whip through the Caribbean each summer, Miami has always been the eye of its own hurricane. Its winds suck in the curious from all points of the compass. To dreamers in New York and Bogotá alike, the city sends out its drum beat of self-promotion. And who gets seduced? A red-hot mix of Cubans and Haitians, Jewish immigrants and American blacks, Central American refugees and retirees from Cleveland.

It doesn't take them long to see that the place is as much a parade as it is a working city. In fact, it hits them right in the face. Which is precisely where the town's vanity first pops up.

Looking good

Miami is the land of the 120-minute nose job. At the film festival benefit one year, they auctioned off a complimentary face lift. Fat recycling and tummy tucks are big business, too. For over 30 years, the annual Cosmetic Surgery Symposium has drawn the *crème de la crème* of the world's plastic surgeons to Miami.

Miami shares with California the North American copyright on the fine art of Flaunting It. Calling attention to oneself is Miami's

PRECEDING PAGES: cycling near the surf. **LEFT:** posing on Ocean Drive. **RIGHT:** On South Beach, body consciousness knows no gender barriers.

favorite pastime; teenagers install 150-watt speakers in their car trunks, then blast music so loud it sets off school alarms. Then there's that ill-fated poster proposed for the tourist bureau, featuring a photo of a female snorkeler, taken from behind, *sans* bathing suit top. "Miami," it proclaimed. "See It Like A Native."

This love of self carries over into love of wealth. Status symbols – racing boats, self-cleaning backyard pools, fine Cuban cigars – are practically a cottage industry in South Florida. In the early 1990s, Miami was BMW's top growth market in the United States. Forever in capitalistic heat, every Miamian is a bit of a gold-toothed pimp. Some of the Miami "River Cops," on trial a few years back for ripping off drug dealers while on duty, appeared in court decked out in their finest gold neckware. Key Biscayne lifeguards, valets outside Joe's Stone Crab restaurant and steakhouse busboys in Little Managua drip with those same 10-carat icons of contemporary Miami. Miami is driven by a sort of underground economy of vanity. People go out on Saturday night to South Beach and Coconut Grove to see and be seen; grabbing a bite to eat is almost an afterthought. They schmooze in the skyboxes at Pro Player Stadium and loiter for hours at Little Havana's Domino Park for the same reason. Even the architecture here is pretentious and corny. There are minarets rising from Opa-locka's City Hall; there's Coral Gables' grandiose hole in the ground, the Venetian Pool, and there's the famous Atlantis, a condominium with a gaping hole in the side.

What gives? How on earth can a town where 5,000 people attend an annual festival dedicated

narcissism, a fine anesthesia for mortality, comes so naturally to Miamians. Maybe it's in the water. Then again, the town does sit on the youngest piece of land mass in all of America. Fisher may have known that when he called Miami Beach a place "where the old could grow young and the young never grow old."

Fisher arrived in South Florida with deep pockets and the prototype of the modern Miami man: part visionary, part exile, part huckster. By dredging his dreamland in a place eternally suspended between ocean and land, he set the tone that things here would never be what they seemed, always a little too superficial.

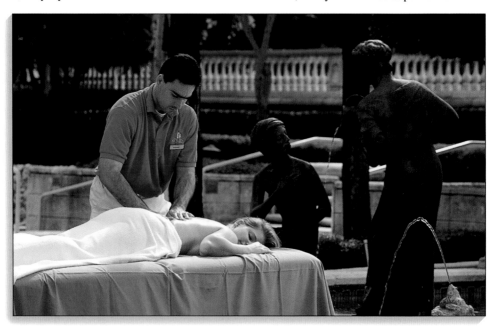

to nothing less than addiction to chocolate ever survive without suffocating on its own hedonistic excess?

History of hedonism

Just watch. Today, as in 1913 when Carl Fisher arrived to suck up enough muck from Biscayne Bay and create that perfect symbol of self-promotion, Miami Beach, this end of the Florida peninsula has made a cash crop of dreams, many of them too good to be true.

As far back as Ponce de León and his fabled "fountain of youth," people have always come to Florida to defy the aging process, and to pretend they'll never die. It's small wonder that

From the beginning, appeals to the ego were shameless. And the train was only leaving the station. Over the years, to a steady rattle of boom-bust, boom-bust, Miami has clung to its eternal present, a picture-perfect postcard of itself. "The whole creation of the Beach was to appeal to escape," publicist Hank Meyer once said. "You were dealing with subliminal suggestion – moods, desires, dreams, fantasies."

Miami's founders had plenty to work with, not the least of which was its weather. For

ABOVE: open-air massage at the Doral Spa.
RIGHT: toned stripper in a gay nightclub.
FAR RIGHT: mannequins tempt the fashion victim.

nearly a century, that average temperature of 75°F (24°C) has coaxed Americans into moving as far south as they could and starting over. It's easy to do: Miami's a flat, timeless place where seasons blur and the imagination soars. It's moist, warm, womblike. The search for the fountain of youth is still stuck in overdrive.

Bronze is beautiful

Here's a classic image: 20 elderly apartment dwellers, lined up in lounge chairs across the front deck of a 1930s hotel, eyes closed, faces skyward, each holding a reflecting fan just below the chin to catch the rays. Day in, day out, year after year, retirees and seasonal tourists spend hours at these altars practicing Miami's official religion: Sun Worship. Largely ignoring Florida's status as the state with the highest cancer rate in the United States, people keep going for the bronze.

Since so few clothes are necessary, skin here is also quite the status symbol. People even come here just to talk about it: Miami hosted the first International Congress of Esthetics, a meeting of beauticians who specialize in skin care. And the first thing visitors to Miami see, either driving in along Interstate 95 or leaving the airport, is a legendary, decades-old advertisement for

FASHION SHOOT CAPITAL

We've come a long way since the 1890s, when South Florida's founding mothers, undeterred by heat, humidity, insects and Native Americans, took to the beach in thick black stockings and closed-toed bathing shoes.

Now models are baring as much as possible for the annual swimsuit edition of *Sports Illustrated* or *Ocean Drive Magazine*. They come from all over the world and converge on South Beach and Coconut Grove, where the rich natural light perfectly reflects their youth and beauty. They're doing it for European catalogues, American stores, magazines and other outlets. It's hard to spend a day in Miami Beach without seeing at least one fashion shoot, especially in winter.

Portfolios under their arms, models strut up and down Ocean Drive on their way to castings. They get their signals from modeling agencies such as Elite Model Management, John Casablancas, Ford, Barbizon and many others.

However, before they strike a single pose and the camera starts clicking, they've got to do the rounds of casting calls, sometimes up to three a night during the season. About 25 percent of those calls result in actual jobs.

A typical shoot might start at 7am and last until sunset, with much of the day spent waiting around. During a good week in the peak winter season, a young model who may still be in school could earn over $10,000.

suntan lotion: a billboard featuring a puppy tugging at the swimsuit bottom of a cocoa-skinned toddler. "Tan. Don't Burn," the billboard says. "Use Coppertone."

The perfect body

Assuming one's tan is suitable for framing, a firm body is in order. Miami comes through: it's hard to jog along a city block without passing a tennis court, health-food store, golf course, martial arts school, yoga club, diet center, dance studio or workout gym. Bicycle and jogging paths

> **EXPENSIVE ITALIAN MUD**
>
> The luxurious and exclusive spa at the Doral Country Club flies in plankton-rich mud from hot springs in Italy to use as face-packs on its pampered guests.

line grand winding routes like Old Cutler Road and the causeway to Key Biscayne.

Rollerbladers by land, windsurfers by sea. They are members all of Miami's Sweat Set. But it's the almighty spa that bottles this *esprit de corps*. These cathedrals of callisthenics have mushroomed in the subtropical heat. There are even spas on the cruise ships that sail from the Port of Miami.

Flaunting it

Once tanned and taut, Miamians take to the streets. And beaches. And clubs. Topless bathing on Miami Beach, if not officially sanctioned, has become *la mode*. Dressed to kill, party-goers descend 5,000-strong on some South Beach and Grove nightclubs. One spot changes its decor every four or five months; owners say club-goers are easily bored. They dance all night in old Art Deco dance palaces, where intermission includes lingerie and swimsuit shows. At other nightspots, huge video screens project images of 2,000 people cramming the dance floor.

Men don't hold back either. One club owner is renowned for his collection of 60 pairs of shorts, often worn with tuxedo jacket and no socks. It's ego-dressing: the women don low-cut tops, silk nightgowns, skirts slit up to the thigh. Heavy on floral patterns, leopard skin and leather, worn tighter on the women than by the cows who made it possible. By day, fashion models stalk the town, but even non-fashion models are always posing. It's not uncommon to see Miamians carrying parrots on their shoulders, or even boa constrictors.

It's that kind of place. *Maître d's* are cult personalities. Fantastic arched bridges lead to luxurious residential islands. It was on one such island that one Arab sheik, His Royal Highness Prince Mohammed al-Fassi, threw up a garish mansion. With mosque. And bowling alley. Not only are streets here named for the showbiz stars of yesteryear – Arthur Godfrey, Jackie Gleason, Ed Sullivan – but also for the people who helped construct their fame. In 1984, even publicist Hank Meyer – assembly line foreman in this factory of dreams – got his name up there on a street sign.

They should have called it Me-ami. On one tiny stretch of the Grove, 18 sidewalk cafes give people 721 seats from where they watch everyone else. "We thought about getting entertainment," says one owner. "But we don't need it. People have people."

So it goes. Non-stop entertainment. Over a stage backdropped by fruit salad sunsets and palm tree props, the curtain has risen faithfully each dawn for 100 years. And there it stands, tongue firmly in cheek, hogging the spotlight – the show-off of American cities admiring itself in a full-length mirror.

Me-ami, indeed.   ❏

LEFT: happy hour cocktail at the end of the day.
RIGHT: the perfect piña colada.

'SHOPPORTUNITIES' IN PARADISE

Thousands of South Americans can't be wrong.
They flock to Miami to shop, and return home
exhausted and laden with bulging suitcases

Miami's mega-malls can be a day-long experience in an environment that weds shopping and entertainment. Food courts, multiplex theaters and hundreds of stores keep you stimulated and in a spending mood. All the major malls are anchored by national retailers. The largest, for now, is the Aventura Mall, in the northern part of the city. It has six major stores, including Lord & Taylor, Bloomingdales, J.C. Penney's and Sears. It is also home to the newest Burdines, the only department store founded in the city. The Falls, in southern Miami, was designed with water in mind. The shops are arranged beside waterfalls and rock-strewn pools. If money is no object, then there is the elegant Bal Harbour Shops. Here restaurants will even feed the poodles of Miami's moneyed set. Or try the cluster of fashionable shops around Collins Avenue and Seventh Street in South Beach. *(See pages 301–2 for mall locations.)*

TREASURE HUNTING

If you're looking for knick-knacks and bargains, there is the Opa-Locka Flea Market – an open-air bazaar of more than 1,000 booths where a shopper can find anything from jeans to plastic toys. Downtown's Flagler Street remains the mecca for shoppers looking for export-ready electronics and jewelry. Be wary, though. Some of the more than 300 stores have been known to switch merchandise while they pack your purchase in the back room. If you want to haggle, then you've come to the right place; otherwise you're better off at a big-name chain that has fixed prices and money-back guarantees.

▽ **VODOU AND SANTERIA**
Need spiritual help? You can find lotions, potions and statues to aid your prayers at *botánicas* in Little Havana and Little Haiti *(see page 225).*

△ **COCOWALK**
This mall is one of Miami's hangouts for the young, who come to shop for music and clothes, see a movie, grab a bite and sip on a margarita.

◁ **CASUAL CHIC**
For "ladies who shop" there are malls, designer boutiques and outlet shops all over Miami.

▷ **TUTTI FRUITY**
Ever since Julia Tuttle sent an orange blossom to Henry Flagler, Florida has been synonymous with fruit. Try an orange, pineapple or mango.

THE BEST OF MIAMI'S MALLS

⊲ **DOWN BY THE BAY**
Bayside Marketplace houses Hard Rock Cafe, the Disney Store and much more. Its plaza sees street performers and nightly entertainment.

△ **A GOOD SMOKE**
In Little Havana factories that recall Old Cuba, cigar aficionados can see their stogies being rolled and then come away with a souvenir box.

● Aventura Mall: recent expansion includes an outdoor piazza, a 24-screen theater and restaurants.
● Bal Harbour Shops: upscale boutiques – Tiffany, Gucci, etc. – and charming cafes in a lush setting.
● Bayside Marketplace: over 150 shops, restaurants and bars that stay open late in downtown Miami.
● CocoWalk: a cluster of bistros and boutiques with a village ambiance.
● Dadeland Mall: a collection of department stores and small shops, including Florida's largest Burdines.
● Dolphin Mall: opening in 2001, this is to be Miami's largest mall.
● The Falls: open-air mall around waterfalls, with over 100 shops, including Macy's and Bloomingdale's.
● Loehman's Fashion Island: a specialty mall, anchored by Loehmann's and Barnes and Noble.
● Prime Outlets at Florida City: this offers over 60 factory outlets with prices below regular retail levels.
● Streets of Mayfair: recently renovated, this popular mall offers an array of shops and restaurants and is home to the posh Mayfair House Hotel.

△ **BEYOND MIAMI**
Worth Avenue in chic Palm Beach is Florida's answer to Beverly Hills' Rodeo Drive. If you have to ask the price in the exclusive designer shops, you shouldn't be there.

▷ **END OF THE ROAD**
Key West is the place to go for those island-theme souvenirs – shells, flowered shirts, coconut ashtrays.

VICE AS VIRTUE

Over the years Miami's reputation for law and order has been far from spotless.

Recently, though, crime figures have fallen, and the city is getting safer

There was a time when crime defined Miami. It was the fertilizer for what someone once called "the Garden of America." That someone was the notorious mobster Al Capone. He knew what he was talking about. He and his chums milked a wide-open Miami for all it was worth. They muscled in on the illegal casinos and nightclubs. They scooped up politicians into their pockets like car keys. They ran the joint.

The town was risky then, rotten to its core. The underworld flourished above ground. Everyone looked the other way. No sweat. This was Miami. This was a kick.

Things haven't changed much. Today, as they did back then, people love living on the edge. Miami is America's edge, geographically and morally. And crime, in all its ghoulish glamor, keeps it there. There's a certain *laissez-faire* to living in these subtropics. That's not to say Miamians weren't embarrassed in 1981 when their city became Murder Capital USA and 621 people died violent deaths in the county.

Still, as major American cities go, Miami is as safe as the next, assuming one's not involved in drugs or looking for trouble – synonymous endeavors in this modern frontier town. In any given year, other cities may even be statistically more dangerous. It's just that Miami wears its crime like a cheap perfume. It's hard to ignore.

Nonchalance

The good citizens of Miami, despite living in a place where there's a sort of one-upmanship to criminal acts, have learned to carry on. Or maybe they're just jaded. In 1986, when 12 corpses were recovered from the rear of automobiles, you could almost hear county medical examiner Joe Davis's patience wearing thin: "There seems to be no let-up in people found in trunks. We've become used to it," the doctor mused.

PRECEDING PAGES: drug-sniffing police dog. **LEFT:** the unashamedly 1980s look of hit TV crime show *Miami Vice*. **RIGHT:** Chicago-style gangsters set the tone in Miami in the early 1930s.

As it entered a new millennium, Miami could certainly boast that it had seen it all:

● A proliferation of handguns – 220,000 sold between 1977 and 1981 alone.

● A crush of immigrants, first in the 1980 Mariel boatlift that landed 125,000 Cubans in Miami practically overnight, and later 50,000

Haitians and 75,000 Nicaraguans fleeing their respective rulers. That, added to what had long been not so much a "melting pot" as a "boiling pot" of bad vibes, spawned several major racial disturbances over two decades.

● A cocaine ring at Eastern Airlines that ran more than one ton of coke a week through the airport – a quarter of all the cocaine smuggled into the United States in 1985.

● A spate of attacks on tourists in the early 1990s that hit the headlines all round the world.

● The murder in 1997 of Italian fashion designer Gianni Versace, gunned down by Andrew Cunanan on the steps of his Miami Beach mansion.

But despite this latest high-profile murder, things have definitely improved in the city. The worst years were the 1980s and early '90s. Now, like a child of the hippy era who has tired of the parties, Miami has settled and matured. Don't be fooled, though, the fantasy is still around. But now it's more common for police to raid suburban homes where marijuana is being grown rather than shoot it out with cocaine cowboys.

When things were bad

In those earlier years of rampant crime there were a million telling tales from Sin City: one motorist fatally shooting another for making a left turn too slowly. A naked man arrested after he threw the severed head of his girlfriend at a police officer. A bar patron who was shot five times in the head – and survived. A health-spa prostitution ring. People robbed on the freeways. In their driveways. In their living rooms. Sometimes by intruders masquerading as cops. Even gory stories of people being fed to alligators.

Forget yellow journalism. This town's stories called for an entire rainbow.

Tying them all together were jaw-dropping statistics that could raise the dead: agents estimated that in the late 1980s there were 700 "free-base" houses in Miami-Dade and neigh-

SAFETY IN THE CITY

In the early 1990s, attacks on tourists in Miami were making the news worldwide. In one year, five of the 10 tourist killings in Florida took place in the city. In 1996, for example, a Dutch tourist was murdered after getting lost in the inner city and stopping to ask for directions.

It was a wake-up call for Miami officials. Police took extraordinary measures to beef up patrols and crack down on troublemakers. There was a concerted campaign to educate tourists and keep them away from unsafe areas.

Now, Miami is no more dangerous for visitors than any other metropolitan area in the US. But there are a few things to remember *(for more tips see page 281)*:

● Avoid neighborhoods that are generally not tourist destinations. If you must venture into one of these areas, go with someone familiar with the neighborhood.

● Being alone at night on the beach may seem romantic, but can invite robbery. In the daytime, don't leave valuables on the sand or beside the pool when you go for a dip.

● Remember this is a big city. For example, when changing money or using an ATM, be aware of your surroundings.

● When you're on the road, don't stop to help stranded motorists – that's the job of the Highway Patrol, who come to the rescue quickly – and don't pick up hitchhikers.

● Above all, use common sense.

boring Broward counties. In 1987, police seized 69,000 lbs (31,000 kg) of cocaine in the Miami area, worth $464 million, even at Miami's then relatively low wholesale price. In 1985, some $6 billion more in cash came in than left the Miami branch of the Federal Reserve. The Internal Revenue Service estimated that the average coke deal in Miami at that time netted at least $300,000.

COKE RAIDS

In one period during the 1980s the police busted an average of 13 cocaine-processing labs per year in South Florida.

Toss in crooked politicians, pot bales washing up on the beach, drug couriers ingesting and then smuggling condoms full of cocaine into the country, self-styled freedom fighters shooting bazookas off at Polish freighters and Russians trying to deal submarines to drug dealers, and suddenly, Miami's reputation as America's Casablanca made perfect sense. Bad news, right? Wrong. Just when things were getting really low down and dirty, just when the murder rate popped the national crime barometer in 1980 at no fewer than 70 homicides per 100,000 population, a funny thing happened.

Miami got hot. And not just weatherwise. In a curious about-face, the national critics were suddenly documenting a veritable renaissance unfolding at the foot of Florida. Just as they had loved kicking the city when it was down and out, the nation's journalists, now cheering on the underdog they had helped breed, rejoiced. Miami, they said, was "bouncing back."

Aided and abetted by the MTV-ish soundtrack and slick pastels of *Miami Vice* every Friday night, a new national consensus about Murder Capital USA was forged. But, although the hype was hip, it was only skin-deep. After all, the city was still located at that convenient crossroads for Caribbean and South American misadventures; and the city was still fermenting its unusual mix of dumb rednecks, macho Latins, scam artists and hotheads who couldn't hack it in the rest of the United States – people who had bailed out for balmier climates and the curious heritage Miami offered: anonymity and glistening acres of white sand.

Nowadays, the city's murder rate may have slipped from the top of the charts, but is it any place to spend a summer vacation?

LEFT: a mourner lays a wreath on the steps where Gianni Versace was shot dead in front of his villa.
RIGHT: a police motorcade.

A "safe" city

To find out, go to the experts. Edna Buchanan, *Miami Herald* reporter turned crime novelist, has said that "solid citizens who stay alert are usually safe. There are no tail-gunners on bread trucks. Life in Miami is simply life in the big city... nowhere near as bad as some people think." Buchanan should know. She won the coveted Pulitzer Prize for documenting over 5,000 violent deaths in 16 years.

Fact is, most deadly violence is either the result of domestic strife or a soured drug deal.

Fact is, a handful of neighborhoods are notorious for their street crime. By steering clear of them, visitors to Miami can leave safely on the same airplane they came in on.

A few years ago, the *Miami Herald* looked at each of the city's 438 homicides. The investigation revealed that most murder suspects were accused of killing someone they knew, and that police figured a third of them were drug-related.

There are experts, too, who say that not only are innocent bystanders safe in Miami – but they have never been safer. One local historian points out that the town's crime rate per capita in 1925 was three times greater than it was during the tumultuous 1980–81 era.

Such authorities, though, do have a point. In 1926, one in every 908 residents was murdered. Sixty years later, it was a mere one in every 2,600. The latest figures available for 1999 show Miami's murder rate as one in 5,797. Only 63 murders were recorded that year in the city and 200 in the county. At this rate, Miami may soon become the safest vacation bet in the world. Until then, the weirdness marches on.

It always has. This corner of the country has a legacy of violence. Long before Miami was legally incorporated in 1896, American forces waged a terrorist campaign to "liberate" Florida from the Indians and the independent souls who

had settled on the peninsula. To win Florida for the United States, Andrew Jackson massacred American blacks who had sought freedom here, then burned and destroyed Indian villages, strung up chiefs and brutally slaughtered Indian women and children.

Crimewise, it was downhill from then on. In the 1930s and '40s, thanks to such bootlegging bad boys from the Midwest as Al Capone, Miami really got a taste of what was to come over the next half-century. Mafia bosses, far from the bridle of those who knew their tricks, went on a feeding frenzy on the Beach. They bought up nightclubs and hotels and took over the gambling industry already in place.

Cocaine cowboys

Like the Mafiosi of the 1930s, the cocaine warriors of the 1970s received at least a *de facto* open-armed welcome in Miami. They were, like their predecessors, good for the bottom line. Yacht dealers took cash for $250,000 "cigarette" boats, sleek vessels equipped with radar scanners and infra-red night-vision scopes that were perfect for bringing in coke from "mother ships" offshore. Real estate experts bemoaned the fact that rich drug smugglers were buying up the land, especially prime waterfront lots, thus jacking up the cost of home-ownership for the law-abiding set. But they sold to them, nevertheless.

During the so-called "cocaine wars" in the late 1970s, some 35 drug killings were recorded in a single six-month stretch. But it was the infamous Dadeland Mall shoot-out in 1979 that made people take notice. In the heart of one of the county's most popular shopping centers, a bastion of suburban safety, drug war assassins sprayed 60 bullets into a liquor store, killing two and wounding another two bystanders. The getaway vehicle was nothing less than a war wagon, equipped with reinforced steel, gun portholes and bulletproof vests. Now *that* was a bit too much.

Then, there's the more recent case of Miguel Moya. He never smuggled a gram of cocaine in the United States, but was convicted in 1999 on charges of bribery, conspiracy, obstruction of justice, money laundering, tax evasion and witness tampering. He was the jury foreman who took a bribe to fix the case of Willie Falcon and Salvator Magluta, acquitted of drug smuggling in 1996 but later convicted of bond jumping, passport fraud and weapons charges.

Over the years, anti-crime groups have often become popular with residents. The tidal wave of crime that washed over Miami a few years back, most of it drug-related, also inspired countless solo acts of heroism and, its awkward bedfellow, vigilantism.

But the crime that dogged this town for the better part of six decades was never able to douse its spirit. Neither voodoo curses, baseball bats nor Uzi machine guns can stop this city from pulling through. In fact, the Miami mystique seems to thrive on chaos. ❑

LEFT: an officer accepts a snack.
RIGHT: gangster-style car parked on Ocean Drive.

The birdcage

ROBIN WILLIAMS
NATHAN LANE

A
MIKE NICHOLS
FILM

GENE HACKMAN
DIANNE WIEST

Come as you are

MIAMI IN FICTION

With a reputation as a modern-day frontier town painted over with glitz, Miami is a prime location for tales of lawbreakers, jet-setters and cross-dressers

More than sun and sand, Miami is full of good stories. Sitting on the edge of the continent, it is a place that has drawn all types, including the eccentric, the rich and the not so rich looking to make a fast buck. The lure of scantily-clad women, gambling and accessible drugs mixed with a palpable fear of something unknown, yet evil, in this foreign land within the United States' borders, has been a potent formula for suspense and intrigue.

The glimmer of infinite mischief has caught the eyes of writers and movie producers who have used the city's palm fronds and blue ocean as a backdrop for books, movies and television shows. On film, Al Pacino portrayed a Mariel refugee turned crazed cocaine boss in the 1983 version of *Scarface*. And the following year, Hollywood conferred star status on the city with the linen-and-pastel, oh-so-hip television series *Miami Vice*. It was hard to tell whether life was imitating art or the other way around. In real life, cocaine cowboys were shooting their way around Miami's highways. On television, two tie-less and sock-less undercover detectives, hair greased back, were fighting their share of the bad guys. The city fathers didn't seem to mind. In the fast-moving opening credits of *Miami Vice*, viewers could peek at fluttering flamingoes at Hialeah Racetrack, modern high-rises on Brickell Avenue and speeding cigarette boats on the glittering bay. It was priceless publicity.

Crime between the covers

The statistics have been going down steadily in recent years, but Miami's reputation as a city of sin, a place where the bizarre and exotic are commonplace, continues to be fodder for writers such as Edna Buchanan, Carolina Garcia-Aguilera, Carl Hiaasen, Dave Barry and Elmore Leonard, among many others.

Although Leonard lives in Detroit, one of his favorite settings for his best-selling novels is

---

LEFT: poster for South Beach cross-dressing movie *The Birdcage*. **RIGHT:** Elmore Leonard, who has set many of his hard-boiled crime novels in Miami Beach.

Miami Beach. He loves the edginess South Florida gives to his characters. His most famous novels set here include *Get Shorty*, *Maximum Bob*, *Swag*, *Gold Coast*, *The Switch* and *The Moonshine Wars*.

Carl Hiaasen, a columnist for the *Miami Herald*, has made an international name for

himself with his satirical, funny and off-beat works. Playing off Hurricane Andrew, former Florida governor Lawton Chiles walking across the state, greedy developers, wacky environmentalists and the state lottery, he has written *Stormy Weather*, *Skin Tight*, *Native Tongue*, *Strip Tease* and *Lucky You*.

Buchanan, the Pulitzer Prize-winning former *Miami Herald* police reporter, has summed up Miami's image in one of her books, *Miami, It's Murder*. Considered by some her best effort, her first book, *The Corpse Had a Familiar Face*, was based on her hardcore beat. In a *New Yorker* magazine profile of Buchanan, Calvin Trillin wrote, "In Miami, a few figures are regularly discussed by first name among people they have never actually met. One of them is Fidel. Another is Edna." She showed up at the 1999 Miami Book Fair sporting gold pistol earrings.

Other Miami-based crime novelists include Paul Levine and his Jake Lassiter series – *Mortal Sin*, *To Speak for the Dead* and *9 Scorpions*; James W. Hall's *Under Cover of Daylight* and *Body Language*; and Les Standiford's novels featuring building contractor John Deal – *Deal to Die For*, *Done Deal* and *Book Deal*.

Hollywood has been tapping into this well of South Florida-inspired creativity. Many of these books have been made into films, including Leonard's *Get Shorty* and *Rum Punch*, which became *Jackie Brown* on the silver screen, and Hiaasen's *Strip Tease*, among others.

Tinseltown, Florida

As early as 1919 D.W. Griffith saw the appeal of filming in South Florida. The well-known director of *The Birth of a Nation* set up cameras on Fort Lauderdale's New River to film his South Seas-themed *The Idol Dancer*. Half a century later Connie Francis was singing *Where the Boys Are* just blocks away at the Elbo Room in Fort Lauderdale, helping make the area a hot spot among college students on spring break.

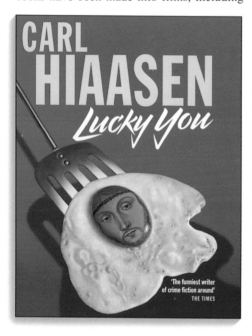

NAKED CAME THE MANATEE

Borrowing on the story-building children's game, in 1996 an editor at the *Miami Herald* came up with the idea of asking the city's best fiction writers each to pen a chapter of a story. The only requirement was that it be set locally.

Humorist Dave Barry kicked off and handed on to crime writer Les Standiford, who was followed by Carl Hiaasen, Elmore Leonard and nine other writers.

After the 13 installments were published, the novella *Naked Came the Manatee* was complete. The result was a romp across land and sea from Coconut Grove to Havana in pursuit of severed heads and a love-starved manatee. It was expanded into book form and published by Putnam.

Now it's hard to go anywhere and not see or be somewhere from a movie. Strolling down Miami Beach's Ocean Drive you're on the set of *The Birdcage* or the jogging path of Cindy Crawford in *Fair Game*. Drive across the MacArthur Causeway and you're where Jeff Goldblum had his flat tire and Eddie Murphy came to his aid in *Holy Man*.

Go for a drink at the Wreck Bar in the Sheraton Yankee Clipper in Fort Lauderdale. The giant aquarium may remind you of Billy Crystal and Robert De Niro's *Analyze This*. Or stroll down Hollywood's Broadwalk to the Hollywood Beach Theater. Seeing that bandstand and faded building may get you feeling a bit steamy if you saw the sultry Kathleen Turner and lustful William Hurt in *Body Heat*.

You can try your hand at hitting golf balls into the water just like Cameron Diaz did in *There's Something About Mary*. Go to the Aqua Golf Driving Range in Pembroke Park. You probably won't see Diaz or co-star Matt Dillon but the range's golf pro David Breslow will tell you about their swings. The building used for Diaz's apartment, now back to its run-down condition just a block off Biscayne Boulevard in down-

MIAMI FILM FESTIVAL

In early February, the Miami Film Festival puts on movies by up-and-coming local talent as well as international hits. It is held downtown at the Gusman Center.

Other films featuring South Florida include the Marx Brothers' *The Cocoanuts*, *Key Largo*, *Ace Ventura: Pet Detective* and three James Bond movies – *Dr No*, *Live and Let Die* and *Goldfinger*.

Small screen efforts

South Florida's TV history stretches over four decades, from Jackie Gleason's *Honeymooners* to the detective show *Surfside Six*, from Ivan Tors' *Flipper* and *Gentle Ben* to the glory days of *Miami Vice*. Those days ended in 1989 and other attempts to cap-

town Miami, sits looking out over Biscayne Bay.

True Lies, starring Arnold Schwarzenegger and Jamie Lee Curtis, featured the old Seven-Mile Bridge in the Florida Keys and a fighter jet protruding from a downtown office building. *Caddyshack*, the crude golf movie with Bill Murray and a gopher was filmed at the Grand Oaks Golf Club in Davie, just north of Miami. *Miami Rhapsody* with Sarah Jessica Parker includes a scene in the Bal Harbour Shops.

FAR LEFT: Carl Hiaasen is a popular local novelist. **LEFT:** Al Pacino in the 1983 remake of *Scarface*, set in Miami. **ABOVE:** John Travolta and director Barry Sonnenfeld on the set of *Get Shorty*.

ture them have not caught on. Other successful shows set in Miami have included *Golden Girls*, which portrayed four elderly women retired in South Florida; and MTV's *Real People*, among others. But in the 1990s, the area reinvented itself as a Latin American Hollywood, the production center for Spanish-language television shows aimed at Florida's southern neighbors.

But the Miami area still hasn't caught on as a true partner in the film and television industry. Some say the red-tape of dealing with the many municipalities is stifling, others say the pool of talent isn't as deep as that of west coast Hollywood. But there's still no substitute for the natural beauty of Miami and its beaches. ❑

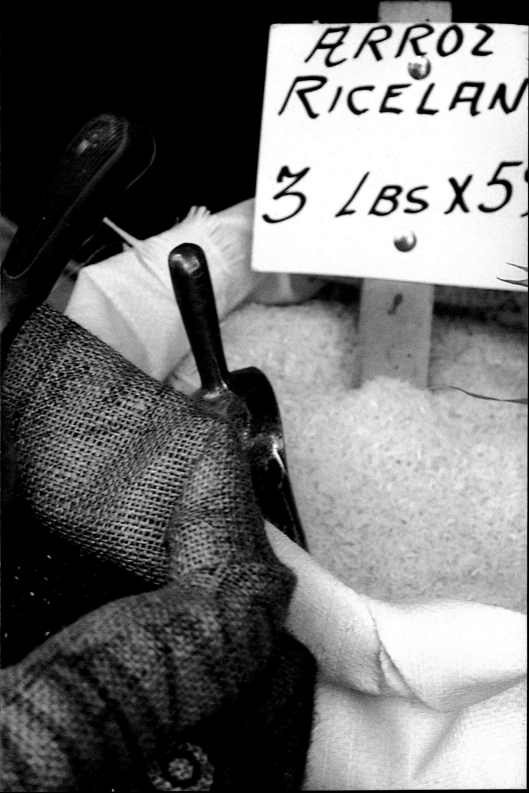

A TASTE OF MIAMI

Caribbean and South American culinary styles combine with seafood and fresh Florida produce to make eating in Miami a memorable experience

Dining out in Miami is like choosing a vacation destination. Name a country, name its cuisine. You can find it somewhere in Miami. The choice is overwhelming and mouthwatering.

One of the choices is Floribbean. That's the term coined to describe the unique flavors created by the gang of Miami chefs daring enough to invent a new taste. It's a fusion of Florida, Caribbean and Latin flavors. Mangos mingled with snapper and lemon grass; cilantro merged with curry, coconut and citrus. You'll find these mouth-watering treats at spots such as Chef Allen's, Norman's and Nemo.

Latin spices

A popular Miami flavor is that most humble of foods, the bean. Not just any bean, but the earthy black bean. Full of Spanish heritage, it is a basic of culinary Cuba. Poor man's food, beans and rice combine to a nearly perfect protein, the equal of red meat but without the fats. Black beans and rice cooked together is called *moros y cristianos,* after the famous collision of Charles Martel and the Arabs in AD 732.

The beans are also used in soup, in stews, served cold in salads, simmered with an onion and a bay leaf to be poured over rice as a side dish. In recent years cooks have drained cooked black beans, mashed them into a paste, flattened it and fried the result into black bean cakes, served with salsa and a dot of sour cream. Black beans are even found in stuffing. *Bolichemechado* is a beef dish stuffed with rice and beans.

Many foods identified with a culture often become clichéd, but in Miami young cooks improvize with the staples to produce gourmet Cuban food. This can be found at a few pricey spots such as Yuca on Lincoln Road and Victor's Cafe in Coral Gables. Elsewhere basic fare rules.

But Hispanic Miami is more than just Cuban cooking. The city's large Nicaraguan population has also spawned numerous restaurants. In the heart of Little Havana is Guayacan. The specialty of the house is steak, grilled and served with a pungent *chimichurri* sauce, made from parsley and garlic. Another is *pescado a la*

PRECEDING PAGES: black beans and rice, key ingredients of *moros y cristianos.* **LEFT:** Florida mangoes ripe for picking. **RIGHT:** oversized *paella* cooked up at the Calle Ocho Festival.

CUBAN ESSENTIALS

- *boniato:* a tasty tuber not unlike sweet potato.
- *carne asada:* roasted pork.
- *flan:* a dessert similar to creme caramel.
- *mojo:* a sauce made of oil, garlic, herbs and lime juice, often used as a meat marinade.
- *palomilla:* a thin steak with fried onions.
- *piccadillo:* minced beef with peppers and olives.
- *plátanos:* plantains – cooking bananas – sliced and fried as a side dish. Some prefer the sweeter *maduros.*
- *ropa vieja:* "old clothes" – shredded beef in tomatoes.
- *yuca:* the essential Cuban tuber, boiled or fried as a vegetable, or cut in chunks for stews.

Tipitapa, worth trying just so you can say the name when ordering. It's deep-fried red snapper drenched in an onion and pepper sauce.

Several Argentine restaurants also satisfy the beef-lover's palate. The *parrillada* is a treasure trove of meats hot off the grill – steak, chorizo, blood sausage, sweetbreads. Las Vacas Gordas in North Beach has the feel of a neighborhood restaurant in Buenos Aires filled with the smell and warmth of the wood-burning grill.

With a sexy samba beat playing in the background, try the Brazilian national dish, *feijoada*. It's a slow-cooked black bean stew full of pork loin and smoked sausage, accompanied by

tains and *griot* – fried pork chunks – that will fill you up for the rest of the day. Unlike Cubans, Haitians eat red beans with rice. Cooks from northern Haiti spice the bean sauce with cloves. Some might put more peppers in their version of *legume* – the standard vegetable stew. Whole red snapper can be had either fried, or cooked in a light tomato sauce with onions.

Or go upscale Haitian at Tap Tap in South Beach. Every inch of the place is covered with color, like a vibrant Haitian painting.

Jamaican food is hot and spicy. Try the jerk chicken, curried goat, oxtail stew and the famous patties, filled with meat and hot sauce.

farofa, sauteed ground *yuca*. Porcao off Brickell Avenue is where local Brazilians go.

One of Miami's little secrets is its authentic Mexican food found in the Homestead area. Even less known, but just as tasty is the Colombian fare, such as plantains cut in thick slices, fried and used to hold concoctions of meats, shrimps and sauces.

Island eats

The Caribbean islands have contributed a lot more than just Cuban cuisine. Haitian food in Miami is the best in the world. Little Haiti offers many storefront restaurants where for $5 you can get a plate of beans and rice, fried plan-

Bahamian restaurants serve butterfly fish with Johnny cake, the island's version of corn bread. Then there's lots of conch – the queen of the mollusks that inhabits a large spiral-shaped shell. Conch meat must be tenderized, usually with a severe beating, and is often further broken down by a soak in lime juice. But the result is delicious, slightly chewy but with a flavor unlike any other seafood. Cracked conch, a sort of conch cutlet, is breaded and then quickly fried, served sizzling hot with a wedge of lime. Conch also makes a superlative chowder and,

ABOVE: tasty morsels to go. **RIGHT:** sun-drenched peppers growing near Homestead, south of Miami.

for the faint of heart, can be disguised in fritters.

Even a cliché like Key lime pie, a dessert served everywhere in Florida, has a distinctive side. Originally made without refrigeration, consisting of little more than the juice of tiny, yellowish Key limes, eggs and sweetened, condensed milk, the pie must be yellow, not green.

Simmering seafood

Remember that nothing goes into this city's big pot without first being brought from some place else and the sea is the factor that binds it all together. The bounty making the leap from the Atlantic and the Gulf of Mexico to Miami's

kitchen is impressive. Look for fresh yellowtail, a smallish snapper with moist, elegant meat that doesn't have an abundance of bones. A ceviche, which is raw fish marinated in freshly squeezed lime juice and flavored with hot peppers, onions and cilantro, is wonderful if it is made with local yellowtail. It can be found in large servings and in varieties like shrimp, octopus, squid or a combination, especially at Peruvian restaurants.

Dolphin, listed on many menus, is a lean, blunt-headed fish and no relative of the famous mammal. Lobster in Florida is really a clawless crawfish, a seasonal food that may be legally

HOW TO MAKE KEY LIME PIE

- Mix together 2 cups of cracker (or sweet biscuit) crumbs, 8oz (225g) of melted butter and half a cup of granulated sugar and press into a buttered pie dish. Preheat the oven to 350°F (180°C) and bake for 10 minutes.
- Beat 5 egg yolks until smooth. Add 15oz (425g) of sweetened condensed milk and beat until smooth. Then stir in half a cup of fresh Key lime (or ordinary lime) juice and 2 tbsp of grated lime peel.
- Fill the pie crust with the mixture and chill for at least one hour. Garnish with a slice of lime or lemon and serve chilled.

caught from August to March. It is completely unlike Maine lobster, not as rich and tougher.

One of the best places to enjoy Miami's seafood bounty is alongside the Miami River, watching the barges go by at East Coast Fisheries or Garcia's Seafood Grille.

But all this is mere warm-up food to the main course, to be had at Miami's most famous restaurant, Joe's Stone Crab in South Beach. People lust for stone crabs, most often served chilled. The fat claws are plump with firm, pure white meat. And if the meat has little flavor and most of the taste comes from the mustard sauce or the melted butter dip, no one seems to notice. Stone crabs are exotic, part of Miami.

Southern roots

If modern Miami dining is an international buffet, old Miami is more connected to Dixie. For real roots, look toward the Everglades. Of the indigenous creatures found in early Miami, the alligator was the only marginally edible item on the list. Millions were killed for their hides, and by the 1960s the alligator's survival was threatened, and hunting was prohibited. Quickly, the alligator came back. By 1988, it was again legal to hunt alligator and it became a menu item, especially the tail.

Alligator tail is all lean white meat and people often say it tastes like chicken. In fact, alli-

gator tastes the way it is cooked. Most often it is breaded and fried, served as an appetizer with a red tomato sauce like fried clam strips. It is also stewed like conch or made into sausage.

Venture into the swamp and one finds the cook fires of Miami's native Americans, the Miccosukee Indians. Many of the Miccosukee ceremonies are kept a secret but their cooking is an open book. Two items, if you can find them, are worth the trek: Everglades frogs' legs consist of delicate, alabaster meat that gently pulls away from the tiny bones. The Indians' own fried bread – dough dropped in hot oil and fried to a golden puff – is another seldom-sampled taste of Miami.

Part of the southern roots that may not be as deep come from Miami's African-American community. Its contributions have been gathered under the term "soul food," which describes fried fish, collard greens, black eyed peas, and, best of all, barbecue. Oil drums cut in half are converted into grills and set up on street corners in Liberty City or Overtown, smoke wafting and aromas enticing.

Despite its southern locality, Miami also fosters a few northern traditions. Jewish food like bagels and lox, matzo ball soup and New York deli-style pastrami and corned beef sandwiches are found in a few neighborhoods. The tradition lives on most notably at Rascal House in Sunny Isles Beach and Wolfie's in South Beach.

Garden of Eden

If Miami is sea and swamp, it is also a bountiful garden. Certain exotic fruits, all brought from elsewhere, grow on the southern tip of Florida and in no other region of the US. While the rest of the country is cold and gray in winter, Miami is growing strawberries, tomatoes, beans and squash. Once citrus was the coveted crop, the rest of the world breathlessly in awe of oranges, tangerines and grapefruit in January. But most of the early citrus is gone, limited now to backyard growers.

What still flourishes in Miami is virtually the whole US crop of Persian limes, that plump little twist of green that is dropped into a gin and tonic. The sour orange is another tiny little fruit, but it plays a catalytic role in producing one of Miami's most flamboyant dishes, whole roast pig. People spend hours squeezing these baby oranges to make a marinade for the pig, called *lechon*.

But the biggest exotic cash crop in Miami is the sacred fruit of India, the mango. Called the apple of the tropics, the mango comes in red, orange, yellow and purple, with the sweet flesh yellow to golden orange. Once an import, it is now a thriving export and has been adopted as part of the flavor of Miami. Mango trees, 40 ft (12 meters) tall at maturity, line streets and pop up in side yards, their heavy fruit hanging down in clusters. In India, they sing songs of love to the mango. In Miami it is part of the movable feast, part of the exotic landscape. ❑

LEFT: sweet treats in the sun.

Café Cubano

At Cafeteria El Pub on Miami's Calle Ocho, a dark-eyed waitress slides a thimble-sized paper cup across the clean counter. Sweet and heavy, the dark brew is raised to the lips and a local ritual begins. Soon, the caffeine and sugar infusion that is café Cubano will sharpen the mind and loosen the tongue. The steamy antithesis to a soothing shot of bourbon, Miami's favorite drink transforms a 10-second sip into a cerebral celebration that winds you up instead of down.

From the chrome-and-glass skyscrapers of downtown Miami to the ham-and-cheese lunch counters of Little Havana, the potent aroma of Cuban coffee percolates throughout the city. While across the country many Americans have become caffeine conscious and sugar phobic, Miamians have adopted this coffee beverage, rendering it as much a local staple as sweet Florida sunshine and salty sea air.

Imported from Latin America, the beans used in Cuban coffee are roasted at a slightly higher temperature and for a longer time than beans used in American coffee. Brewed in traditional, red-and-white espresso machines, each cup is individually prepared with extreme care and precision. Three scoops of freshly ground coffee are dropped into the filter. In about 10 seconds, an ounce of scalding water pushes through the tightly packed coffee and a foamy, molasses-thick nectar drops into a tiny metal pitcher below. Two teaspoons of sugar are stirred in and the liquid is poured into a tiny paper, plastic, or china *demi-tasse*.

At home, many of Miami's older Cubans still brew the coffee the old-fashioned way – in a cheesecloth funnel, or sometimes an old sock, filled with coffee and boiling water. To create the foam, a drop of coffee is added to two spoonfuls of sugar and mashed into a paste. The grounds are then saved for the flower garden.

Coffee and sugar, the ingredients of café Cubano, have been two of the main ingredients of the Cuban economy for the past 200 years. The coffee bean, which grew wild, was first cultivated by European settlers as early as the 1500s. By the 1800s, *cafetals* – coffee plantations – flourished throughout the island's fertile, mountainous land. Concurrently, sugar plantations prospered.

During the early 1900s, cafes along the elegant boulevards of old Havana sold the local drink from

RIGHT: Cuban coffee stall.

enormous machines that clamored and chimed with each freshly brewed batch. Later, cafes improvized their own Pavlovian call by ringing a bell on the streets to entice people in.

The popularity of café Cubano took hold in Miami in the 1960s, when the first wave of Cuban immigrants peppered the streets with hand-painted signs advertising the potent brew. Café Pilon, one of the major suppliers in Miami, services over 1,500 restaurants, along with supplying beans, grinders and machines to almost 5,000 Miami businesses.

Café Cubano is served ubiquitously, from the lace tablecloth restaurants to the beauty parlors, dress shops, Art Deco hotels, hospitals and funeral

homes. Take-out windows sell it in large plastic containers with a supply of tiny paper cups. Even the McDonald's restaurant in Little Havana offers café Cubano to go with the Huevo McMuffins. While the decor varies, the coffee is a constant.

Taken alone as a pick-me-up, or with a guava-filled Cuban pastry, café Cubano is sipped throughout the city from morning till night. Sometimes, bite-size pieces of bread dipped in sugar are dunked in the coffee. After meals, it is served in the company of a hand-rolled cigar. While *café con leche* – Cuban coffee with warm milk in a regular-size cup – is often served and frequently given to children, in true café Cubano, cream is a sacrilege, a social taboo. ❏

FESTIVALS

Miami's hedonist spirit is nowhere more evident than in the vibrant street parties and outdoor events that pepper the city's calendar

In a recent year, with compelling drum beats, 119,986 people in Miami's Little Havana squeezed, shoved and sweated into the longest Conga line on record. Why? Because, in Miami, especially in high season, it's a civic duty to party.

Year-round, unlike cities of chill, Miami hosts its parties in the street – with sunshine and sensuality guaranteed. Visitors have always come for "fun in the sun" – tourists believing the sales pitch, college kids starting a break, senior citizens outlasting winter's wrath. And if weather is no concern, why not party outdoors?

This street-party tradition started years ago as revelers gathered for sport, art and business. As early as 1915, cars bedecked with plants rolled through the Magic Knight of Dade's Mid-Winter Festival parade, advertising arrowroot starch as the locally supplied ingredient.

Lots of noise

With verve from Cuban immigrants, Miami has pumped these festivals over the past decades with ethnic flair. Now, with lots of noise and no subtlety whatsoever, Miami tells the world: "We're here. Come celebrate with us!"

Carnaval Miami/Calle Ocho, a week-long festival in mid-March, typifies this boast. When Miamians conga-ed into the *Guinness Book of World Records*, they turned a neighborhood block party into an *event*. Touted as America's biggest Hispanic bash, the celebration reveals the city's Hispanic soul – its pride and hospitality – through scents and sounds, color and chaos.

From the start in 1978, the festival outstripped expectations, spilling over 15 blocks. And, by the mid-1980s, with a million visitors due, planners added five more. At the last count filling 23 blocks, the all-day party offers "dance 'til you die" on Calle Ocho (SW Eighth Street) between Fourth and 27th avenues. Other Car-

naval salsa overflows to stadiums and sites throughout the city. Fame spawned size: a beauty pageant, masquerade ball, big-name performers like the Miami Sound Machine, Celia Cruz, José Feliciano and, more recently, heartthrob Enrique Iglesias. Fame also spawned oversize: a huge marathon and bike race, and

supposedly the world's largest *arroz con pollo* (chicken and rice) dinner.

Growth has not always been graceful. The Calle Ocho organizers, the civic-minded Kiwanis Club, exposed provincial roots in the late 1980s. They twice banned entertainers who had performed in Cuba, claiming insult to Miami's staunchly anti-Castro exile community. Protests and lawsuits followed. But the music lingered, on *Calle Ocho* albums that – surprise! – included blacklisted stars.

Dubbed the largest black heritage festival in the United States is the Miami/Bahamas Goombay Festival. This summer street party celebrates Bahamian slaves' independence and the

---

PRECEDING PAGES: performers at the Bahamian Goombay Festival in Coconut Grove. **LEFT:** more Goombay festivities. **RIGHT:** posing in a convertible at Miami Beach's Art Deco Weekend.

long-standing ties between Miami and the Bahamas. Goombay transforms Coconut Grove's Grand Avenue into Nassau's Bay Street.

The weekend romp in early June, dating from 1977, captures the joy of *junkanoo* – dancers, costumed in gaudy crêpe-paper concoctions, swaying to the clamor of cowbells, whistles and washboards. On the street and on stage, rappers' words compete with steel band sounds from "The Islands." In noon-time parades, the Royal Bahamian Police Marching Band conducts precision drills, in uniforms starched bright white.

More than 400 vendors of arts, crafts and food line Grand Avenue – with conch fritters and Bahama Mama's salads already legendary. In just a few short blocks, thousands of would-be Bahamians or real Bahamians (who make up the largest national group of tourists to Miami) are near to home.

The Orange Bowl

But Miami's oldest festivals are linked to sporting and arts traditions, not ethnic roots, especially the largest, oldest and arguably most traditional: the Orange Bowl, the college football classic that frequently decides national championships. Since 1935, the annual King Orange Jamboree Parade on New Year's Eve has mated

THE TOP TWELVE

- Orange Bowl: New Year's Day.
- Art Deco Weekend: mid-January.
- Coconut Grove Arts Festival: mid-February.
- Miami Film Festival: mid-February.
- Carnaval Miami/Calle Ocho Festival: early March.
- Coconut Grove Bed Race: mid-May.
- Miami/Bahamas Goombay Festival: early June.
- Columbus Day Regatta: mid-October.
- Miami Book Fair International: mid-November.
- Orange Bowl Festival: December–January.
- King Mango Strut: mid-December.
- King Orange Jamboree Parade: New Year's Eve.

with the Orange Bowl on New Year's Day, to send football fans into ecstasy for the year.

The jamboree regularly tallies 80,000 fans in bleachers along the downtown route, plus millions of viewers on television. Promoted by organizers as family entertainment, it's a parade where bands playing spirited John Phillip Sousa marches and school fight songs stir onlookers.

The mythical King Jamboree often takes physical shape as a huge smiling balloon face – sometimes buoyed by helium, sometimes anchored by stick or human legs. The Orange Bowl queen is also regal, but definitely human.

With behemoth floats elaborately lit inside and out, the parade claims to be the largest night-time fanfare in the world. Paced for a half-hour's local television coverage and an hour on a national network, it moves slowly and deliberately along a 2¼-mile (3.5-km) route along Biscayne Boulevard, and back again.

Planning extends year-round for the Orange Bowl Festival, a December-to-January hoopla that includes a sailing regatta, international tennis tournament, fashion show, and offspring like the Junior Orange Bowl Parade, which holds its own celebrations in Coral Gables.

When Miamians leave the streets, they head to special alternatives – water parties, such as the Columbus Day Regatta, which floats in mid-

dips in the water. Exploding fireworks and bellowing conch shells keep the crews alert.

Other major sports events congregate in the early spring. February sees the Miami International Boat Show, the Key Biscayne Tennis Championship and the Homestead Championship Rodeo, while the popular Miami Grand Prix is held every March in Homestead,

Art in the streets

Many of Miami's street festivities center on art, with the mid-February open-air Coconut Grove Arts Festival cited as the largest, oldest and most diverse in the entire state. In 1963, at its

October from Coconut Grove to Elliott Key and back. Early on Saturday, boats lurch to a start through Biscayne Bay, and television and radio stations record the quantity of beer drunk and the number of topless bathers spotted.

The cruising regatta regularly logs up to 650 participant and 2,000 spectator boats, with, admittedly, some doubts about who's who. A mainstay from the early 1950s, the weekend is a non-stop event, more camaraderie than competition. Docked overnight at the half-way point, sailors turn into swimmers with sociable skinny

start-up, a few dozen local artists casually chatted with a few thousand neighbors. Now, art exhibitors and art lovers still talk, one on one, but over the din of a crowd "guesstimated" at between 800,000 and 1 million people.

Saturday through Monday, the Grove hyperventilates to accommodate festival-goers. With nationwide competition for 300 display spots, familiar sites disappear. The Bad Portrait booth, for example, got ousted.

Art lovers also head to Miami Beach, where Art Deco Weekend in mid-January tints South Beach pastel colors. Cafe-hopping on the promenade, strollers drift along, eyeing booths on Ocean Drive from Fifth to 15th streets.

LEFT: marching with a message at the King Mango Strut. **ABOVE:** dress-up for grown-ups.

Even the elite "Moon Over Miami" fundraiser for Art Deco preservationists tumbles into the street, closing Collins Avenue between 10th and 11th streets. Amid Big Band revivals, conservative black tuxedos brush up next to Art Deco T-shirts, sometimes even found on the very same body.

An afternoon parade winds from Miami Beach City Hall through the mile-square, pastel-painted architectural district. Rhythm and blues, reggae and *lambada* merge with poolside chatter. Crowds easily top half a million.

FUN FOR FOODIES

A Taste of the Grove, an outdoor food fest hosted by dozens of Miami's finest restaurants, takes place in Coconut Grove's Peacock Park in mid-January.

It's here that Deco dominates. Street theater sets scenes at 1930s beach resorts or 1940s railway stations. Auctions offer stylized doors salvaged from modern renovations. Activists chide owners of dilapidated buildings, suggesting a coat of whitewash "for the image." And the Miami Design Preservation League sells plastic sandpails with "I dig Deco" in appropriate hues: pale blue, pink or even white.

There are a couple of other arts festivals worth checking out. Beaux Arts, an arts-and-crafts show on the University of Miami's Coral Gables campus, clamored for "first festival" status in 1990, moving to an early-January slot after almost four decades of being held in March. Also

in January Art Miami, held at the Miami Beach Convention Center, features works from 100 of the most respected art dealers from 18 countries, representing emerging artists, photography, contemporary and modern art.

Cultural highlights

Even events normally indoors, like book and film festivals, take to the streets in Miami. Plus they offer a cultural, even an intellectual twist, just enough to confuse those who think Miami is all beach and bare bottoms and little or no brain.

At the Miami Film Festival in February, film buffs and directors from around the world congregate at the downtown Gusman Center for the Performing Arts and small art theaters across the city for this star-studded local event. It is recognized as one of the leading international film festivals. In 2000, festival organizers broke rank with Cuban exile hard-liners, risking the future of the event's county funding, and dared screen a film made in Cuba. Although the film was critical of Castro, just showing it goes against a Miami-Dade rule that borders on its own foreign policy.

Also on Miami's screens are the Hispanic Film Festival and the Gay and Lesbian Film Festival, held in early May and July, respectively.

In 1984, local booksellers, a community college and the public library invented a book fair, which has blossomed into eight days of show-and-tell about books. In November the annual Miami Book Fair International attracts more than 300 exhibitors and half a million browsers.

A week-long conference features prominent writers such as Alice Walker or Norman Mailer, sometimes hawking a book, sometimes a heritage, such as the Latin or Caribbean traditions appropriate to Miami. Over the closing weekend, books spill, with sellers and buyers shoulder to shoulder, on to the downtown Wolfson Campus of Miami-Dade Community College.

Planning for spontaneity

In the past few decades, partying has become serious business in Miami. Promoters supply street antics, security, and assurances that thousands will get invited and actually attend. Competition now forces organizers to fix dates early.

But not everyone loves a party. Local residents complain that out-of-towners and traffic tangles bar them from their own streets. And cutbacks may be inevitable. Miami commissioners are now obliged to consider citizens' petitions to limit the number and size of festivals.

With 17-page agreements to handle details like disposing of trash and providing toilets, planning spontaneity in Miami gets more and more challenging.

But this is irrelevant niggling for those bound for the streets. Parking is *always* impossible, but homeowners rent the front lawn and radio DJs provide tips

discourage those who like intimacy. Indeed, people phobic of large crowds should stick to the side streets, where Miami's smaller communities – the Haitians and the Jamaicans, among others – have their own special days.

Or be philosophical, like King Mango Strut paraders who each December offer a fresh perspective on a year of nonsense. Half party, half satire, the Strut evolved when the Mango Band, playing kazoos and conch shells, was rejected by Orange Bowl organizers in 1981.

GLAD TO BE GAY

Gay public events include the Winter Party, a wild fling in South Beach in March, and the six-day White Party in November, which raises money for Aids and ends with a formal do at Vizcaya.

on available car space. Public transport like Metrorail just adapts, and festival shuttles and trains move crowds from their stops.

Party-goers just arrive early, bring patience, and hunker. When partying or planning gets too exhausting, they consider lying down – at the Coconut Grove Bed Race, for instance, where one Sunday each May four-member teams push and pull beds to raise money for local charities.

Attendance estimates, bulging from corporate sponsors who think bigger-is-better, may

The following year, band members started a tradition, instantly, Miami-style. Committed to wackiness and a late start, their colorful half-hour parade in Coconut Grove struts two blocks from Commodore Plaza to Peacock Park.

And it abandons all propriety. Such "irregulars" as the Synchronized Briefcase Drill Team, Flamingo Freedom Band, and Marching Freds highlight festival foibles. As Strut founder Glenn Terry put it: "We like to show that Miami has a sense of humor. We like to make people happy. And we like to have fun and enjoy ourselves."

As Miamians know, allow people into the streets to eat, drink, dance and gawk – and there's no reason to go home. ❏

LEFT: thousands head for Little Havana's Calle Ocho Festival every year. **ABOVE:** spontaneous street dancing, a Miami specialty.

Nightlife

I f the club scene's your thing, head straight for South Beach. It's hard to miss the hot spots. Just follow the music – house, progressive, trance, tribal or garage – that thumps out from the darkened halls onto the sidewalks along Washington and Collins avenues on weekend evenings. Or look out for the lines of young men and women dressed in their finest along the sidewalks. They'll be trying to get inside one of the clubs by catching the eye of the doorman, who ultimately decides their fate for the evening.

On the wild side

All the clubs operate on the concept of triage, which means not everyone gets in. The elite clubs, such as Level and Crobar on Washington Avenue, keep a list at the door. If you're on the list, you get in. If not, you stay out and watch others file inside while you hope to get noticed. This can get messy.

Luckily, there are ways to avoid the hassle. Most hotels on Miami Beach have connections with the clubs, and the concierges have access to the people who keep the lists. Having a word with your concierge should guarantee you entry.

If you're short of a hotel connection but are prepared to brave the crowds, you need special gear. No, not mountain-climbing shoes; just attention-grabbing duds. The advice from seasoned clubbers is to be extremely well dressed. By this we mean a suit and tie. Dressing crazy will help, too, but be original. It's a tricky balance: you want to be subtle, but you also need to be noticed.

Once you're in, be cool. Don't be shocked at the $25 cover charge and the $7 drinks.

If you have the time, you won't be short of clubs to check out in a 20-block area on South Beach, with names like Liquid, Groove Jet, Shadow Lounge, Amnesia and Bash, among many others. Some are live-music venues, while others feature celebrity DJs. Occasionally DJs and traveling bands take over hotel ballrooms and throw their own parties. If they're playing your kind of music, these can be as fun as the established clubs.

To find out what's happening while you're in town, pick up a copy of Friday's *Weekend* section in the *Miami Herald*, or the free *Street* or *New Times* publications that hit the racks on Thursdays.

Gays and lesbians

South Beach is a gay and lesbian meeting-place – for visitors and residents alike. There is freedom here to live and play uninhibited. That also means a good selection of clubs. Check out Salvation, a watering hole with DJs on West Avenue; Twist, a club with outdoor lounge game room and dance floor on Washington Avenue; and, also on Washington, Pump, good for partying until breakfast. Across the bay, try Cactus, an ideal place to shoot pool or see a drag show, on Biscayne Boulevard, or Splash, a dance club in South Miami.

Bars and lounges

If you don't want to do the club thing, either because they're too loud or too expensive, or because they're too difficult to get into, Miami Beach has many good lounges and bars. Lola Bar at 23rd and Collins, for example, has a cool interior and is a lot more laid back than the typical club.

In addition, Ocean Drive is lined with restaurants with outdoor seating, many offering live jazz or Latin music. Alternatively, you can take salsa lessons like actor and singer Will Smith did at Starfish on West Avenue. Or how about Cuban-influenced jazz at Cafe Nostalgia in the oh-so-trendy Forge restaurant in mid-Miami Beach?

Away from the beach

Luckily for those who want to get away from the South Beach scene – traffic tie-ups along Washington and Collins avenues can stretch for miles on weekend nights – more and more people looking for a dance floor have been crossing the causeway to downtown Miami. The newest hot spot is Space, in the Park West district.

On the mainland, there are many choices. CocoWalk in Coconut Grove is a popular night spot, chock full of bars, restaurants, shops and movie theaters. Live music has been featured at Tobacco Road down by the Miami River for more than a century. Churchill's, a Brit pub incongruously found in Little Haiti, draws crowds with off-beat bands such as Plutonium Pie and Buddha Gonzalez, to name just a couple of the acts that grace its stage seven nights a week. Power Studios in the Design Dis-

The tamer side

There is much more to Miami's nightlife than music. The monthly openings of new art shows at clusters of galleries around the city are often an excuse for very serious socializing and schmoozing. On Lincoln Road in Miami Beach, the openings on the second Thursday of every month are augmented by live performances and various art-related events. In the Design District, the second Friday of the month is the night for sampling the new art on a gallery walk.

Coral Gables tends to draw a more affluent and older crowd to its established and pricey galleries on the first Friday of the month. It even lays on a

trict offers an eclectic musical experience. It is able to host three different bands on three stages within its restaurant-bar-studio complex.

Jazz clubs are scattered throughout the landscape, from Satchmo's in Coral Gables to O'Hara's Pub in Fort Lauderdale to the Van Dyke Hotel on Lincoln Road and Jazid on Washington Avenue.

Feel like Flamenco? Casa Panza in Little Havana has live flamenco on Tuesdays, Thursdays and Saturdays. It's a tiny place, so get there early and dine on a few plates of Spanish *tapas*.

LEFT: dancer at Club Bash on Washington Avenue, South Beach. **ABOVE:** the outdoor bar at the Clevelander Hotel on Ocean Drive.

shuttle bus to take you from venue to venue.

If literature interests you, find out what's going on at Books & Books where authors regularly appear for signings and to read from their latest works. The main store, which has the fullest schedule, is in Coral Gables, but the Lincoln Road branch has its own share of events.

Live theater offers a wide variety of choices from Spanish language plays to off-beat productions staged in small venues throughout the county. The Coconut Grove Playhouse and the Jackie Gleason Theater put on traditional Broadway-style shows.

The city also offers opera productions, a ballet company and the New World Symphony to please lovers of the classics. ❏

SPORTING MIAMI

From football to ice hockey, from windsurfing to golf, there is a sport,
a venue and often a professional team for every taste in Miami

For those who prefer participating to spectating, South Florida offers an unlimited choice of activities. Wake up with the sun as it rises above the ocean and take off for a jog on the sand with the waves lapping at your feet along the 7 miles (11 km) of shoreline on Miami Beach. If you prefer a harder surface, there is the wooden oceanfront boardwalk between 21st and 47th streets in mid-Beach or the paved pathway along Ocean Drive.

Ocean Drive is also a popular spot for rollerblading, South Beach's transportation mode of choice. If you haven't brought your own wheels, you can rent at Skate 2000, with locations on Ocean Drive and Lincoln Road.

Another popular spot for outdoor activities begins as you cross the Rickenbacker Causeway toward Key Biscayne. Here, you can rent sail boards and learn to windsurf on the gentle swell of Biscayne Bay. Farther along, on Virginia Key, are stands that rent bikes, jet skis and motor scooters. The road leading to Key Biscayne is one of the most popular bicycling routes, with several miles of paths leading across the palm-lined island. When you get to Bill Baggs State Recreation Area you can choose: either hand over the entrance fee and continue to the tip of the island to get a glimpse of the restored lighthouse, or just turn around and head back.

While on the Key, if you're into tennis you can hit the ball where Pete Sampras and Andre Agassi duke it out once a year at the county-owned Key Biscayne Tennis Center. There's even an old-fashioned grass court. Or if you prefer to sweat it out on South Beach, try Flamingo Park on 11th Street, where there are plenty of clay courts and pickup partners. Like tennis courts, golf courses abound throughout the county, from the famous Key Biscayne links, where former President Richard Nixon and his pal Bebe Rebozo played, to the Blue Monster at Doral on the western edge of the county.

Wanna go fishing? Charters leave for the deep blue sea from a number of marinas stretching from Haulover Park to Black Point. For the best snorkeling and scuba diving, head south to Biscayne National Park, or just about anywhere in the Keys. Here you can get a close-up view of the spectacular reefs inhab-

ited by a breathtaking array of tropical fish.

Or paddle a kayak or canoe through the uninhabited mangroves along South Florida's shores and enjoy the ibis, heron and anhingas as they take flight. Rentals are available at various sites, including Oleta River State Recreational Area to the north and, of course, the town of Flamingo in the Everglades National Park to the south.

The opportunities for sporting activities are endless. Your only limit will be time.

Spectator sports

Once you tire of taking part, it may be time to sit back and watch the professionals demonstrate how it should be done. For a long time, it

PRECEDING PAGES: windsurfers on the bay.
LEFT: water-skier carving a turn. **RIGHT:** rollerbladers take to the sidewalks by the dozen in South Beach.

seemed as if Miami only had two seasons for avid sports spectators: football season and football training camp. That's because for many years, the only professional sports team to call Miami home was the Miami Dolphins football team. The team came into existence in 1970, and just two years after coach Don Shula promised fans he would be "subtle as a punch," he led the team to the first and only perfect season in National Football League history. That year (1973) the Dolphins won 17 games without a loss, including their first Super Bowl victory.

As suburbs sprang up and the team's fan base spread, the Dolphins abandoned their inner-city Orange Bowl in Little Havana for bigger and better digs on the border between Miami-Dade and Broward counties. The stadium was named after team owner Joe Robbie, and later renamed Pro Player Stadium.

Then, an explosion of other sports franchises appeared on the scene in the following decades. The first new kid on the block was the Miami Heat basketball team, which hosted its first regular season game in 1988 at a sold-out Miami Arena, filled with fans wearing tuxedos. It only took a dozen years for the Heat to outgrow its home. Fans now watch the hoopsters at the American Airlines Arena, an architecturally

MIAMI'S KING OF SPORT

In 1994 Wayne Huizenga, then owner of the Blockbuster Video empire, bought the Miami Dolphins, the most successful of Florida's three NFL teams. One person is not supposed to own more than one major team; however, at the time Huizenga also owned the Marlins baseball squad and the Panthers hockey team. He recently sold the Marlins to businessman John Henry.

Huizenga also has control of the 75,000-seat Pro Player Stadium, home to both the Dolphins and the Marlins, and South Florida's top sports arena. Since 1997 the college football classic Orange Bowl has also been played here. Call (305) 623-6100 for information.

dazzling structure on the bay. A woman's professional basketball team, the Miami Sol, began playing in 2000.

Spring training

Another spectator sport that lures fans in droves to Florida is the all-American, apple-pie institution of baseball. Careers are reborn every spring here as baseball bursts out all over the state when many of the country's Major League teams head south for spring training.

Although Miami itself does not currently have a visiting team, other nearby towns get in on the action. Fort Lauderdale plays host to the Baltimore Orioles, West Palm Beach accommodates the Montreal Expos and Fort Myers is shared by the Boston Red Sox and the Minnesota Twins.

It all begins in early March, when most of the country is still scraping ice off their driveways, and lasts for two months. The skies are their azure clearest and the temperature seems locked at 70°F-plus (21°C). Author Pat Jordan wrote: "Spring training is like a big summer picnic, where everyone's playing softball and eating barbecue. It's like a big country fair with people all around the ballpark."

And even though nothing counts for real in the training games, the multi-million dollar star for spring games, they cost considerably less than at a real-world Major League game.

Miami, long the home of a minor-league team, began playing with the "big boys" in 1991, when Major League baseball awarded the city a franchise. The team was named the Florida Marlins and began playing at Pro Player Stadium. Within six years, they were the proud winners of the World Series.

Other options

Golf and tennis seem made to be watched or played in South Florida. Every week there is a golf tournament somewhere. Because it is home

players attract tens of thousands of fans from across the country who eat mediocre hot dogs, drink warm beer, and scream and shout with excitement at the thought of scoring a foul ball tossed over a chain link fence or an autographed baseball cap. There's something about getting a baseball player's autograph that dates back to the childhood rush of getting close enough to touch and talk to someone who never before seemed real. While ballpark seats are not free

LEFT: cycling is a great way to avoid the traffic, see the sights and get some exercise, all at the same time. **ABOVE:** the 18th hole at Doral Country Club, a venue for high-profile golf tournaments.

to a number of world-class links, South Florida has hosted championships at Key Biscayne, Doral Country Club's Blue Monster and several other courses in Palm Beach County. Tennis hit the big time here when the Lipton International Players Championship debuted in 1985. Two years later, it moved to Key Biscayne, where it is still played, now under the sponsorship of the Swedish phone company Ericsson.

Who would have thought that a game on ice would ever hit the subtropics? In 1993, the Florida Panthers made their National Hockey League debut in the Miami Arena. The team made it to the Stanley Cup final two years later. They had a new stadium built for them – the

National Car Rental Center – in Broward County on the edge of the Everglades.

Soccer is also getting a foothold in the area, with the Miami Fusion of Major League Soccer. Since its 1998 inaugural season, the team has been playing its games 30 miles (48 km) north of downtown Miami at Lockhart Stadium in Broward County.

In addition to the professional teams in various sports, Miami's universities and colleges also get in on the action. In fact, in this part of the US, college sports are as

> ### SNOB SPORT
>
> Those with champagne tastes can watch polo being played at the Palm Beach Polo and Country Club and Boca Raton's Royal Palm Polo Club, both north of Miami.

South." Since then stock-car races, especially the big NASCAR (National Association for Stock Car Auto Racing) events, have been a highlight of the Florida sporting scene. Although the races at Daytona and Sebring draw the biggest crowds, the Miami area got in on the act with street races, until 1995 when the speedway was built. The 1½-mile (2.4-km) oval, situated on the eastern side of Homestead, south of downtown Miami, has five major weekend events per year, including three NASCAR races and the Miami Grand Prix.

popular as, if not more popular than, their professional counterparts. The University of Miami's teams, known as the Hurricanes, are the local favorites.

Skidmarks and gasoline

To the south, those who love the smell of gasoline and the rush of speed can indulge in both at the Homestead-Miami Speedway.

Stock-car racing, born in the North Florida hill country, was made legitimate in 1959 when the first race was held at the Daytona International Speedway, on Florida's central east coast. Soon after, the entire nation grew curious about the doings of "those crazy rednecks down

Taking a gamble

If the incessant roar of engines is not enough to sate a craving for a sports-induced high, Miami offers the intoxicating thrill of legalized gambling. While casinos have yet to win statewide voting approval, Florida is a haven for those who love the excitement of pari-mutuel betting, in which all those who pick the winners take home a share of the total amount put down.

Throughout the state, more than 15 million people a year wage over $1.6 billion on jai alai (*see box*) and horse racing. Generally, pari-

ABOVE: cheerleader for the Miami Dolphins football team. **RIGHT:** racehorses training at Hialeah Park.

mutuel sports attract two distinct types of fans: the serious player who approaches his or her gamble of choice with a steadfast dedication and desire to win, and the second type, vacationers or residents betting for fun rather than for profit.

Florida is one of the few states in the US where you can wager on human beings – as long as they are playing jai alai. In Miami, the jai alai arena (known as a fronton) is near the airport. Along the Gold Coast there are two more, in Dania and Palm Beach. Connecticut and Rhode Island are the only other states in the nation where you can watch the game.

The wagering concepts common to other pari-mutuel sports hold for jai alai. Win, place, show, quinela, perfecta, trifecta – all apply to the men who play this version of handball.

Down at the track

Thoroughbred racing, however, dominates the local gambling industry. Horseracing's tradition of glamor, high-society and heroes is known throughout the world and earned it the sobriquet the "Sport of Kings." The Miami area has been a winter mecca for the nation's best horses and jockeys for years, and in a routine winter season, every important thoroughbred in training east of the Mississippi River is likely to be stabled somewhere in South Florida.

Years ago, prominent sports, entertainment and political figures made South Florida's horse tracks a place to see and be seen. These days, those memories still have a ghostly hold over some of the more elaborate tracks – Calder and Gulfstream Park – but for the most part the crowds are more pedestrian than genteel. Gulfstream Park itself, in Hallandale, north of Miami Beach, is now more urban and sits in the middle of a high-rise condo community. Pompano Beach, just north of Fort Lauderdale, also has a first-rate track.

Between October and April, South Florida is also the focal point of the nation's harness racing. The opening of Pompano Park in Pompano Beach about 30 years ago served as the catalyst for what has become an annual southern migration of big name harness horsemen to Florida. Virtually all of the sport's superstars ship their stables to Pompano for winter racing. They also prepare young horses being developed for the next summer's races in the north.

Along with horses, Florida's greyhound racing industry is without peer. The state is by far the most important greyhound area in the nation if for no other reason than sheer volume. Miami and Palm Beach both have their own track, where the sleek canines can be watched as they are lured around the course by an artificial rabbit, to the cheers of bettors. The modern version of greyhound racing is believed to have evolved from a coursing meet held in 1904 in North Dakota. Anthropologists claim that Cleopatra fancied greyhounds, a trait she shared with most Egyptian royalty. In England, the sport reached its great popularity during the Tudor period, in the reign of Queen Elizabeth I, who inspired the slogan the "Sport of Queens." ❏

JAI ALAI: THE RULES OF THE GAME

The sport of jai alai originated in Spain's Basque Country and reached the US in the early 20th century. It came via Cuba, so it is no surprise that Florida has more jai alai arenas than anywhere else in the country. Terms used in the game are a blend of Spanish and Basque.

Similar to handball, the game is played on a large, three-sided court *(concha)*, using a curved basket *(cesta)* and a very hard ball *(pelota)*. Games are played between two teams of one or two players *(pelotari)*, and last about 15 minutes each: there are usually about 14 games in an evening. Jai alai is simple but super-fast, with players hurling the ball at over 150 miles (240 km) per hour.

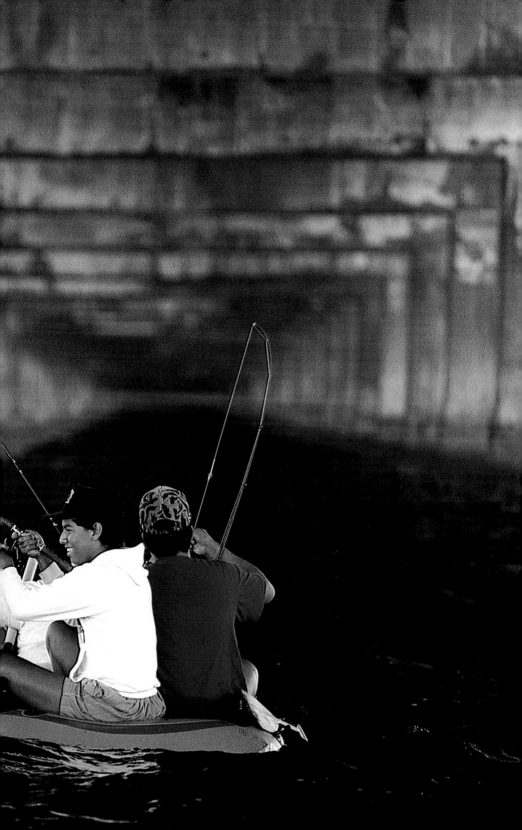

PLACES

*A detailed guide to the entire city, with principal sites
clearly cross-referenced by number to the maps*

At dawn, a red-headed rooster crows his morning call through the inner-city neighborhood of Little Haiti. Across the bay, the Art Deco dreamland of South Beach is waking up to another glorious day beside America's hippest stretch of sand. Miami's cityscape is a picture of incongruity – part American dream, part Third World struggle.

The Places section that follows is designed to evoke that often-elusive "sense of place." It is a portrait of Miami's neighborhoods and nearby cities and the quality of life within them – from the high-powered offices of downtown Miami to the low, lush strawberry fields south of the city.

The section has been subdivided into various chapters.

● The island of Miami Beach is the first port of call for most visitors, and all the action takes place in South Beach, with its famous Art Deco district. The action generally involves looking good – it's the place to see and be seen.

● Back on the mainland is Downtown Miami, the commercial and financial hub of the city, with its own share of architectural delights from Miami's early years.

● Across the Miami River from downtown is Little Havana, peopled day and night by the city's influential community of Cuban exiles.

● The next two chapters cover the quieter but distinctive neighborhoods of Coral Gables and Coconut Grove, which have both played crucial roles in the city's development.

● Back across the bay is the island of Key Biscayne, hiding place of some of the best beaches in the Miami area.

● The next two chapters, Heading South and Northern Miami, take in the outskirts of the city, including the Redland, the city's bountiful fruit basket, and the Caribbean enclave of Little Haiti.

● Finally, the Excursions section will guide you through the Miami environs, from the old-money mansions of extravagant Palm Beach and the stunning beaches of Florida's west coast to the womb-like wonders of the Everglades and the laid-back islands of the Keys.

In between visiting the principal sights, it's worth making time to uncover hidden corners of the city that are very different from your own home town, and to bask in its simple secrets of where to find the best fried bananas or the most enticing *salsa*-filled nightclub. In essence, the things that make a place a place. ❏

PRECEDING PAGES: Deco style in South Beach; leafy residence in Coral Gables; fishing for an urban catch. **LEFT:** satellite image by NASA of the Miami coast.

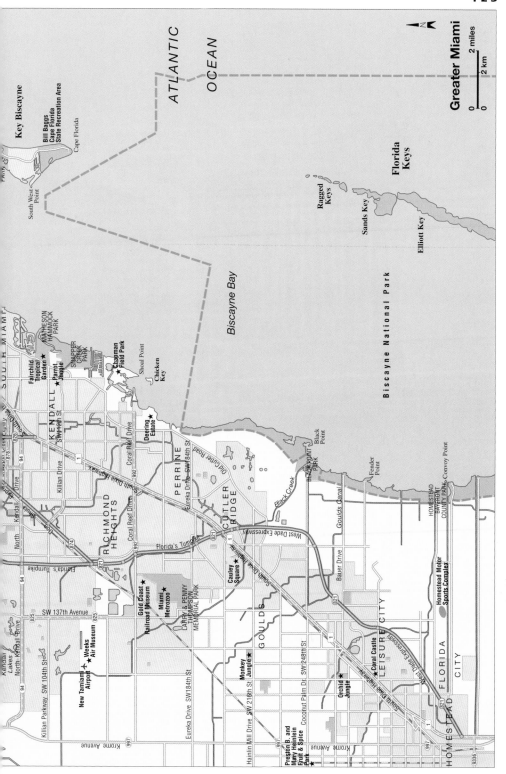

Greater Miami

N

| 0 | | 2 miles |
| 0 | | 2 km |

ATLANTIC

OCEAN

Key Biscayne

Bill Baggs
Cape Florida
State Recreation Area

Cape Florida

South West
Point

Florida
Keys

Ragged
Keys

Sands Key

Elliott Key

Biscayne Bay

Biscayne National Park

SOUTH MIAMI

MATHESON
HAMMOCK
PARK

SNAPPER
CREEK
PARK

Fairchild
Tropical
Garden ★

Parrot
Jungle ★

★ Chapman
Field Park

Shoal Point

Chicken
Key

KENDALL

SW 104th St

Killian Drive

Coral Reef Drive

★ Deering
Estate

Old Cutler Road

Eureka Drive SW 84th St

RICHMOND
HEIGHTS

Coral Reef Drive

Killian Parkway

Kendall Drive

South Dixie Highway

Florida's Turnpike

PERRINE

CUTLER
RIDGE

Black Creek

Black
Point

Fender
Point

West Dade Expressway

BLACK POINT
PARK

Goulds Canal

SW 137th Avenue

★ Gold Coast
Railroad Museum

★ Miami
Metrozoo

LARRY & PENNY
THOMPSON
MEMORIAL PARK

Cauley
Square ★

South Dixie Highway

GOULDS

Bauer Drive

HOMESTEAD
BAYFRONT
COUNTY PARK

Convoy Point

Weeks ★
Air Museum

New Tamiami ★
Airport

SW 137th Avenue

Eureka Drive SW 184th St

Monkey ★
Jungle

SW 216th St

Coconut Palm Dr. SW 248th St

Orchid ★
Jungle

★ Coral Castle

LEISURE CITY

West Dade Expressway

Homestead Motor
Sports Complex

FLORIDA
CITY

Krome Avenue

Hainlin Mill Drive

Preston B. and
Mary Heinlein
Fruit & Spice
Park ★

Krome Avenue

HOMESTEAD

MIAMI BEACH

The appeal of Miami Beach lies in its miles and miles of unbroken sands and in fun-loving South Beach, where you can relax and party to your heart's content in an Art Deco wonderland

Map on page 128

T he Bulgarian artist who calls himself Christo was prophetic when it came to Miami Beach. After more than a year of battling environmentalists, politicians and tourism honchos, Christo convinced the doubting dozens to allow him to use gleaming Biscayne Bay as the backdrop for his art. On May 7, 1983, when Miami Beach was for the most part a has-been Riviera of the South, Christo and a band of loyal subjects finished wrapping 11 islands in Biscayne Bay in 6½ million sq. ft (600,000 sq. meters) of flamingo-pink plastic.

For two weeks, the islands floated among the shiny pink fabric for all to see. The grim opposition had given way to gasps of delight and civic pride. After decades of being ignored, Miami Beach was once again in the pink.

Soon after, *Miami Vice* arrived and Miami Beach, particularly South Beach, with its white-sand beaches and cotton candy-color hotels with whimsical Art Deco designs, never looked better.

In fact, Miami Beach has reinvented itself many times over the years. Since Carl Fisher shaped it out of a snake- and rodent-infested sandspur and cut Lincoln Road through dense mangrove using circus elephants in 1915, golden days in Miami Beach have come, gone and come again. Once the dream-vacation mecca of every red-blooded American, it fell into disrepair as families spurned it for central Florida and Walt Disney World during the 1970s.

PRECEDING PAGES: sunset colors and Deco lines. **LEFT:** South Beach's Breakwater Hotel. **BELOW:** playground for young and old.

In the early 1980s, residents knew and tourists were warned not even to drive through blighted and deserted South Beach at night. Then preservationists began to campaign for restoration of the Beach's unmatched collection of Deco hotels, and they met with remarkable success. Parks were cleaned up and improved. Dredgers put the beach back where it belonged, behind the solid wall of overblown hotels along Collins Avenue. Now, tourists not only drive through; they stop, stroll, eat, drink and dance the night away. When it's time to turn in, they sleep in renovated and historic hotels. South Beach is no longer the place to avoid. It's the place to be – and be seen. Tacky is still trendy here, kitsch is still cool, but South Beach has now morphed into sophisticated and hip. And the beach beckons all year-round.

Developers have spent hundreds of millions of dollars transforming run-down and forgotten hotels and apartment buildings – inhabited for decades by retired Jews from cold northeastern cities – into chic buildings where artists create, yuppies entertain, and tourists vacation. South Beach has made another kind of comeback, this time as a trendy urban neighborhood of Art Deco apartments, nightclubs, restaurants, oceanfront cafes, upscale boutiques, art galleries and theaters. It even has a spiffy nickname: **SoBe** –

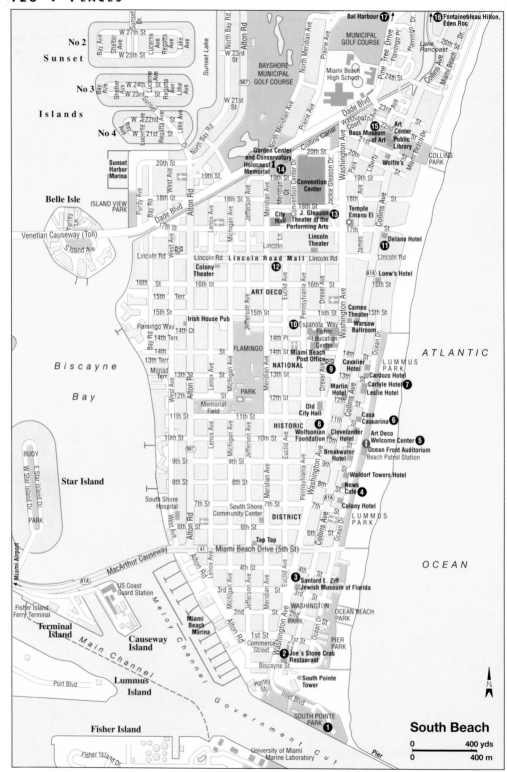

No 2
Sunset

No 3

Islands

No 4

W 27th St
Bay Ave
Shelter Ave
Lucerne Ave
Regatta Ave
Lake Ave
W 25th St

Bay Ave
Shelter Ave
Lucerne Ave
Regatta Ave
Lake Ave
W 24th St
W 23rd St

W 22nd Ave
Bay Ave
Lucerne Ave
Regatta Ave
Lake Ave
W 21st Ave

Sunset Lake
Sunset Dr.

W 23rd St

North Bay Rd
Alton Rd
North Meridian Ave
Prairie Ave
Collins Ave

MUNICIPAL
GOLF COURSE

Pine Tree Drive
Flamingo Dr.
Flamingo Pl.

Bal Harbour **17**

Fontainebleau Hilton, **16**
Eden Roc

Lake
Pancoast

26th St
25th St

Collins Ave
Miami Beach Dr.

BAYSHORE
MUNICIPAL
GOLF COURSE

(907)

Miami Beach
High School

24th St

Dade Blvd

23rd St

Washington Court

22nd St

Art
Center
Public
Library

COLLINS
PARK

Belle Isle

Sunset
Harbor
Marina

ISLAND VIEW
PARK

Parrey Ave

Venetian Causeway (Toll)

S Island Ave

20th St

19th St

18th St

Purdy Ave
Bay Rd
West Ave
Dade Blvd
Alton Rd

17th St

West Ave

Garden Center
and Conservatory
Holocaust **14**
Memorial

Lenox Ave
Michigan Ave
Jefferson Ave
Meridian Ave
Meridian Ct
Convention Center Dr
Jackie Gleason Dr.

Collins Canal

20th St

19th St

18th St

Convention
Center

J. Gleason **13**
Theater of the
Performing Arts

City
Hall

Lincoln
Theater

Temple
Emanu El

Washington Ave
Liberty
James
Collins Ave

Bass Museum **15**
21st St
of Art

Wolfie's

20th St

19th St

Delano Hotel **11**

Lincoln Rd

Lincoln Rd

Colony
Theater

16th
St

15th
St

15th
Terr.

15th
St

ART DECO

Lincoln Rd
Lincoln Road Mall
Lincoln Rd
12

Irish House Pub

14th Ct
14th
St
14th
Terr.

13th Terr.

Monad
Terr.

Flamingo Way

Bay Rd

FLAMINGO

14th Pl.

Espanola Way **10**
Fisher
Education
Center

Miami Beach
Post Office

NATIONAL

Colony
Theater

Loew's Hotel **(A1A)**

Cameo
Theater

Warsaw
Ballroom

Ocean Dr.

16th St

15th St

ATLANTIC

Cavalier
Hotel

LUMMUS
PARK

Biscayne

Bay

13th Terr.

West 12th St

13th
St

PARK

Memorial
Field

Lenox Ave
Michigan Ave
Jefferson Ave
Meridian Ave

12th
St

Old
City Hall

13th
St

9

Marlin
Hotel

Casa
Casuarina

Cardozo Hotel
Carlyle Hotel **7**
Leslie Hotel

Drexel Ave
Pennsylvania Ave
Euclid Ave

6

BUOY

Star Island

E Star Island Dr.
W Star Island Dr.

PARK

11th St

10th St

9th St

8th St

South Shore
Hospital

Lenox Ave
Michigan Ave
Jefferson Ave

11th St

10th St

9th St

8th St

South Shore
Community Center

HISTORIC

Wolfsonian **8**
Foundation

DISTRICT

Clevelander
Hotel

Breakwater
Hotel

Washington Ave
Pennsylvania Ave
Euclid Ave

Art Deco
Welcome Center **5**
Ocean Front Auditorium
Beach Patrol Station

Waldorf Towers Hotel

News **4**
Cafe

Colony Hotel

LUMMUS
PARK

Collins Ave
Ocean Dr.

OCEAN

Miami Airport

(A1A)

MacArthur Causeway

(41)

Miami Beach Drive (5th St)

4th
St

3rd
St

2nd
St

Alton Rd
Michigan Ave
Jefferson Ave
Meridian Ave

4th
St

3rd
St

Tap Tap

Euclid Ave
Washington Ave

Sanford L. Ziff **3**
Jewish Museum of Florida

WASHINGTON
PARK

Ocean Dr.

OCEAN BEACH
PARK

Fisher Island
Ferry Terminal

Terminal
Island

US Coast
Guard Station

Causeway
Island

Miami Beach
Marina

Meloy Channel

Alton Rd

Commerce
Street

1st
St

Biscayne St

Harley
St

Washington Ave

2 Joe's Stone Crab
Restaurant

South Pointe
Tower

1st
St

PIER
PARK

Port Blvd

Lummus
Island

Main Channel

Government Cut

SOUTH POINTE
PARK

1

Fisher Island

Fisher Island Dr.

University of Miami
Marine Laboratory

Pier

South Beach

0   400 yds

0   400 m

N

inspired by Manhattan's SoHo. The Beach still cultivates a more-vice-than-nice image, which makes it a frustrating, yet exciting place to live, but it is an astoundingly beautiful spot to visit.

Map on page 128

A gay renaissance

Along with the arrival of developers, Miami Beach has also experienced substantial growth in its gay population. The *Miami Herald* once reported that gay tenants occupy one-third of the Art Deco District apartments.

In addition to finding South Beach an ideal gay vacation destination where same-sex couples can check into gay hotels, dine in gay restaurants, and kiss in public without scornful looks, hundreds of gays and lesbians have invested in the area, opening book stores, cafes and boutiques. They have also played a major role in the urban gentrification of the area.

Miami Beach police officers are generally friendly and helpful, and use a variety of vehicles on patrol.

Businesses owned by gays, or by those who are supportive of the gay movement, place a rainbow in their storefront windows as a symbol of welcome. There's even a well-established gay chamber of commerce and several support groups to help newcomers. So important is the gay population to the city, that some Miami Beach commissioners take their campaigns into gay bars as a way of garnering votes, and the Miami Beach Police Department now requires its officers to attend gay sensitivity training programs.

South of Sixth Street

The narrow island of Miami Beach runs parallel to the coast and is separated from mainland Miami by the broad expanse of Biscayne Bay. Although there are several bridges linking the mainland to the Beach, the **MacArthur Causeway**, which joins downtown Miami with the southern tip of the island and the heart of vibrant South Beach, also offers the best view of the Port of Miami, the bay and its mansion-lined islands *(see Biscayne Bay chapter, page 150)*. Formerly a drawbridge that was often lifted for passing boat traffic, the causeway was rebuilt in the mid-1990s and is now a massive expanse of concrete above the bay.

BELOW: flamboyant entertaiment.

Once you've crossed the bay and passed the islands, the teasing is over: the real Miami Beach has been reached. Beyond the U.S. Coast Guard station is the 400-slip Miami Beach Marina, from where dive boats depart for artificial reefs offshore, and charter fishing boats, filled with knowing captains and eager anglers, head out to catch The Big One.

On the southern tip of the island is **South Pointe Park ❶**, a 17-acre (7-hectare) slice of meandering sidewalks, grassy walkways, a beach (although this is not really the park's strong suit) and a fitness course. The 150-ft (45-meter) South Pointe Pier, which joins the long jetty at the mouth of Government Cut, is a prime spot for fishing and watching the cruise ships head out to deep water. South Pointe Park also has benches along the water, an observation tower, charcoal grills, picnic pavilions and a playground for children.

Across from the entrance to the park, at 227 Biscayne Street, is **Joe's Stone Crab Restaurant ❷**, a

TIP

The ocean off South Beach is very calm, but surfers keen to ride a wave should head just north of South Pointe Park. Board rentals can be arranged at X-Isle Surf Shop, 437 Washington Avenue.

BELOW: the Ziff Jewish Museum, in a renovated synagogue.

South Beach institution since 1913. Only at Joe's is pride given over to pleasure. Only at Joe's do Miami's politicos and movers-and-shakers wait with the common folk – sometimes for as long as four hours – for a table. Joe's takes no reservations, although a little cash placed in the palm of the *maître d*'s hand has been known to hurry things along a bit.

And only at Joe's do otherwise reserved adults allow themselves to have huge paper bibs tied around their necks and tucked over their clothing by waiters in tuxedos. To what end? After they've dipped the first succulent claw into butter or mustard sauce, customers understand that there are no better stone crabs' claws to be had than at Joe's. And they are grateful for those claws, despite the fact that they've waited for hours, donned bibs, and depleted their wallets. If you want to share the delectable claws with friends who couldn't be there, Joe's will ship anywhere in the United States.

On the beach at First Street is lively **Penrod's**, a big, relaxed, waterfront complex where you can choose from four bars and three restaurants, or order a picnic from the deli and have it brought to you right on the beach.

The area between the southern tip of the island and Sixth Street to the north has lagged behind in South Beach's rise, but is now slowly catching up with the renaissance of the Art Deco District. Until recently, this southern portion of the island was home to some of the oldest and poorest people in the country. Up until World War II, Jews – who became a driving force in the vitality and development of the city – were not allowed north of Fifth Street.

In the early 1970s the City of Miami Beach had this portion of the island designated a redevelopment area – bureaucratic parlance for urban renewal. The city put a moratorium on building improvements and came up with a plan

Map on page 128

to hire a master developer to create a Venice-like community in the 250-acre (100-hectare) area, complete with canals and gondolas. That idea, not surprisingly, fell apart.

The elderly Jewish retirees, many of whom fled Eastern Europe during the 1930s and 1940s are mostly gone, now that the neighborhood is being transformed into an upscale yuppie urban quarter with townhouses, skyscrapers, shopping, and, of course, trendy restaurants.

At 301 Washington Avenue is the renovated **Sanford L. Ziff Jewish Museum of Florida** ❸ (open Tues–Sun; entrance fee; tel: (305) 672-5044), housed in a handsome 1930s synagogue complete with Art Deco features. One of the stained-glass panels is in memory of the notorious gangster Meyer Lansky. Another reminder that the new coexists with the old are the flying fish and octopus that adorn the bright blue building across the street at 248 Euclid Avenue.

Fifth Street, the main road that leads from the MacArthur Causeway to the beach, has had a makeover in recent years. Health food stores and restaurants are popping up, and the entire street is slowly, but surely, coming to life.

Between Jefferson and Meridian on Fifth is **Tap Tap**, a combination Haitian restaurant, art gallery, and popular gathering spot for artists, journalists and film-makers. Amid floor-to-ceiling murals of bold, primitive art, Tap Tap is the only authentic Haitian restaurant on the Beach. Along with photo exhibits, lectures and televised soccer matches, it hosts some of the best live Haitian music this side of Port-au-Prince.

The building on the next block to the east, now housing renovated apartments and stores, is the site of the former Fifth Street Gym where boxing greats Muhamad Ali, Sonny Liston, Joe Louis and Roberto Duran trained.

BELOW: Tap Tap restaurant – Haiti meets South Beach.

At the corner of Fifth and Washington is **The China Grill**, a New York transplant famous for its Asian/New World cuisine. Dine here and you may rub shoulders with a celebrity or two.

Deco delights

From Sixth Street to 23rd Street the look of the Beach drastically changes. In the 1960s and 1970s, this area fell out of vogue and became a crime-ridden, seedy retirement ghetto. With so many ailing elderly people living here, it was often referred to as God's Waiting Room. But thanks to committed Art Deco lovers who petitioned and lobbied and fought with politicians and state and federal agencies, in 1979 this portion of Miami Beach, with more than 500 playful, rounded Deco buildings built in the 1930s, became the youngest historic district in the nation. Its official name is the **Miami Beach Art Deco National Historic District**.

Soon after, developers, salivating over the potential of owning a piece of what was now being heralded as "The American Riviera," sunk millions into renovations. Since the late 1980s, fast-talking speculators have treated the Deco District like a Monopoly game, gobbling up properties as quickly as they can. Without the capital to live through the off-season, many have found themselves entangled in financial fiascoes, and end up filing for bankruptcy.

A notoriously fickle business, nightclubs and restaurants in this part of South Beach have high mortality rates, and the "in" spot of today may very likely be gone by tomorrow. Even international celebrities have gotten caught up in the high-stakes action. Among them are Mickey Rourke, Michael Caine, Madonna, Gloria and Emilio Estefan and Prince. Some have had better fortune than others.

Fidel Castro, the most hated man in Miami, spent his honeymoon in Miami Beach in 1948.

BELOW: Deco hotels on Collins Avenue.

As SoBe grew to become an international playground of the rich and beautiful, area rents and taxes skyrocketed. Many locals, who for years lived in low-rent heaven, were forced to move elsewhere. New Yorkers, accustomed to high-rent high-rises, bought relatively inexpensive condos for use as weekend retreats, and made dirt-cheap apartments a thing of the past. Although the city government is indeed happy with South Beach's transformation, there is a certain amount of local resentment toward the SoBe phenomenon, which has resulted in increased traffic, noise and parking hassles.

A street with a view

For the most historic, modern and dramatic architectural view of the SoBe Art Deco revival, head up **Ocean Drive**. To the east is **Lummus Park**, eight blocks of glorious beach with white sand that stretches 300 ft (90 meters) to the Atlantic Ocean. Little old ladies in sensible shoes and umbrellas, surfers in slick gear and teenage sun worshippers in tiny bathing suits, sprawl on towels or sit in lawn chairs.

Beach-goers listen to boom boxes – suitcase-size radios – fly kites, play paddle ball or go rollerblading on the busy sidewalk. Refreshment vendors hawk snow cones and sodas.

To the west are restored hotels and apartment houses, as well as chic little European-style outdoor cafes, restaurants and stores. The sidewalks have been enlarged and painted. The color: pink, of course.

As a popular cruising street, the traffic on Ocean Drive is horrendous. The parking situation is even worse, with overly zealous meter maids constantly prowling for tardy parkers. Adding to the congestion – and to the view – is the ubiquitous row of Jeeps, BMWs, convertibles, Harley Davidsons and other fashionable vehicles that trawl along Ocean Drive. Drivers peer into restaurants and onto porches, and people in the restaurants and porches stare back; dates have been known to be secured this way.

SoBe is also a place where people walk, a rarity in car-addicted South Florida. The colorful locals – such as the eccentric gentleman who wears a 6-ft (2-meter) boa constrictor around his neck, or Haydee and Sahara Scull, buxom Cuban twins who are as well known for their campy Carmen Miranda-style outfits as for their brightly colored street-scene collages – blend easily with half-naked rollerbladers and the growing number of sophisticated European tourists who converge on the beach.

Model society

Several modeling agencies and professional film processing shops occupy Ocean Drive, creating a constant beautiful-people alert. A few trendy cafes appear to employ only models. Each waiter and waitress is more stunning than the one who came before. Problem is, they spend a lot of time flaunting their looks, forgetting about the customers completely.

By 7am, there's a photographer on almost every Ocean Drive corner, taking advantage of the bright morning light. Reflectors in hand, they shout instructions

Map on page 128

The quirky Scull twins are often spotted around town in identical outfits.

BELOW: the News Cafe, an Ocean Drive institution.

On Miami Beach even the lifeguard huts are eye-catching. This one is opposite 10th Street.

in German, French, Italian and English, as the models toss their hair in the air. Huge, air-conditioned motor homes line the streets, and serve as changing rooms and resting spots for the women. The modeling business has in fact become a multi-million dollar industry for Miami Beach, with magazines like *Vogue* and *Paris Match* vying for the best locations.

Between Sixth and Eighth streets, Ocean Drive sports a gaggle of brightly colored Deco hotels that culminates with the famous **Colony Hotel**. The Colony's neon sign is a SoBe landmark. Just beyond, the sea of green umbrellas on the corner of Eighth Street is the **News Cafe ❹**, one of Ocean Drive's big winners in the restaurant business. Since it opened in 1988, the News has been jam-packed day and night. With jazz playing in the background, and an assortment of foreign magazines and newspapers, it has a faithful European and local clientele. Italian designer Gianni Versace, an habitué, had his last breakfast here before being gunned down on the steps of his mansion up the street.

On the same block is **Larios on the Beach**, a Cuban restaurant owned by Miami icons, singer Gloria Estefan and music producer-husband Emilio.

Heading up the street, more Art Deco hotels shout for attention. There is the yellow and white **Waldorf Towers Hotel**, and the blue and white stripes of the **Breakwater Hotel**, at 940 Ocean Drive, while the **Clevelander Hotel** hops all night with its sprawling outdoor bar.

Directly on the beach at 10th Street is the **Miami Beach Ocean Front Auditorium**. Here, beach residents both young and old gather for music, lectures and lunches. Nearby is the **Art Deco Welcome Center ❺** (open daily; tel: (305) 531-3484), operated by the Miami Design Preservation League, the non-profit group responsible for the movement to preserve the Art Deco properties and for

BELOW: distinctive Deco styling at the Cavalier Hotel.

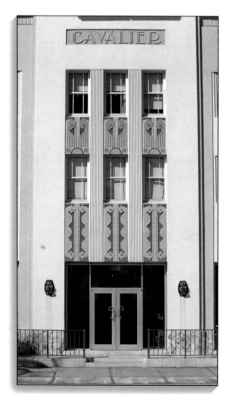

DECO WALKING TOURS

The beauty of the Art Deco buildings is in their details – flamingo and pelican motifs, windows shaped as portholes, stucco stylized friezes in geometric designs, tropical pastel shades of pink, aqua and yellow. So, park the car, put on comfortable shoes, grab the camera and head over to the Art Deco Welcome Center at 1001 Ocean Drive, just across from the Clevelander and Edison hotels.

Choose between a self-guided audio tour and a group tour led by a member of the Miami Design Preservation League. The 1-hour 40-minute group tour leaves the center on Saturdays at 10:30am and Thursdays at 6:30pm. Cost is $10 per person. The self-guided tour is available daily from 11am until 4pm. For $5 you're loaned a Walkman. You'll hear the history of Miami Beach, from its earlier days when the hotels were built, to the fight in the 1970s and '80s to save the decaying structures.

You can buy books and souvenirs relating to South Beach and Art Deco at the MDPL's gift shop at the Art Deco Welcome Center. The center has another shop on the corner of Lincoln Road and Drexel Avenue, but all tours leave from the Ocean Drive location.

For more information on the tours or to make reservations, call (305) 531-3484.

Map on page 128

listing them on the National Register of Historic Places. The Welcome Center offers a wealth of Art Deco information. It also sells maps, books, postcards, souvenirs and Art Deco antiques and jewelry. This is the place to buy presents, because a portion of the asking price goes back into preserving the district. The center also sponsors informative and entertaining walking tours of the district.

About one block north on Ocean Drive is **Casa Casuarina ❻**, a magnificent Mediterranean-style mansion hidden behind towering pine trees. Formerly a run-down apartment building, this structure was designed to resemble Christopher Columbus' home in the Dominican Republic, complete with 15-ft (5-meter) high antique wooden doors. Gianni Versace bought it in 1992 for $2.9 million. A year later, he bought its neighbor, the Revere Hotel, for $3.7 million, then tore it down to put in a private courtyard and pool. After his death in 1997, the Versace family put it up for sale. Asking price: $23–25 million.

A little farther north on Ocean Drive is another line of Deco darlings. On the corner of 13th Street is the **Carlyle ❼**, one of the first Art Deco hotels to be refurbished. It, like many of the other small hotels on Ocean Drive, has been used as a backdrop for movies, videos and modeling sessions. On either side of the Carlyle, the **Leslie** and the **Cardozo** were also restored early. Just beyond the Cardozo, the **Cavalier**, with its soaring windows and small Deco lobby, is rented regularly by photography crews from other cities. The Cavalier and the Casa Grande (also on Ocean Drive, but back near the News Cafe) are owned by Jamaican-born Island Records founder Chris Blackwell. A shrewd entrepreneur, Blackwell has also brought his Island Trading Company, an art and clothing boutique with a Caribbean flair, to Ocean Drive. It is housed on the ground floor of the Netherland Hotel.

Versace was in on the act from the beginning of the Miami Beach renaissance: many of his outrageous designs were used on the hit show Miami Vice.

BELOW: a South Beach welcome.

Away from the beach

There is more to SoBe than Ocean Drive. The two streets that run parallel to it should not be missed. Two blocks west is **Washington Avenue**, a frenetic, clamoring kind of thoroughfare that feels and sounds more New York City than Miami Beach. A walking avenue, Washington is a dichotomy of new and old. The recent arrivals – nightclubs, over-priced antique and Art Deco shops and trendy restaurants serving sushi and Thai cuisine – rub shoulders with more established residents – fruit markets, second-hand stores, Kosher shops, junk outlets and tattoo and body-piercing parlors.

But it's the people who bring vibrancy to Washington Avenue. Cuban men who stand at outdoor cafes sipping cafe Cubano, businessmen, bag ladies, New Wave punks, Hip Hop kids – they're all here. On weekend nights, teens from far and wide turn it into a scene, converging in a procession of slow-moving cars with blaring stereos, ogling each other as they try to pick up a date.

Between Washington and Ocean Drive is **Collins Avenue**, one of the most scenic and strangest thoroughfares in SoBe. As the Beach's main drag, it continues northward, out of the SoBe area, all the way to Bal Harbour and beyond. Designer boutiques such as Armani, Versace and Kenneth Cole have sprouted up at the southern end of Collins from Sixth to Eighth streets. At 801 Collins is **The Hotel**, built as the Tiffany in 1939. It was forced to change its name in 1998, after its renovation by fashion designer Todd Oldham, when the famous jeweler got huffy.

Heading north again and back on Washington, look out for the **Wolfsonian Foundation ❽** (open daily except Wed; Sun pm only; entrance fee; tel: (305) 531-1001), housed in the pretty, renovated Mediterranean-Revival Washington

TIP

Parking can be a nightmare in South Beach. There is a big parking lot just north of Lincoln Road Mall, but otherwise you must rely on meters. For an easy life, take a bus or a cab.

BELOW: the Clay Hotel, a travelers' meeting place.

Storage Company building, at the intersection with 10th Street. Beginning in the 1920s, when Beach residents lived here seasonally, they stored their precious possessions here – everything from curtains to cars – before heading back north. One of the clients was Mitchell Wolfson Jr, heir to the Wometco movie theater fortune. He bought the building in 1984 and established his Foundation here two years later.

Opened in 1995, the Wolfsonian is his pride and joy. For more than three decades, Wolfson has traveled the world collecting objets d'art, especially propaganda artworks of the 19th and early 20th centuries. Now, his eccentric collection of more than 70,000 pieces is on display, including such oddities as Hitler propaganda posters, bronze busts of Mussolini, furniture designed by architect Frank Lloyd Wright, and metalworks, industrial products, trains, appliances, comic books, ceramics and paintings that have had an impact on modern design techniques throughout the world. The collection even spills out onto the sidewalk where a bridge tender's house sits, used at times to house surplus exhibits. At other times it sits empty.

On the corner of Collins Avenue and Espanola Way is the Beach's oldest and best-known gay club, the Warsaw Ballroom. It is housed in a "Nautical Tropical Deco" building that started life as Hoffman's Cafeteria.

Local institutions

A block to the north of the Wolfsonian is a local landmark, the **Old City Hall**, a 1920s Mediterranean-style building that towers over the surrounding streets. Behind it is the Miami Beach Police Station, an aqua and white Streamline structure with a glass brick front. Another Chris Blackwell property, the **Marlin Hotel**, is back on Collins Avenue at No. 1200. The front porch of this Deco gem is a great place to sit and sip a martini. North again, on the corner of Washington and 13th Street is the **Miami Beach Post Office ❾**. Built in 1937, this building is crowned by a marble and stained-glass lantern. Inside, murals and bronze grillwork decorate a vast rotunda.

BELOW: the area used to belong to the elderly.

Continuing to 1445 Washington Avenue, you reach the **Cameo Theater**, the premier hall for international films when it opened in 1938. After years of refurbishing, the 980-seat theater now draws the younger set to concerts given by Latin and reggae bands, and club nights featuring techno and trance music.

At 1438 Washington Avenue is the gaudy **Clay Hotel and International Youth Hostel**, with flamingo-pink facade and wrought-iron balconies. A clean, cheap and interesting place to stay, the hostel is filled with people from other countries. Hand-written notices on lobby bulletin boards are clearly penned by people who speak English as a second language. The European-style hostel is only two blocks from the ocean.

The entrance to the hostel is actually on **Espanola Way ❿**, a narrow street of Mediterranean-Revival buildings, with white buttresses and gas lamps, which was constructed in 1925. A charming little street that was often used as a set for *Miami Vice*, Espanola has the distinction that Desi Arnaz, the Cuban bandleader and TV star Lucille Ball's husband, played in the Village Tavern (now the youth hostel) in the 1930s. In recent years it has attracted artists, who rent tiny studios on the second and third floors. At street level are

The electric-powered Electrowave shuttle is an easy way to get around SoBe. It runs all day and most of the night, from Alton and Lincoln, via Washington, to Fifth and Alton, and then back again. The fare is just 25 cents.

BELOW: terrace of the Delano Hotel.

several expensive but interesting Deco-era clothing and furniture stores, coffee houses, restaurants and art galleries. On Sundays, Espanola bustles with a different crowd shopping for fresh vegetables, flowers and arts and crafts at its eclectic open-air market.

At 16th and Collins is a new 800-room hotel, **Loew's**, designed to blend with the restored Art Deco hotels surrounding it. Just across the street is another shopping cluster, the Anchor Shops. Up the block at 1685 Collins is one of the most interesting hotels on the Beach, the **Delano ⓫**. Built in 1947 and topped off with a modernistic finned tower, the Delano was remodeled in 1995 by French designer Philippe Starck and his partner Ian Schrager, the *haute* hotelier who founded New York City's famed nightclub Studio 54. Austere but elegant, the Delano has white walls, white floors, white beds, white chairs, and even white TV sets. It has become a darling of the rich-and-famous set. In its lobby is the Blue Door, a restaurant and bar operated by the same people who run the China Grill.

Added culture

Known in its heyday in the 1950s as the Fifth Avenue of the South, the **Lincoln Road Mall ⓬** has recently awakened from a long, sad slumber. Designed by Morris Lapidus, Miami Beach's flamboyant "architect of joy," Lincoln Road is a pedestrian-only thoroughfare that was neglected for years. A few cheap luggage and trinket stores remain, but they're being rapidly squeezed out by upscale chain stores such as Williams Sonoma and Pottery Barn. There's even a Deco-style McDonald's and Burger King in the neighborhood. The Road, as it is called by locals, has become a victim of its own success. Sky-

rocketing rents have pushed out the younger, artsy and more creative crowd that brought it back from the dead.

Three blocks of storefronts, known as the **South Florida Art Center**, have been transformed into galleries, boutiques, cafes, and 52 studios where more than 100 artists work and display their art. The main office is at 924 Lincoln Road, but there are several galleries that belong to the center.

Several one-of-a-kind restaurants on the Road make dining here a treat, and a stroll around will produce intriguing results. Left over from the original Lincoln Road is a Morris Lapidus fountain studded with broken plates. Take a load off your feet a few blocks down on a black-rubber chair made from truck tires by Spanish artist Miralda. The road is further brightened up at No. 818 by Britto Central, a gallery devoted to Brazilian pop artist Romero Britto.

Once the home of the Miami City Ballet, which moved to bigger digs at 2200 Liberty Avenue, the area still hosts a few small dance troupes: Ballet Flamenco la Rosa at 555 17th Street, and the Mideastern Dance Exchange at 350 Lincoln Road, which offers African, Caribbean, and belly-dancing classes to the public.

At 1040 Lincoln Road is the **Colony Theater**, a former movie house, now a city-owned performing arts center. Also on the Road (at No. 555) is the **Lincoln Theatre**, home to the New World Symphony, America's only national training orchestra for musicians from ages 21 to 30. These 90 young musicians have played to wide acclaim in Paris and at New York City's Carnegie Hall. No longer is that tired, old joke true: "What's the difference between Miami and yogurt? The answer: yogurt has culture."

In 1993, MTV Latino, the Spanish language version of the popular music video TV station, moved in to Lincoln Road and established a state-of-the-art

Map
on page
128

Actor Michael Caine has also been drawn to Lincoln Road. He opened his South Beach Brasserie in a former synagogue here in 1996.

LEFT: cyclists and pedestrians only on Lincoln Road Mall. **BELOW:** Miami Beach beauty.

Although the Miami City Ballet has moved from rehearsal studios that were visible to a fascinated public on Lincoln Road, you can still watch the dancers practising, as the new facility at 2200 Liberty Avenue includes a number of studios with so-called "storefront windows."

BELOW: harrowing images on the Holocaust Memorial.

studio in a remodeled Deco building. Soon after, Sony's Latin Music Division did the same. Together, the two have triggered a boom in the production of Spanish-language music videos in the SoBe area. They've been followed by an influx of Spanish-language "dotcom" companies doing business with Latin America via the Internet.

Books & Books, a sister of the Books & Books store in Coral Gables, is on Lincoln Road, and is South Beach's favorite literary hang-out, with book signings and lectures by prominent authors.

A few blocks away from the Road is Hank Meyer Boulevard. In Miami Beach, streets are not named for presidents or war heroes, but for entertainers and publicists. Also known as 17th Street, Hank Meyer Boulevard was named for a publicist who encouraged comedian Jackie Gleason to broadcast his television program from Miami. Gleason did so – for 22 years.

A 3,023-seat performing arts center is named for the popular entertainer who immortalized Miami Beach as the "sun and fun capital of the world" on his weekly show. Broadway shows and major ballet and symphony productions are held in the **Jackie Gleason Theater of the Performing Arts** ⓭ (more commonly known as TOPA), at 1700 Washington Avenue, the Art Deco building where the national show originated. In front of the theater is *The Mermaid*, a sculpture by Roy Lichtenstein.

On Meridian Avenue is the **Holocaust Memorial** ⓮, a somber testament to the tragedies of World War II. Situated near the Miami Beach Garden Center and Conservatory, the memorial, designed by Kenneth Treister, is a 42-ft (13-meter) bronze sculpture of a hand reaching towards the heavens. Set against a backdrop of photographs of Nazi death camps and the names of those who died, the sculpture has life-size renditions of terrified victims struggling to the top.

There is one art museum on Miami Beach. Just one. The **Bass Museum of Art** ⓯ (open Tues–Sun; entrance fee; tel: (305) 673-7530), at 2121 Park Avenue, is a fine museum with a diverse collection of European art. This includes major paintings from the 15th century through the 20th century, tapestries, religious pieces such as ecclesiastical vestments and artifacts, and some sculpture. Highlights to look out for are *The Holy Family*, a painting by Peter Paul Rubens, and a 16th-century Flemish tapestry called *The Tournament*. The Bass has also become a repository of architectural photos and drawings documenting Miami Beach history, and there is an architectural and design collection with works from the U.S., the Caribbean and Latin America.

Extensive renovation and expansion work at the Bass, under the watchful eye of world-renowned Japanese architect Arata Isozaki, was due for completion in late 2000. The museum is now part of the new Miami Beach Cultural Campus, bounded by 21st and 23rd streets, which includes the new headquarters and rehearsal facility for the **Miami City Ballet**, designed by local architectural firm Arquitectonica, as well as the planned Miami Beach Regional Library.

Nearby, at 21st Street and Collins, sits a Miami Beach eating (not dining) institution: **Wolfie's**. The menus here are as large as tabloid newspapers, the waitresses wear name tags and eavesdrop on conversations, offering unsolicited advice along with a basket of free rolls and pastries. Wolfie's is an old-fashioned delicatessen where you can still find a steaming bowl of matzoh ball soup and pastrami sandwiches that are almost four inches thick.

Once you've had your fill of SoBe "culture" you'll need a cold beer to wash it all down. Two bars that couldn't be more different or more South Beach are the **Irish House Pub** and **Club Deuce**. The Irish House, at 1430 Alton Road, is a real neighborhood bar with a great jukebox, greasy food and locals – from sailors based in the area to reporters. Deuce, at 222 14th Street in the heart of South Beach, is a tougher and funkier nightspot whose clientele ranges from aging transvestites to fresh-faced kids on spring break from college. A pool game at Deuce is not to be undertaken lightly. If you get hungry, step outside for a great snack at La Sandwicherie, an open-air counter jutting from the alley just across the street.

Beyond SoBe

Miami Beach doesn't end with South Beach. Collins Avenue continues north, and running parallel to Collins Avenue is something that has endeared Miami Beach politicians to the people – a public boardwalk, stretching 1.8 miles (2.9 km) along the ocean from 21st to 47th streets. The action that takes place on the boardwalk is a study of the people of Miami Beach. Hasidic Jewish families stroll around, couples jog, teenagers hold hands and gaze at the water and each other. The view from the boardwalk can't be beaten. With the ocean on one side and fancy high-rise hotels and apartment buildings on the other, it's both a

Map on page 128

The boardwalk that runs northward from 21st Street is popular with Miamians of all stripes.

BELOW: beach business.

tropical paradise and a voyeur's dream. Though well-lighted, portions of the boardwalk are not recommended at night, so take care.

In this part of town there are a couple of great accommodation options just the right distance from the madness to the south – a kitsch 1950s hostel, the Banana Bungalow, at 2360 Collins Avenue, and the serene Deco-era Indian Creek Hotel, at 2727 Indian Creek Drive. But the most celebrated hotel in Miami Beach has always been the **Fontainebleau Hilton Resort and Spa** ⓰, situated about 20 blocks to the north, at 4441 Collins Avenue. Built in 1954, it reeks of post-war confidence, a time when large families drove to Florida in big gas-guzzling cars for a winter retreat of sun and fun, away from the frozen, gray north. Everyone who was anyone in those days, including Frank Sinatra and Bob Hope, either performed or stayed at the Fontainebleau.

Excess personified, the hotel consists of two curving 14-story buildings that face the Atlantic, along with marble staircases, crystal chandeliers, 1,206 rooms, two pools (one a two-story lagoon with a floating bar) and an entire indoor shopping center. Because of its size and amenities, the Fontainebleau also does a brisk convention business.

If the hotel itself is too much to bear, try a mirror image of it painted on one of its walls at 44th Street and Collins Avenue. Covering 10 stories is a *trompe l'oeil* of – that's right – the Fontainebleau Hilton. The hotel is expensive, but a peek at the mural is free. Unfortunately, the mural is about to come down, a casualty of the condo-development craze sweeping the beach. A 40-story skyscraper is going up on that spot.

The Fontainebleau is the grandest of the dinosaur hotels of the era, but it is by no means the only one. Next door is the **Eden Roc**, with its multi-million

TIP

North of 21st Street the beaches become more family-friendly than the poseurs' paradise to the south. The sands at 53rd Street even have a playground and public conveniences.

BELOW: mural at the Fontainebleau.

Map
on page
128

dollar refurbished lobby. It's been restored to its original 1950s design, and meets the approval of the original architect and designer, Morris Lapidus. As he put it, "I did elaborate, not gaudy." From about 42nd Street and Collins Avenue to the north are wall-to-wall hotels and high-rise condominiums, a testament to post-World War II America's "bigger is better" philosophy.

Running along Collins Avenue on the west side is **Indian Creek**, behind which lie stately mansions with kidney-shaped pools and boats moored on private docks. For one week every February, hundreds of pricey yachts bob on the creek across from the grand hotels, up for sale in the Yacht and Brokerage Show.

West of Collins at 71st Street is the Normandy Fountain area, a burgeoning neighborhood with an eclectic collection of restaurants – Argentinian, Colombian, Japanese and French.

From 79th to 87th streets on the ocean is the **North Shore State Recreation Area**. You don't have to be a diehard swimmer or sunbather to enjoy this serene beach. A fitness trail winds its way through groves of trees, and there's a series of boardwalks that meanders into natural surroundings. There are picnic tables and grills for family outings.

The other Miami Beach

The towns and villages in the north portion of the island of Miami Beach are vastly different in scope and style. **Surfside** was a 1930s settling ground and winter destination resort for French Canadians. Every spring since the mid-1960s, it has thrown a week-long bash, Canada Week, to honor its Canadian population.

Today, Surfside is a comfortable, low-key neighborhood where young and old, established and still-striving, mingle. The Surfside Community Center, at 9301

BELOW: away from South Beach the sands are more deserted.

TIP

The sleepy town of Surfside has a few of its own architectural gems, including examples of Tropical Deco. The Miami Design Preservation League offers special tours of the area. Call (305) 531-3484 for details.

BELOW:
upscale shopping at Bal Harbour.

Collins Avenue, bustles with locals and tourists playing canasta and chatting. In a new development, which has brought a bit of glamour to the area, the Rubell family, hoteliers and art collectors, have opened their latest elegant inn, Beach House Bal Harbour, at 9449 Collins Avenue.

Along Harding Avenue, Surfside's main commercial street, mothers stroll with baby carriages, and retirees gather for coffee. A flashback to small-town America, the street still has a beauty parlor where a shampoo and set cost less than you imagine. At the corner of Harding and 95th Street is **Sheldon's Drug Store**, an old-fashioned lunch counter that sells ice-cream sodas and egg creams. It was after eating bagels and eggs at Sheldon's that the late Isaac Bashevis Singer learned he had won the Nobel Prize for Literature *(see page 148)*. Singer lived for about 20 years in Surfside, and 95th Street is now known as Isaac B. Singer Boulevard.

The international crooner and most tanned man alive, Julio Iglesias, lives nearby in **Indian Creek Village**, as does former Miami Dolphins football coach Don Shula. Just west of Surfside, Indian Creek has a lush – and private – golf course and 27 lavish mansions.

For art galleries in the area, head for **Bay Harbor Islands**, a tiny town made up of two islands on the Intracoastal Waterway, with small-scale apartment buildings and private homes. The most unusual collection here is housed in the **Kenneth R. Laurence Galleries**, at 1007 Kane Concourse. Mr Laurence, a retired builder with a penchant for what he calls "aesthetics collecting of historic documents," has on display framed documents, diaries and letters signed by Napolean, Ghandi, Churchill, Kennedy, Pasteur and Chopin. Also in Bay Harbor is the Palm Restaurant, which is under the same ownership as its well-known namesakes in New York and Los Angeles.

To the northeast of Bay Harbor is **Bal Harbour** ⓱, a 250-acre (100-hectare) enclave of concrete condos and lavishly landscaped medians. A flashy and ultra-upscale town, Bal Harbour is home to the **Bal Harbour Shops**. This exclusive mall is a haven of elegance and opulence. Fine outdoor eateries in the mall offer designer foods to go along with the designer fashions.

Haulover Park, north of Bal Harbour and south of Sunny Isles Beach, is a mile (1.5 km) long beach uninterrupted by high-rises – a rarity in South Florida. Just over the bridge, the sky is dotted with colorful kites of all shapes and sizes available for sale. Kayaks can be rented at the marina on the western side of Haulover to explore the mangroves lining Dumbfoundling Bay.

To the east is the beach. In recent years, the northern part of Haulover Park has become a mecca for nude sunbathers. It's the only nude beach in the county. Although park officials are uncomfortable about the bounty of exposed body parts, they have allowed it to continue because, they say, at least it is contained. Shielded from the highway by sea-grape trees, the nudists are not narcissistic, just happy to enjoy the beach *au naturel*.

Sunny Isles Beach, about 2 miles (3 km) long, is covered in rocky sand. The winds and rough surf here lure surfers and sailors. The Newport Beach Pier, built in 1936 and thrice destroyed by hurricanes, is a great fishing spot.

Capping Miami-Dade County's northernmost beaches is **Golden Beach**. Like its name, the coastal community here is wealthy and the beach is private. Residents live in palatial, Venetian-style homes along 2 miles (3 km) of Atlantic shorelines. There are about 300 homes in Golden Beach, the most famous being 461 Ocean Boulevard, which rock star Eric Clapton immortalized by naming his album after the house in which he was staying. ❑

Map on page 128

BELOW: beach bums in the making.

ART DECO: SOUTH BEACH STYLE

The exotic, colorful buildings on Ocean Drive and nearby streets are the product of Miami's unique interpretation of the Art Deco style

The splendid Art Deco buildings in Miami Beach were built to raise the spirits of Americans during the Great Depression. Many decades later, preservationists say that they are among the most architecturally significant structures in the US.

The roots of Art Deco go back to 1901, when the Société des Artistes Décorateurs was formed in Paris with the goal of merging the mass production of industrial technology with the decorative arts. It was proudly introduced to the world in 1925 at the Paris Exposition Internationale des Arts Décoratifs et Industriels Modernes. The nickname "Art Deco" came about only in 1966, when it was dreamed up for a retrospective of the 1925 Paris show.

The Art Deco style was thoroughly evocative of the new Machine Age, which was inspired partly by the aerodynamic designs of aeroplanes and cars. However, Art Deco combined all kinds of influences, from the swirls of Art Nouveau to the hard lines of Cubism.

TROPICAL DECO

In the 1930s and '40s, hundreds of Deco structures were built in South Beach. Art Deco's stark, white exteriors were already well suited to Florida's hot climate, but architects in Miami soon developed their own style, which was later dubbed Tropical Deco. Many features, from the design of the windows to the choice of colors, were inspired by South Florida's weather and its seaside location. The more futuristic Art Deco style known as Streamline Moderne, which replaced some of the detail characteristic of traditional Art Deco with smoother lines and sweeping curves, was particularly popular in Miami. Several elements, such as "porthole" windows and tube railings, were borrowed from the design of sleek ocean-going liners.

△ **WINDOWS**
Long bands of windows, often continuing around the corner of a building (as seen here, on the Park Central Hotel on Ocean Drive), allowed in plenty of natural light and refreshing sea breezes.

▽ **SPEED AND MOTION**
Ocean Drive's Breakwater Hotel, illustrated here on a Deco-style postcard, has a tower like a ship's funnel and horizontal, colored "racing stripes" that give a feeling of speed and movement.

◁ **TROPICAL DECORATION**
Many exteriors, elevator doors and windows feature typical Tropical Deco motifs, such as pelicans and sunbursts.

▽ **FRIEZES OF COLOR**
Bas-relief stucco friezes, featuring stylized natural forms or geometric designs, decorate many facades.

△ NEON CITY
The Art Deco architects in Miami tried out all kinds of new materials, including chrome, glass blocks and terrazzo – a cheap, imitation marble. Neon lighting was used for the first time and is one of the most distinctive features of South Beach. It means that the architecture can be enjoyed day and night.

△ FANTASY TOWERS
The Ritz Plaza on Collins Avenue is one of several later Art Deco hotels, built in South Beach in the 1940s, whose design was influenced by the science-fiction fantasies of *Buck Rogers* and *Flash Gordon*. This is noticeable particularly in the thrust of its tower.

▽ MARVELOUS MARLIN
This hotel on Collins is a classic Streamline building. Notice the rounded corners and "eyebrows" – canopies that shade the windows against the sun. Deco roofs were generally flat but often broken by a raised central parapet or pointed finial.

THE FIGHT TO SAVE MIAMI DECO

The Art Deco hotels of South Beach provided a welcome refuge for visiting northerners for some time, but by the 1960s they had begun to decay. Several of the area's once-glamorous hotels became low-rent housing for the elderly, and much of the district became run-down and crime-ridden.

In 1976, Barbara Capitman (1920–90) set up the Miami Design Preservation League to stop the demolition of the Art Deco buildings and to encourage their restoration. In 1979, 1 sq mile (2.5 sq km) of South Beach was listed on the National Registry of Historic Places. It was the first 20th-century district to receive such recognition.

In the 1980s, a designer called Leonard Horowitz endowed South Beach with a new color scheme, nicknamed the Deco Dazzle, by painting many of the old buildings in bright colors; originally most would have been white with just the trim picked out in color.

Media interest in Miami's Art Deco enclave gradually increased, and then rocketed after South Beach became one of the favorite backdrops in the hit TV series, *Miami Vice*. Fashion photographers were drawn south to Florida too, Bruce Weber being one of the first to be lured both by the stylish and colorful location and by the climate. In the late 1980s, developers and other entrepreneurs moved in, opening nightclubs and model agencies and renovating hotels.

My Love Affair With Miami Beach

Before he died, Isaac Bashevis Singer, winner of the Nobel Prize for Literature, recalled his early days in the area.

In 1948 when my wife, Alma, and I visited Florida for the first time, the face of Miami Beach resembled a small Israel. From the cafeterias to the streets, Yiddish resounded around us in accents as thick as those you would hear in Tel Aviv. It was remarkable: Jewishness had survived every atrocity of Hitler and the Nazis. Here, the sound of the Old World was as alive as ever.

Alma and I had not had a vacation since 1940, when we were married. (I was lucky to have a wife who did not resent being married to a poor writer.) But it was a particularly cold winter in New York in 1948, so we decided to buy two train tickets to Miami.

All night we traveled, sitting up in our seats, until the early morning, when the conductor told us to step out of the train at Deerfield Beach for a glass of fresh orange juice. That first sip was nothing less than ambrosia. In my native Poland, orange juice was considered a most healthful drink. Even today, Alma carries home oranges from the grocery and squeezes fresh juice for breakfast.

When we arrived at the train station in Miami, a taxi took us to Miami Beach. As we rode over the causeway, I could hardly believe my eyes. To me, being at a summer place in winter was a great event. It was almost unimaginable that in Miami it was 80°F while in New York it was 20. Everything – the buildings, water – had an indescribable glow and brightness to it. The palm trees especially made a great impression on me. The driver let us off at the Pierre Motel. Owned by the brothers Gottlieb, it was a modern place but still had its own charm and good clientele. We were given a nice room with a balcony, where I worked every day. It was in those years that I wrote chapters of the *The Family Moskat*, my first big novel, which ran as a serial in the *Jewish Daily Forward*.

In the 1940s and 1950s, Miami Beach was in its so-called heyday. During the day, planes with long streamers flew over the beach advertising dinners with seven courses for $1.50. Rather than eat in the hotel, we often had dinner with acquaintances and old friends at one of the many cafeterias. We ate heartily: borscht, sweet-and-sour cabbage, salad, bread, coffee and dessert.

The cafeterias were nostalgic places for me, and I loved going to them. They reminded me of the Yiddish Writers Club of Warsaw, where I had rubbed elbows with not only some of the greatest Yiddish writers and poets but English and German writers as well. The same food was served and the same conversations took place. I noticed that often people met here again accidentally after a long separation during the Hitler era and a lot of tears were shed.

LEFT: the late Nobel Laureate Isaac Bashevis Singer, who lived in Surfside, in north Miami Beach.
RIGHT: an early postcard of Miami Beach.

For some reason we stopped coming to Miami Beach in the 1960s. Then, in 1973, I was invited to give a lecture in downtown Miami. A former neighbor of Alma's in Munich happened to come to my lecture. Afterward, she invited us to her apartment on Collins Avenue.

By then, we had fallen in love with Miami Beach all over again, and we considered buying an apartment. For five days, we struggled with the decision: Should we, could we, afford to buy an apartment? In the end, we bought one with a splendid view of the ocean where we live all year round today.

One morning in 1978, I went to Sheldon's Drugstore to have eggs and bagels. Earlier, a friend had called to tell me she had heard on *Good Morning America* that I had won the Nobel Prize, but I had dismissed it as just a nomination and not the real thing.

When I returned after breakfast, Alma was calling out to me excitedly. My editor at the *Forward* was on the telephone. He told me that he had heard on the transatlantic wire that I had won the Nobel. My hands grew cold and Alma says I turned as white as a sheet. Two months later, after many hectic shopping trips to buy clothes for the big event, we flew to Stockholm. It was an ecstatic moment for me when the King of Sweden handed me the prize.

But just because someone has won the Nobel Prize does not mean that life changes dramatically. After the ceremonies had ended and the rush of interviews was over, life went on as before. Alma and I returned to our apartment and I continued to write each day.

From this oasis of comfort, I have pondered the many changes that have taken place on Miami Beach since 1948, not all of them for the best.

Nevertheless, for me, Miami Beach is still one of the most beautiful places in the world. Nothing can equal the splendor of nature. Every day, as I sit on the beach looking out at the ocean, each palm tree, each wave, each sea gull is still a revelation to me. After all these years, Miami Beach feels like home. ❑

Map
on pages
122–3

BISCAYNE BAY

*The expanse of water that separates Miami Beach from the
rest of the city is dotted with exclusive residential islands
and home to the largest cruise port in the world*

Driving over Biscayne Bay, tourists and even some locals cannot help but
stare transfixed at the yachts, sailboats and condominium-sized cruise
ships that ply the waters below. Either that or they gaze in wonder at the
panorama of Miami's downtown skyline.

A good view of all this can be had from the MacArthur Causeway. Coming
from Miami Beach, the first thing you'll notice is the **US Coast Guard Station**,
a launching point for cutters patrolling the seas looking for rafters or drug runners. To the south is **Fisher Island**, separated from Miami Beach by Government Cut, a man-made channel leading out of the bay. The island is one of the
highest priced pieces of real estate in South Florida. It draws part of its exclusivity from being linked to the causeway by ferry only. Second homes to celebrities such as Oprah Winfrey, condos here sell in the $6-million range.

Farther along, on the north side of the MacArthur Causeway are bridges leading to **Star**, **Palm** and **Hibiscus** islands. These posh islands, dotted with mansions with yachts moored in their backyards, have had their share of famous and
infamous residents. Al Capone, the notorious gangster who terrorized Chicago
in the 1920s, lived at 93 Palm Island. Fiction writer and journalist Damon
Runyon lived at 271 Hibiscus Island. Nowadays Gloria Estefan and Miami
Heat basketball stars call these islands home.

Isolated on a dot of land north of Star Island is the
Flagler Memorial Monument, an obelisk honoring
Henry Flagler, considered the single-most influential
person in South Florida's development.

The Port of Miami

On the other side of the causeway are **Lummus** and
Dodge islands, home to the **Dante Fascell Port of
Miami**, named after a powerful congressman who
steered a great deal of money toward the port's construction. The old port facilities stretched from the
Freedom Tower to the *Miami Herald* building in
downtown Miami. They were replaced in 1964 by the
complex on these islands, which has since captured a
huge chunk of the cruise ship market. Well over 3
million passengers pass through the port each year. It
also handles close to 50 cargo lines.

There is no better spot to watch the huge cruise
ships slowly make their way out to sea than **Watson
Island**, farther to the west on MacArthur Causeway.
At night the view is even more spectacular, when
lights in the cabins and lamps on the decks are glow-
ing on the liners, all moored in a long row at the port
– as you drive along the causeway the effect is almost
magical. Thursdays and Fridays are the best days to
catch a glimpse of these floating hotels as they load up
for weekend sailings.

BELOW: a yacht
cruises alongside
the MacArthur
Causeway.

On the northeast side of Watson Island is the future home of Parrot Jungle, to open in 2001 *(see page 213)*. The island, more than anything, looks like an advertising campaign for the wonders of modern transportation. The sounds are diverse: the drone of jets flying overhead to Miami Airport, the whoosh of helicopters that lift tourists above Miami Beach, the bellow of horns from cruise ships, the slap of tug boats dragging cargo ships across the choppy cut, and, on the causeway, the ever-present sound of cars. It's a symphony of engines.

The most startling sight are the bulbous airplanes that circle the Miami skyline and splash into Biscayne Bay, only to crawl up to Watson Island. These seaplanes belong to Chalks International, the world's oldest airline, headquartered on the island. Chalks, founded in 1919, had some rough times recently, when its owners threatened to shut it down because it was losing money. The very idea that the chubby planes would fly no more so upset Miamians that many of them wrote angry letters to the editor of the *Miami Herald*. One *Herald* columnist began an unofficial campaign to keep the airline on Watson Island. The public outcry worked. In early 1996, Chalks merged with Pan Am, a new company that bought the rights to the defunct airline's name, and it is now officially called the Pan Am Air Bridge. Chalks, however, has a loyal fan club and most customers and locals insist on calling it by its original name.

Seeing the bay from your car is one thing, but you'll get much closer to the action on an evening cruise. Choose from gambling, dining or just gawking. Boats such as *The Island Queen* and *Casino Princesa* leave from Bayside Marketplace, Watson Island or the Port of Miami. Fishing and sailing charters leave from the Biscayne Bay Marriott marina or the Miami Beach Marina. There are also day trips to the Bahamas or cruises beyond US waters, to allow gambling. ❑

When the upper-crust residents of Fisher Island catch the car ferry to the mainland, workers at the ferry station hose their cars down as they arrive, just in case they got splashed with sea water during the 10-minute crossing.

BELOW: the *Fantasy* cruise ship casts off.

DOWNTOWN MIAMI

On the lively downtown streets, behind the street vendors, cut-price emporia and throngs of people from all corners of the globe, are architectural reminders of the city's brief history

Map on page 156

t is a toddler in the family of America's big cities. Some of downtown Miami's older buildings are younger than many of the folks who have come here to retire. But since April 15, 1896, when Henry Flagler brought his East Coast Railway into Miami, literally putting the town on the map for subsequent waves of settlers, the little devil has turned into a spunky, scrappy city. With its notable, excitable Latin edge, downtown feels more like the northern tip of the southern hemisphere than the other way around.

From a distance, especially at night, downtown Miami looks like a throbbing megalopolis, its bank of skyscrapers floodlit and twinkling in colored neon, creating a magic-show skyline quite unlike any other in the United States. Yet, for the visitor walking along Biscayne Boulevard, through the central grid of one-way streets, across the Miami River and into the gleaming Brickell Avenue quarter, Miami runs very much on a human scale.

There are cops walking beats along wide sidewalks; hawkers selling fruit, juices and cakes from corner pushcarts; cabbies dozing in taxis queued up along Flagler Street like bright yellow bonbons; hot-dog vendors and shoeshine men on the steps of the Dade County Courthouse. The city seems more like a street fair than the cultural, political and administrative nerve center of a sprawling metropolis.

PRECEDING PAGES: baggage handlers. **LEFT:** skyline from the Miami River. **BELOW:** nostalgic billboard and the Freedom Tower.

Downtown playgrounds

Just off Biscayne Boulevard – the main thoroughfare that runs parallel to Miami's waterfront – is **Bayside Marketplace ❶**, a 16-acre (6-hectare) extravaganza of more than 140 shops, restaurants and attractions. Since its development, Bayside has been the life of downtown, attracting both tourists and residents at all hours of the day and night. Along the water's edge, private boats dock for lunch and dinner as mime artists, jugglers and bands entertain the crowds. The huge neon guitar in the background marks the entrance to the Hard Rock Cafe Miami, with the emphasis at this branch on memorabilia from the city's Latin superstars, such as Gloria Estefan and John Secada.

To the north stands the **American Airlines Arena**, the new home of the Miami Heat, the city's representative in the National Basketball Association. Hopes are high that the Arena will be a catalyst in bringing new life in the form of restaurants and clubs to the area north of Bayside.

Beyond the Arena, **Bicentennial Park**, former site of the Miami Grand Prix, is mostly desolate. Its Torch of Freedom is often the backdrop for demonstrations. North of the park, at Biscayne Boulevard and 13th Street, is the oldest Art Deco structure in Miami. The

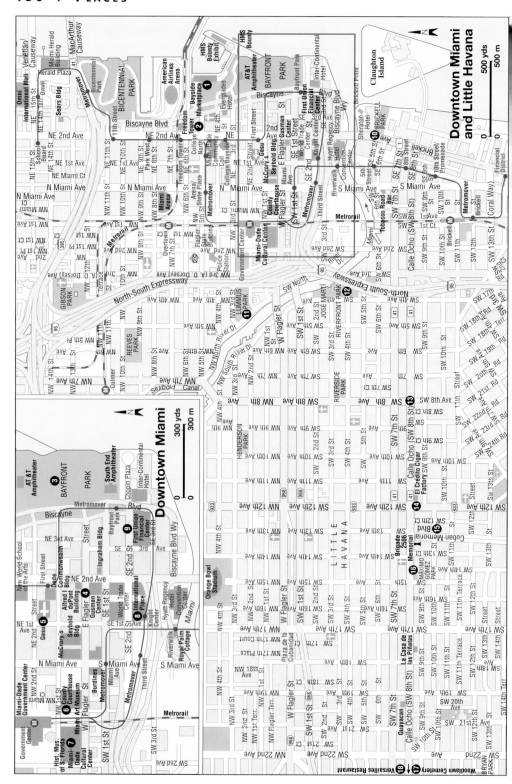

Sears Building, dating from 1929, is now in total disrepair, but preservationists have fought to keep its tower as the linchpin of a planned performing arts complex. At 14th Street is the Boulevard Shops, another fine Art Deco specimen. Behind it on the bay is the *Miami Herald* building.

South again, opposite the American Airlines Arena, the restored **Freedom Tower ❷** rises on the west side of Biscayne Boulevard. Built in 1925 as home to the now defunct *Miami News*, the tower served in the 1960s as a processing center for Cuban immigrants, hence its name. It was abandoned for years, until Saudi Arabian investors in the late 1980s sunk money back into the 17-story gem, once called "Miami's Statue of Liberty," and restored it to its former grandeur. Though empty once again, in 1997 it was bought by the Cuban American National Foundation, which plans to turn it into a museum chronicling the Cuban-American experience.

Farther south, beyond Bayside Marketplace, is **Bayfront Park ❸**, a large greenery built in the early 1920s from earth dredged out of Biscayne Bay. At its southern end stands a memorial built by the late Japanese sculptor Isamu Noguchi and dedicated to the crew of the ill-fated *Challenger* space shuttle. This is the spot where, in 1933, an assassin attempted to kill President-elect Franklin D. Roosevelt. He missed Roosevelt, but mortally wounded Chicago's mayor, Anton Cermak.

The park underwent a $30-million facelift a few years ago and now features a sprawling amphitheater, host to concerts and festivals. At the eastern edge stands a celebrated statue of Christopher Columbus, presented to the city by the people of Italy on Columbus Day in 1953. In the evenings, horse-drawn buggies take sightseers through the park from Bayside Marketplace.

Map on page 156

This gigantic guitar sits atop the Hard Rock Cafe at Bayside Marketplace.

BELOW: the Metromover above a downtown street.

THE METROMOVER

Look up from the downtown streets and you may see the Metromover whisking passengers between the skyscrapers, unhindered by the congested traffic below. This driverless, rubber-wheeled train runs along an elevated 4.4-mile (7.1-km) track, which covers most of the downtown area. The route consists of an inner, central loop and two branches. The branches serve Bicentennial Park and Omni Mall to the north, and Brickell Avenue to the south. Maps explaining the system can be picked up at the main station, Government Center (at 111 NW First Street), or at other visitor information centers.

With 21 stations in a relatively small area and a train every 90 seconds during rush hour, the Metromover is a convenient and quick way to hop from one place to another. Costing just 25 cents a ride, it is also a fun and inexpensive way to get an aerial glimpse of downtown Miami and the waters of Biscayne Bay.

At Government Center and Brickell stations, the Metromover connects with Metrorail, which runs on a higher set of tracks. Metrorail is a high-speed train serving Greater Miami along a 20-mile (32-km) arc that soars above the trees and roofs. It carries passengers northwest to Hialeah, and south to Coconut Grove and Kendall.

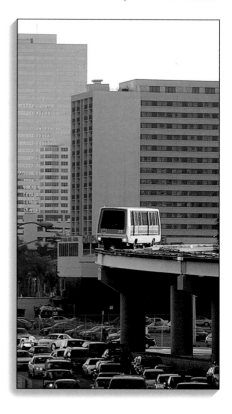

A walker's delight

For the true heart of downtown, head west from here on Flagler Street. The city's geographical center is at the intersection of Flagler and Miami Avenue. The two streets divide Miami-Dade County into the four quadrants of the compass, and it's from here that all of Miami gets its bearings. This is the eye of Miami's urban storm.

Two blocks east of this crossroads is the best place to start a walking tour of downtown Miami's landmarks. Here, at the intersection of Flagler and NE Second Avenue sits a collection of the wonders of the city's brief past. The Streamline Moderne architectural gem on the southeast corner, now a Sports Authority athletic goods store, has a curved facade, and a three-story atrium inside. Until 1995 it was a branch of Walgreens, opened in 1936 as one of the drugstore chain's most attractive shops. Just south on Second Avenue is the classy **Ingraham Building**, a mock Florentine Renaissance beauty that opened in 1926. Its lobby, crowned by an ornate ceiling, has many original features, including the light fixtures, the mailbox and the office directory. Scenes of South Florida wildlife play out on the gold of the elevator.

West along Flagler Street, at No. 174, is the Spanish-Moorish-style Olympia Building, which houses the glorious **Gusman Center for the Performing Arts**. Built as a movie theater for Paramount Pictures in the mid-1920s, this auditorium is a romantic re-creation of what might be an Andalusian patio at night, replete with billowing clouds painted overhead and stars a-twinkling. The tall, smooth organ pipes tower in the cool cavern near the left of the stage. Film lovers visiting in February can catch a first-run movie here during the annual Miami Film Festival.

Many Miami addresses are given according to their location relative to Miami Avenue and Flagler Street: e.g. 1200 NW 26th Street is 12 blocks west of Miami Avenue and 26 blocks north of Flagler Street.

BELOW: a dance company performs downtown.

Opposite the Gusman, the severe lines of the **Alfred I duPont Building** define Miami's ode to New York's Rockefeller Center. An Art Deco jewel built between 1937 and 1939, the duPont served as the southeastern seat of the Florida National Bank and Trust system, and was regional headquarters for the US Navy during World War II. Its appearance has remained relatively unchanged. Inside the lobby, the Deco-styled cafe and directory seem like remnants of a Miami that flared, then faded, over half a century ago. At the foot of the escalator, near the front door, the view up is toward beautiful murals inspired by Florida's history and landscape.

Next, it's back on the street to the buzzing of contemporary Miami. Electronic hardware outlets are everywhere; they are what many Miamians first think of at the mention of "downtown." The shops, lined door-to-door throughout the downtown area, are magnets to shoppers from all around the Caribbean and Latin America. They cart off stereos, TV sets and video recorders by the bagful. Some even come with empty suitcases in order to carry the goods on the next plane out.

A few doors down on Flagler is the **Capital Mall**, a short cut which takes you through to NE First Street. This corridor might be downtown's best-kept secret, with its cluster of architectural delights dating back to the 1920s. Be sure to look up to appreciate the architectural touches on the buildings, mostly obliterated at street level by tacky shop signs. As you exit the mall, look across the street to the **Dade Commonwealth Building** with its majestic eagles resting atop neo-classical columns. Born of the boom era, the Commonwealth Building is really a truncated version of its former self; the killer hurricane of 1926 obliterated the top 10 stories.

West, on the south side of First Street, sits the **Shoreland Arcade**. The arcade once housed the Shoreland Company, a huge boom-era developer. The structure dates to the mid-1920s. The highly ornate, classical design remains intact, its huge arched entranceways boasting elaborately painted friezes. The original chandeliers, decorative terrazzo floors and mailbox also remain.

Carefully cross First Avenue – Miami drivers are notoriously reckless – then turn toward the northeast. A French-inspired mansard roof, rare for Miami, tops off the slim, imposing Capitol Bank Building, at 117 NE First Avenue. Next door is the **Gesu Catholic Church** ❺, the oldest Catholic parish in Miami. This is a beautiful, Mediterranean-Revival structure built in the mid-1920s. Covering the ceiling is a mural, restored in its entirety by a lone Nicaraguan refugee in the late 1980s.

Continuing north one block on First Avenue you reach Miami-Dade Community College's **Wolfson Campus**, the largest community college in the United States. Wolfson has given downtown Miami an extra boost of energy; the campus has hosted huge paella cook-off parties, and each November the Miami International Book Fair sets up camp here. Directly west of the campus is the **United States Post Office** and **Federal Courthouse**. The latter, a 1931 neo-classical edifice, has a mural on the second floor depicting

Map on page 156

TIP

In the downtown electronics outlets be wary of deals too good to be true. For example, when shop owners wrap purchases for the trip home, tourists are sometimes surprised to unwrap a different item than the one they bought.

BELOW: shoeshine with a message.

The top few floors of Miami-Dade County Courthouse, once the tallest building south of Baltimore.

BELOW: gold sold by the inch.

Miami's growth from tropical backwater to booming city. It also houses the small jail cell that in 1990 was the unluxurious home-away-from-home for Panamanian dictator Manuel Noriega, while he awaited trial on drug charges.

Returning to First Street, and heading west again, you pass by the rear of the old Jackson Byron's Pharmacy. A couple of doors past that is the 10-story **Seybold Building**. Built in the 1920s, it's the heart of downtown's booming jewelry business, one of the busiest in the country.

Next door is an empty building that once housed a Five & Dime store called **McCrory's**. It is one of the oldest buildings in downtown – parts of it date back to 1906. The American civil rights movement made history in 1960 when blacks staged a daring lunch-counter sit-in at the cafeteria.

One block south along Miami Avenue – the oldest thoroughfare in the city – is **Burdines**, downtown's flagship department store. Burdines began near this spot back in the late 1800s and today the chain is the largest in Florida. Note the footbridge that crosses Miami Avenue and ties the old Burdines to its newer counterpart. On the south facade of the building is an enormous mural by seascape artist Wyland.

Heart of the county

West on Flagler is the **Miami-Dade County Courthouse ❻**, the unofficial hub of downtown. It was built between 1925 and 1928 in the neo-classical style. The building once housed both the city and county jails, which were stacked safely on the top 10 floors. Earlier, along the building's north side, gallows used to be erected from time to time for executions. Each fall, turkey buzzards that have migrated from Ohio take over the courthouse's roof as their winter home.

To the northwest is the **Miami-Dade Government Center**, headquarters to the county government. Wander the lobby shops and cafes, then hop an elevator to the higher floors for sweeping views of the downtown streets, curling Miami River, turquoise Biscayne Bay and its islands and port.

Across NW First Street is the **Miami-Dade Cultural Center ⑦**, designed by renowned architect Philip Johnson. The Center is home to the Miami-Dade Public Library, the Historical Museum of Southern Florida (open daily; Sun pm only; entrance fee; tel: (305) 375-1492) and the Miami Art Museum (open Tues–Sun; Sat–Sun pm only; entrance fee; tel: (305) 375-3000). Costs are minimal and the library, of course, is free. The plaza connecting the Center's components is an architectural delight, a quiet world unto itself, reminiscent of the piazzas of Italian hill towns. It is best approached around the corner from its southeast entrance. This urban oasis is a great place to bring your lunch and relax in the sun.

South of Flagler

South of Flagler Street are two of Miami's more striking skyscrapers. On the corner of SE First Avenue and Second Street is the 48-story **International Place ⑧**, opened in the late 1980s and designed by the internationally renowned architect I.M. Pei. At night, the tower is floodlit in different colors – red, white and blue on the Fourth of July, emerald green on St Patrick's Day. To the south is the last sloping bend of the **Miami River**, just before it spills into Biscayne Bay at Brickell Point. Near the river is the **Royal Palm Cottage**, a yellow-framed house built in 1897. Today it sits next to a waterfront restaurant at the Riverwalk Metromover station.

Map on page 156

BELOW: a haven of calm – Miami-Dade Cultural Center.

Map on page 156

Before the banks moved in, Brickell Avenue was the corridor for Miami's most beautiful mansions, a veritable millionaires' row.

BELOW: color-coded lighting at International Place.
RIGHT: Brickell Avenue banker.

Closer to the bay is Miami's tallest skyscraper, the **First Union Financial Center ❾**, a product of the early 1980s building boom downtown. Part of the complex rests on the site of an ancient Indian burial mound. Its 55 stories also make it the tallest building in Florida.

SE Second Avenue crosses the river on the newly renovated Brickell Avenue Bridge, adorned with a bronze statue of a Tequesta Indian warrior (by Cuban-born sculptor Manuel Carbonell), and continues south as **Brickell Avenue ❿**, also known as "bankers row." Here, international banks symbolize Miami's strong connections with the South American and Caribbean economies. Rounding the turn at 15th Road, the banks give way to the city's most famous high-rise residential real estate. Arquitectonica, a daring and avant-garde architectural firm, made its mark here. The firm's most famous works are on Brickell Avenue: the **Palace Condominium** (at No. 1541) and the **Atlantis** (at No. 2025); the latter featured in the opening scenes of *Miami Vice*.

One of the most interesting spots in the downtown area is back toward the river. **Tobacco Road**, a bar and restaurant at 626 S Miami Avenue, claims the city's oldest liquor license (1912) and was run as a speakeasy during the Prohibition years. Dark and smoky, with walls covered in old newspaper clippings about the club, the Road cranks out live blues or jazz most nights, as well as occasionally hosting open-mike poetry readings.

Lummus Park

For a little taste of Miami history, head west from the heart of downtown to **Lummus Park ⓫**, which contains two of Miami's most historic structures. The William English Slave Plantation House, a limestone fortress commonly known

as **Fort Dallas**, was built in 1838 and moved to this site in 1925 from just down the river. The **William Wagner House** was crafted from Dade County pine by a 19th-century homesteader. Just to the south, at 360 W Flager Street, is the **East Coast Fisheries**, a Miami institution since 1926, and a fine place for lunch on the river. Grab a table upstairs, order from the large menu, then sit back and absorb the atmosphere.

Another interesting area on the periphery of downtown is the Overtown-Park West development around NW Sixth Street and Second Avenue, the first major redevelopment of a central city neighborhood in South Florida. Backers are still hoping this project, which began in 1988, will bring suburbanites back downtown to live, lured by new apartments and the **Miami Arena** sports stadium.

Just north is **Overtown**, one of the city's oldest black communities. Today, it's a shell of its former self, ripped apart by a freeway system and crippled by poverty and crime. It's not an area to wander into alone, by day or by night. Known in prouder times as Harlem South, it was once home to a largely self-sufficient black community and famous for its lively jazz clubs and theaters. Spotty efforts are underway to bring back some of its luster, such as the Ninth Street walkway paved in a pattern of blue, orange and yellow, and the refurbished 1915 Lyric Theater at 819 NW Second Avenue. ❑

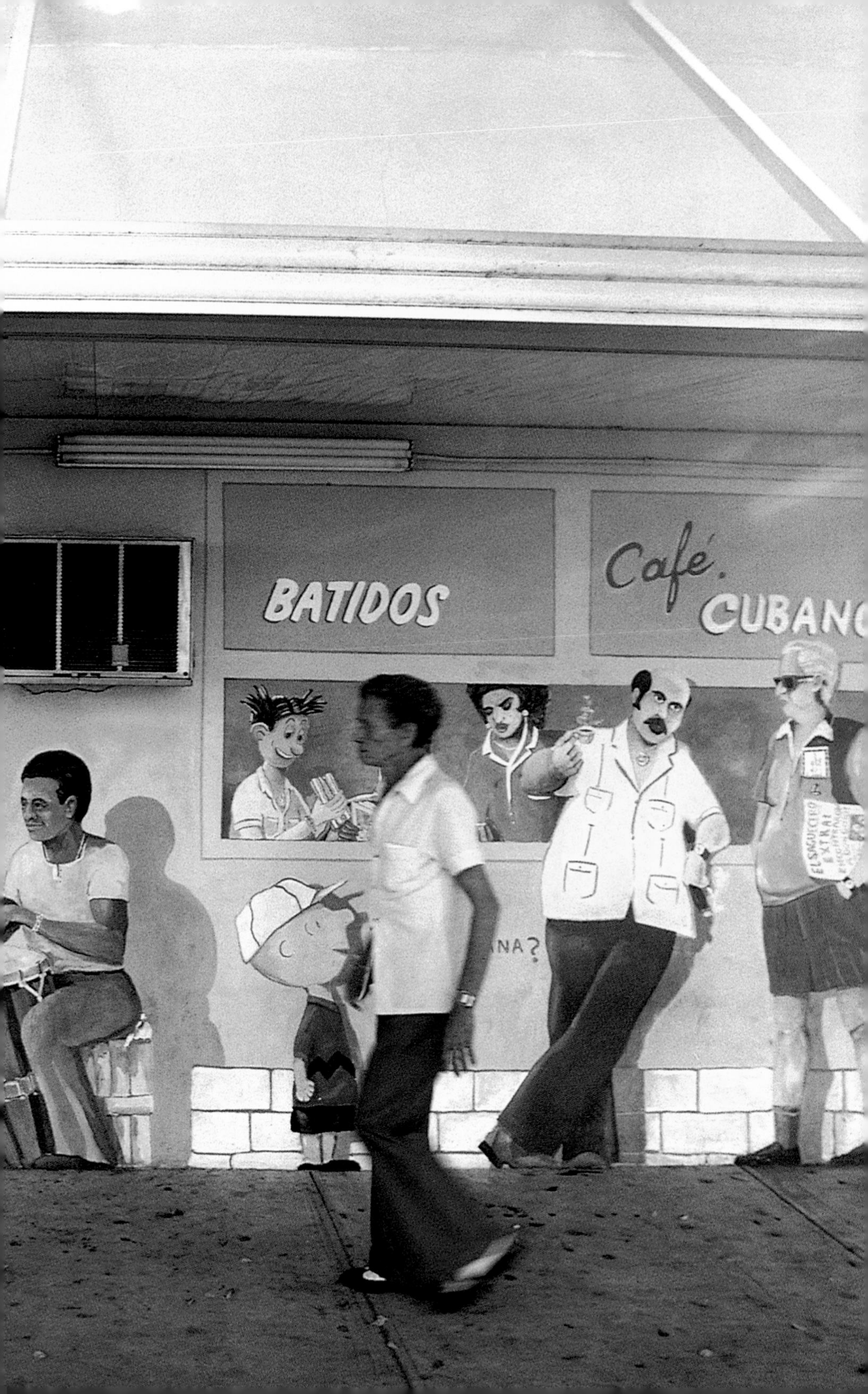
BATIDOS
Café
CUBAN

LITTLE HAVANA

*Immigrants not just from Cuba but from all over the Caribbean
and Central America have made Miami their new home. Here, in
Little Havana, their Latin traditions last longest*

Map
on page
156

Picture a neighborhood where a flame leaps day and night for veterans of
the Bay of Pigs invasion. Imagine a parade where schoolchildren march
proudly for a homeland they never once knew. Picture a fast-food restaurant that features hamburgers, French fries and café Cubano, to go.

At the core of Little Havana beats an exile's heart, scarred with sadness for
a lost homeland, swelled with pride in its past. From pharmacies and restaurants
to car washes and grocery stores, the names here speak of far away and long ago:
Farmacia Camaguey, Frutería Los Pinareños, Managua Medical Center.

Havana, Cuba, never looked like this hodge-podge of car dealerships, strip
shopping centers, furniture stores, flower shops, run-down 1950s motels and
well-kept Mediterranean-style houses. This is Havana, Miami, an immigrants'
launching pad, a constantly changing monument to new beginnings and hope.

Today, one can find *guayaberas* in Hialeah, dance *salsa* in Key Biscayne,
sip *ajiaco* in Kendall. The neighborhood's Cuban flavor has become diluted
in recent years as Central American refugees have taken over entire blocks.
Still, Little Havana remains the symbolic center of South Florida's thriving
Cuban community, a place to savor a good meal or a good memory.

Very roughly, Little Havana is bounded by the Miami River to the east, 37th
Avenue to the west, State Road 836 to the north and
Coral Way to the south. It sprawls over a collection of
old Miami neighborhoods settled after the turn of the
20th century and first known by the names Shenandoah and Riverside.

Cuban exiles first began settling here *en masse* after
their country's 1959 revolution, re-opening boarded-up stores and filling vacant apartment buildings in the
deteriorating neighborhood. As the first Cuban settlers moved up economically, they moved out to more
affluent areas, leaving room for new waves of fellow
Cubans disenchanted with communism.

Since the late 1970s, local merchants and city officials have dreamed of developing the area west of
12th Avenue into a tourist attraction similar to San
Francisco's Chinatown or New Orleans' French Quarter. The 60-block area would have hotels and specialty
shops, and apartments built above businesses to lend
the neighborhood an urban, ethnic ambiance. More
than two decades later, the Latin Quarter has met with
modest success; brick sidewalks lined with olive trees
and scattered shops with white stucco walls and red-tiled roofs are the prime evidence of its existence.

Unprodded by urban planners, change has proceeded at a more rapid pace east of 12th Avenue. In the
1980s, struggling Central American immigrants – the
majority of them Nicaraguans – crowded bungalows
and patronized the corner *bodegas*.

PRECEDING PAGES:
lifelike mural.
LEFT:
Little Havana smile.
BELOW: blind
street musician.

River scenes

To get to Little Havana from Downtown Miami you first have to cross the **Miami River**. Once a waterway to the Everglades plied by Tequesta Indians in cypress canoes, today's Miami River is a busy, gritty shipping center. Spilling on to its banks are boatyards, marinas, terminals and fisheries.

One doesn't need a boat to appreciate the river. Try visiting the public parks that line its banks.Most outstanding is **José Martí Riverfront Park** ⓬ on the eastern edge of Little Havana, a vision of pink stucco buildings and red-brick walks sprawled along the river's south bank. Built on what was once a Tequesta Indian settlement, the site became known in 1980 as Tent City, a temporary shelter for homeless Mariel refugees. In 1985, it became a park dedicated to José Martí, the Cuban writer and philosopher, and leader of Cuba's independence struggle against Spain. The park includes a pool, a fountain, a bust of José Martí donated by the Cuban government in 1952 and a statue of the late South Florida Congressman Claude Pepper.

From 1965 to 1973, so-called "Freedom Flights" brought an estimated 260,000 Cubans from Havana to Miami as they fled Castro's revolution.

Calle Ocho

Little Havana's best-known street is **Calle Ocho (SW Eighth Street)** ⓭, which heads west out of town, eventually becoming the Tamiami Trail, which links Miami with Tampa. In January, Calle Ocho hosts the Three Kings Day Parade, as well as a schoolchildren's march in honor of José Martí. The major annual event is the Calle Ocho festival in March, a mammoth street party that features Latin food and entertainment.

At 1106 Calle Ocho is **El Crédito Cigar Factory** ⓮ (open Mon–Sat; free; tel: (305) 858-4162), the biggest producer of handmade cigars in Miami. Step inside

BELOW: the Brigade 2506 Memorial with its eternal flame.

JOSÉ MARTÍ (1853–95)

A man of action and of letters who was instrumental in the liberation of Cuba from Spain, José Martí serves as an inspiration to Cubans on both sides of the Florida Straits. In Miami they have named a park, streets and even their anti-Castro radio and TV stations after him.

Born in 1853 in Havana, Martí grew into a frail young man. At 16, though, he began his campaign for Cuban independence by founding an anti-colonial newspaper, *The Free Fatherland*. After a stint in jail for denouncing a fellow student for marching in a Spanish procession, Martí was sent into exile in Spain.

He journeyed to several countries but eventually settled with his wife and son in New York in 1881. For 15 years, he organized exiles, lectured and wrote speeches, articles and poetry (in the 1960s, his *Versos Sencillos* were married to the song *Guajira Guantanamero* and became the unofficial Cuban national anthem).

In 1895, he and Máximo Gómez landed in Cuba with the intention of taking the island from the Spanish by force. They took to the hills, where they were joined by hundreds of supporters. A month later, at the Battle of Dos Ríos, Martí was shot as he charged the enemy. Independence was achieved seven years after his death.

and see two dozen men and women nimbly cutting the leaves, rolling them into cigars and squeezing them into wooden presses. Many of these craftsmen learned their trade in Cuba, where, before the revolution, owner Ernesto Perez Carillo's father and grandfather ran the business.

A couple of blocks west of the cigar factory is **Cuban Memorial Boulevard ⑮**, the southern extension of SW 13th Avenue. At the boulevard's junction with Calle Ocho is the **Brigade 2506 Memorial**, which commemorates the ill-fated Bay of Pigs invasion of 1961. On April 17 of that year a team of exile volunteers trained and sponsored by the US Central Intelligence Agency landed at Cuba's Bay of Pigs. The invasion, intended to spark a mass uprising against Fidel Castro, did not succeed. After three days of fighting, almost 1,000 men were taken prisoner, and the remainder were forced to retreat to Miami.

The memorial consists of a flame surrounded by a half-dozen unloaded missiles pointing upwards. On plaques are the names of the 94 members of the invasion team who lost their lives.

Clustered within walking distance of the Brigade 2506 Memorial are a number of Little Havana commercial institutions. To the east, **Casino Records** at 1208 Calle Ocho offers a wide range of Latin music on tape, record and compact disc. There's everything from early 20th-century Cuban *danzons* and spirited *salsa* by Cuban exile Celia Cruz to mambos and *cha-cha-chas* by the late Cuban bandleader Damaso Perez Prado. The variety here includes Dominican *merengues*, Colombian *cumbias*, Brazilian sambas and Argentinian tangos.

Another Cuban institution transplanted from Havana to Little Havana after the revolution is the **Casa de los Trucos**, at 1343 Calle Ocho. This House of Tricks carries strange hats, Uzi machine guns that spit water, maracas, magic

Map
on page
156

Miami-Dade County is officially bilingual. Signs are often in both English and Spanish, and the Miami Herald (the state's most widely-read daily) has a Spanish edition, El Nuevo Heraldo.

BELOW: cigars on display at El Crédito.

tricks and a wide variety of masks, including ones depicting Fidel Castro.

Close by is **Pinareños Market**, a fruit stand, half indoors, half outdoors, whose displays include a variety of tropical delicacies. Depending on the season, one might find papaya, *platanos manzanos* (apple bananas), *boniato* (the Cuban sweet potato) and *malanga*, a white-flesh root that is usually boiled or used in soups.

Local color

Down the street stands a **McDonald's Restaurant** that offers Cuban coffee along with its regular fast-food fare. The real reason to stop here is not the food, but the opportunity to see two pieces of original art by Haydee and Sahara Scull, Cuban-born identical twins whose murals combine painting and sculpture to evoke happy images of 1950s Havana. Hanging here is a charming, bustling scene of the action outside Havana's cathedral: a caped man with a flower; a woman in a tight yellow dress and, in the lower left-hand corner, a pair of brown-tressed women in identical red dresses, the ubiquitous Scull sisters.

Outside, look at the sidewalk to see Little Havana's version of Hollywood Boulevard. Stars embedded in the bricks honor Hispanic performers and artists.

To the west, the rattle of dominoes and smell of cigars pervade what must be Miami's most densely populated park. Located at the corner of Calle Ocho and SW 15th Avenue, **Máximo Gómez Park ⑯** (better known as **Domino Park**) is a collection of games tables covered by red-tiled roofs. Concerned about crime, Miami city officials have limited access to the park to those over the age of 55, and an identification card is required to get in. Exceptions are made for tourists. A large mural at the park shows a portrait of every leader from North and South

During the 1980s, a "miracle" tree thrived on SW Fourth Street in Little Havana. After a 92-year-old man claimed that the tree's sap had cured his cataracts, people flocked to it, hoping to cure their own ills. Unfortunately, an entrepreneur chopped the tree down and sold off the splinters.

BELOW: a father gets a haircut…
RIGHT: …while his son watches.

America who attended the 1994 Miami Summit of the Americas. This might be the only opportunity you get to have your picture taken with Bill Clinton.

A few blocks to the west is **La Casa de las Piñatas**, 1756 Calle Ocho, a shop filled with colorful *piñatas* (bags of toys and candy that kids are supposed to hit with a stick until they burst) and other accessories for children's parties.

About 10 blocks farther west, turn left on SW 27th Avenue. At No. 901 is **Botánica la Esperanza**, a store filled with herbs, candles, dolls and small images of saints. *Botánicas* sell the ingredients and tools required for the religious rites associated with Santería and Vodou. If you stand inside long enough, you're likely to hear customers discussing which herb to use for a particular problem, or which prayer to recite for a loved one. Devotees buy Spanish-made wood-paste statues of Catholic saints, such as St Judas Tadeo, the Virgin of Regla and the Virgin of Charity, Cuba's patron saint. These will then be set in small shrines, often in the worshippers' own front yards.

Botánicas, scattered throughout Little Havana and other Miami neighborhoods, are not designed for tourists. Outsiders are politely tolerated, but not particularly welcomed. Practitioners are sensitive about being sensationalized and misinterpreted. Tact and discretion are advised.

Well worth a visit is **Woodlawn Cemetery ⓱**, at the corner of Calle Ocho and SW 32nd Avenue. Anastasio Somoza, the Nicaraguan strongman unseated by his country's 1979 Sandinista revolution, rests here in a mausoleum marked only with his initials. Carlos Prio Socarras, the Cuban president elected in 1948 and deposed in a 1952 coup by Fulgencio Batista, lies beneath a tombstone that carries the colors of the Cuban flag. Also here is Gerardo Machado y Morales, Cuba's fifth president, a harsh dictator forced to flee Cuba following a 1933 revolt.

Map on page 156

Statue of a deity on display in a Little Havana botánica.

BELOW: a domino game in Máximo Gómez Park.

A recent tomb here is that of Jorge Mas Canosa, founder of the Cuban American National Foundation and the burr under Fidel Castro's saddle for many years. He died in Miami in 1997. Another famous Cuban family is represented: Desi Arnaz Sr., Lucille Ball's father-in-law. In the rear section of the cemetery is another monument to the veterans of the Bay of Pigs.

Successful young Cubans are sometimes called YUCAs – Young Up-and-coming Cuban Americans. Yuca is a popular Cuban food, and a chic restaurant called Yuca in Miami Beach plays on the double meaning.

Spicy fare

Little Havana is at its most accessible through the palate. The area abounds with restaurants and coffee shops serving up a wide range of Latin foods.

Cuban cooking is homey – people's fare – and Calle Ocho offers a variety of options. Starting from the west, at No. 3555 you will find **Versailles** ⑱, one of the most popular eating establishments in town. The large mirrors and bright lights make this place unselfconsciously gaudy, and that is part of its charm. Fast-paced and moderately priced, Versailles attracts a widely varied clientele, from large noisy families and groups of businessmen to theater-goers dropping in for a late-night snack. It is also a favorite stop for politicos courting the Cuban vote. The menu is huge. Neophytes to Cuban cooking might try the restaurant's sampler of Cuban foods: roast pork, sweet plantains, ham croquettes and tamales. Also popular, and with a similar menu, is **La Carreta**, across the street at No. 3632 and one of the only places around that is open 24 hours.

Small Nicaraguan restaurants have abounded in the neighborhood since the late 1980s. **Guayacan**, at No. 1933, is where homesick Nicaraguans go for homemade soups and delectable beef-tongue simmered in tomato sauce.

For a quick and very inexpensive snack, drop in to **El Rey de las Fritas** (at No. 1177). A Cuban version of the hamburger, the *frita* consists of a beef

BELOW: street food, Little Havana style.

patty and *julienne* potatoes doused with spicy sauce and served inside a roll.

Former President Ronald Reagan, wildly popular among many Cuban exiles for his hardline anti-communist stance, made Little Havana history on May 20, 1983, when he stopped for lunch at **La Esquina de Tejas**, at 101 SW 12th Avenue, now also known as Ronald Reagan Avenue. The restaurant, which serves standard Cuban fare (try the Cuban sandwiches), has not forgotten this visit. Reagan's autograph is reproduced on the menus, and the restaurant still serves "The President's Special."

For local entertainment try **Casa Panza**, at 1260 Calle Ocho, which puts on live flamenco Tuesdays, Thursdays and Saturdays. Or venture to a Little Havana theater. At **Teatro de Bellas Artes** (2113 Calle Ocho) you might stumble upon a Spanish tragedy or a contemporary anti-Castro comedy. **Teatro Ocho** (2101 Calle Ocho) is home to the Hispanic Theater Guild. For music shows and Cuban exile comedy-in-the-rough, try **Teatro Martí** at 420 SW Eighth Avenue.

The neighborhood is currently experiencing a fledgling cultural renaissance with the appearance of new galleries, workshops and theaters. The newly renovated **Tower Theater** (1508 Calle Ocho) is home to the annual Hispanic Film Festival. **Performance Space 742**, at 742 SW 16th Avenue, features Rumba on Saturdays and drumming jam sessions. The **Manuel Artime Theater**, at 900 SW First Street, is home to the Miami Hispanic Ballet.

Map on page 156

Little Managua

Twenty years after Cuba's 1959 revolution, upheaval in Nicaragua began sending a new group of refugees to Miami. The result: **Little Managua**. In Miami, Nicaraguans found much sympathy from Cuban exiles, many of whom embraced the anti-Sandinista cause as their own.

By the time the Sandinistas were defeated in Nicaragua's 1990 elections, Miami's Nicaraguan community had grown to an estimated 150,000 residents: former government ministers, ex-Contra fighters, entrepreneurs, professionals and workers, all in turn alienated by the Marxist-led Sandinistas. With the Sandinistas' electoral defeat, the mood on Miami's streets was euphoric as Nicaraguans honked their car horns, waved flags and shrieked with joy. Cubans joined in, hoping Fidel Castro would be next.

Nicaraguan exiles have made their strongest impact in East Little Havana and in the **Sweetwater** area on Miami's western edge, about 7 miles (11 km) west of Little Havana; the latter neighborhood is what has become known as Little Managua.

Today, Little Managua remains a community in transition, its future to be determined as much by events in Nicaragua as the situation in South Florida. But some landmarks are here to stay.

The most famous Nicaraguan eatery around is **Los Ranchos Restaurant**, at 125 SW 107th Avenue in Sweetwater, owned and operated by José Somoza, nephew of Anastasio Somoza, the late Nicaraguan dictator. Savor the *churrasco* steak with *chimichurri* sauce, then finish with *tres leches*, a rich creamy cake that is the house specialty. There are newer branches in Coral Gables, and at Bayside Marketplace. ❑

BELOW: a satisfied coffee shop regular.

CORAL GABLES

George Merrick's planned city is a quiet haven from the Miami hustle and bustle. Explore its oak-lined streets to discover architectural delights from the 1920s land boom

Map on page 178

E ntrepreneur and developer George Merrick called it the City Beautiful, and Coral Gables is certainly that. Its most notable features include towering Mediterranean and colonial-style houses with manicured lawns and carefully tended shrubbery, and quiet, tree-lined streets, monumental gateways, pergolas of flowing vines and ornate fountains that look as if they have been transplanted from a square in Seville.

It is also the City Prosperous. Its 43,000 residents – 92 percent of them whites, half of whom are Hispanic – earn nearly twice as much as their neighbors throughout Miami-Dade County, and an average Coral Gables home is worth over $275,000. The healthy economic atmosphere attracts the headquarters of a number of prestigious firms, including Hilton International, Seagram's Overseas, Texaco, Del Monte Produce and American Airlines.

Easy recycling

It is certainly the City Confusing. Its streets, with small, white, sometimes illegible signs, have mainly Spanish names in no alphabetical or rational order, so that visitors have to contend with a hodge-podge system where avenues like Caligula, Savona and Luenga run randomly one after the other off Le Jeune Road.

Coral Gables is bordered in the north by the Tamiami Trail (SW Eighth Street), and encompasses the next 5 miles (8 km) or so south, through the Granada and Biltmore golf courses (public), the Riviera Country Club (private) and the University of Miami, to Sunset Drive. Then, to the southeast, it also includes the area between Old Cutler Road and the edge of Biscayne Bay, for 3 miles (5 km) south to a few blocks beyond Fairchild Tropical Garden.

It is also the City Fussy. Its strict zoning laws forbid the removal of a tree without city permission, the keeping of more than four cats or dogs per household and the parking of boats or trucks in house driveways (they must be kept out of sight in garages or behind homes). Residents putting out their trash for the weekly pick-up must separate items like milk cartons, newspapers, soft drinks cans and plastic bottles to ensure easy recycling.

But Coral Gables is an immaculate and fascinating city. Its restaurants have architecture as inviting as their fare; its bright shops have red-tiled roofs and arched windows; and at the foot of its sloping gardens are sleek yachts moored on winding waterways. It's a city that, in the words of a former preservation administrator, "tries to maintain the quality of life."

This quality has been around since the 1920s, when George Merrick first imagined turning the area's citrus groves into a flourishing residential community

PRECEDING PAGES: Gables panache. **LEFT:** coral-rock planters. **BELOW:** a secluded home on Coral Way.

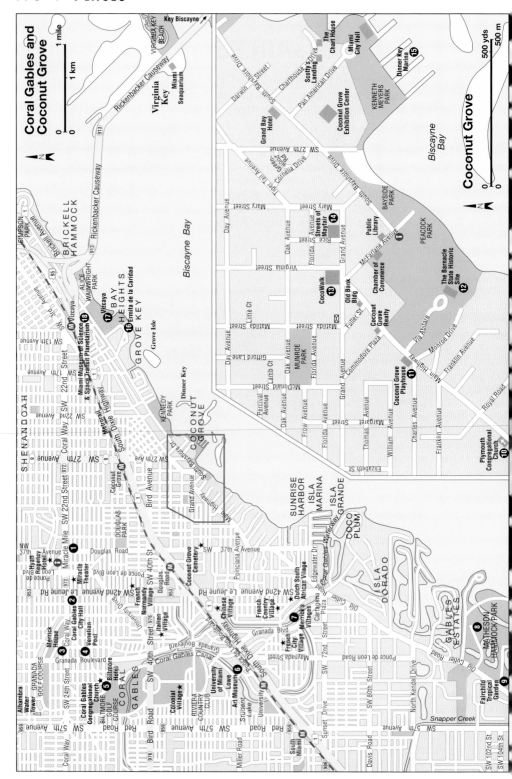

with a Mediterranean theme. By the mid-1920s, 600 homes had been built, roadways had been constructed, and thousands of trees, shrubs and flowers had been planted. It was boom time but not for long. Land values dropped because of artificial inflation and over-speculation; the disastrous 1926 hurricane put a halt to further building; the depression of 1929 ended the frolicking Jazz Age; and the city declined into bankruptcy. Later, though, Coral Gables rose again from the ashes.

Map on page 178

Enter the City Beautiful

For lovers of Mediterranean architecture and tropical landscapes, Coral Gables is an ideal place to wander around. One of the visible features of Merrick's vision is the elaborate limestone arches you drive through as you enter the city from the Tamiami Trail. Entry points are on Douglas Road, Granada Boulevard (a copy of the gate to the city of Granada in Spain) and Country Club Prado (an elegant entrance popular as a backdrop for bridal photographs). Pick one and enter the city. We suggest starting at the graceful, towered building with a 40-ft (12-meter) arch built in 1924 on the corner of Douglas Road and the Tamiami Trail, now incorporated into a modern office complex.

Miracle Mile is only half a mile long. Its 1940s developer justified the choice of name by explaining that the walk down one side of the street and up the other constituted a mile.

Head south until you reach the Gables' main shopping area, **Miracle Mile ❶** (also known as SW 22nd Street or Coral Way). It is only four blocks long, stretching from Douglas to Le Jeune roads, but is packed with 160 shops and cafes, including shoe stores, bookshops and bridal boutiques.

One block north of the Mile, at the corner of Aragon and Galiano, pop into the neat **Chamber of Commerce** building (it has a red-tiled roof) and pick up a sheaf of brochures on area attractions. Ask for the map of the city, as it details an all-encompassing self-guided tour and a bicycle path.

Not far away is a modern-day version of Merrick's baroque dream – the **Hyatt Regency Hotel**, designed by Gables architect John Nichols and opened in 1987 at the corner of Douglas and Alhambra. The location is appropriate, since the 242-room hotel's Moorish architecture is patterned after the ornate Alhambra in Granada, Spain. The U-shaped complex is composed of archways and columns, courtyards and fountains, topped by a red barrel-tile roof. Inside are stone balustrades, huge, elegant mirrors, silk-draped ceiling-to-floor windows, tapestries and landscaped terraces. The Court of the Lions, the hotel's outdoor patio area, modeled on the Alhambra's courtyard.

BELOW: framed in the City Beautiful.

The most dominant structure on the Mile itself is the **Colonnade Building** at the corner of Ponce de Leon Boulevard. Built in 1925, it features a huge baroque front door, a rotunda with marble floors and a central fountain. It is home to the Florida National Bank, but it is also connected to the elegant 13-story **Omni Colonnade Hotel**, at 180 Aragon Avenue.

Near the western end of the Mile, at No. 280, is the **Miracle Theater**, a 600-seat, 1940s Deco movie theater that was turned into a playhouse in 1995 and now has a resident company that performs all year round.

For reading matter on the Gables, or just about any subject under the sun, call in at **Books & Books**, a block north again, at 296 Aragon Avenue. With some

The Alhambra Water Tower, designed by Denman Fink, was built in 1925.

BELOW: courtyard of the Biltmore Hotel.

5,000 volumes, this store has enough to keep the bibliophile entranced for the day. There's not only an old and rare book section, but owner Mitchell Kaplan helps customers track down out-of-print books. Kaplan, co-founder of the Miami International Book Fair, sponsors lectures and book signings at the shop. At the foot of the Mile, on the other side of Le Jeune Road, stands **Coral Gables City Hall ❷**. Built in the late 1920s, it is a semi-circular building with a facade of 12 columns and a Spanish Renaissance-style clock tower.

Continue west along Coral Way and you'll be driving through what looks like a tunnel formed by mature banyan and oak trees hung with Spanish moss. A few blocks west, at 907 Coral Way, is the **Merrick House ❸**, where George Merrick grew up. It was constructed between 1899 and 1906, of oolitic limestone – a rock plentiful in South Florida and often mistaken for coral – with a multi-gabled roof of coral-colored tiles. The house is filled with Merrick family art, furniture and personal treasures and has been restored to its 1920s look. The 2-acre (1-hectare) property is operated by the city as a museum (open Wed and Sun; gardens open daily; donation; tel: (305) 460-5361). Farther west, turn right on Alhambra Circle and drive past the **Alhambra Water Tower**, cleverly disguised as a lighthouse with designs that give it an Moorish feel.

Merrick's legacy

The flamboyance of Coral Gables' heyday is no better exemplified than at the huge **Venetian Pool ❹**, at 2701 De Soto Boulevard (open Tues–Sun: hours vary according to season; entrance fee; tel: (305) 460-5356). With all the construction work that went on here in the 1920s, it is not surprising to discover that this 820,000-gallon (3-million liter) swimming pool was originally a coral-rock

GEORGE MERRICK

Born in 1886, George Merrick was the son of a minister who moved from Massachusetts to South Florida when he was 12. His father, Solomon Merrick, built a home with a gabled roof from what he thought was coral rock and called it Coral Gables. He planted groves of avocados and citrus, and his son would deliver the produce at 2am in a horse-drawn wagon. When his father died George took over the property and built it into Florida's most prosperous fruit and vegetable business. He bought the adjoining land and set about developing his vision of a residential community – a South Florida city with a Mediterranean feel.

To do this he assembled a team that included architect Phineas Paist, landscaper Frank Button and artist Denman Fink, his uncle. The homes and buildings were intended to reflect the best of Spanish and Italian design. He named the city Coral Gables after his childhood home.

By 1926, the one-year-old city had 131 miles (211 km) of paved streets, 2,153 families, 11 schools and six hotels. But in the same year a hurricane and the subsequent property crash sent Merrick and his city into bankruptcy. At the celebration of Coral Gables' 15th anniversary, however, Merrick predicted the city would again see prosperity. He was right, but did not live long enough to see it happen.

quarry. Converted into a pool by Phineas Paist and Denman Fink in 1923, it is now listed in the National Register of Historic Places and claims, with good reason, to be the "world's most beautiful" public swimming pool. It is fed with cool spring water daily, and features waterfalls and coral caves. Surrounding the pool are Venetian-style structures such as loggias, porticos and a cobblestone bridge. Beauty pageants were held here in the pool's early years, and swimming champ-turned-Hollywood star Esther Williams was known to swim here. In 1989, the pool received a $2.3 million restoration.

Nearby is a fine example of how Merrick's legacy continues to be reinforced today. **Venetian Villas**, at 2800 Toledo Street, with its Moorish arches, Spanish tile fountains and wrought-iron balconies, opened in 1926 as a winter retreat for wealthy northerners. It was later converted to a 22-apartment building, then fell into disrepair. But the Edelman Restoration Company, which has gained a reputation for restoring old buildings, gave the villas a $2 million facelift in 1989, and converted the property into six luxury condominiums valued at more than $500,000 each.

Flanking the western edge of the city, at 1200 Anastasia Avenue, is the resort hotel Merrick built for $10 million. The **Biltmore Hotel ❺**, whose tower is modeled on the Giralda in Seville, has gone through several phases since its spectacular opening in 1926. In its prime, the Biltmore attracted celebrities from Al Capone to Judy Garland, and industrial barons who rode gondolas and hunted fox in the hotel grounds. But the hotel fell into disrepair during the Depression and stayed almost fallow until 1943, when it was turned into a World War II army hospital. It was not until 1987 that guests were admitted again to the luxuriously refurbished 286-room hotel. The grand interior with

Map on page 178

TIP

You can treat yourself to an English-style tea at the Biltmore Hotel. To be sure of a table you should book in advance: call (305) 445-1926.

BELOW: service with a smile from the Coral Gables police force.

hand-painted ceilings, Spanish tiles and marble floors is well worth a look, as is the swimming pool, which is said to be the largest hotel pool in the country. Johnny Weissmuller, star of the Tarzan movies, set a world swimming record here in the 1930s. Local lore has it that a ghost resides in the hotel. Weekly tours leave from the lobby.

In 1994, the Biltmore hosted the Summit of the Americas, when heads of state from North and South America gathered to discuss the future of the hemisphere. It has also become the favored hideaway of Miami-visiting movie stars and royalty, and one of the most sought-after fashion-shoot locations in the city.

Directly across the street from the hotel is the **Coral Gables Congregational Church**. This pretty Spanish baroque-style church is host to many lectures, book readings and concerts.

Miami's seat of learning

To the south is the area's most prestigious private university, the **University of Miami**, which boasts one of the best football teams in the US. UM has long discarded its derisive image as Suntan-U, whose students were purportedly more interested in frolicking in the sun than learning, and has an enrollment of close to 14,000 and a full-time faculty of 1,500 on its 260-acre (105-hectare) campus on the north side of Ponce de Leon Boulevard. It opened its School of Medicine in 1952, and the School of Marine and Atmospheric Science in 1969, but the real attraction here is its art museum.

The **Lowe Art Museum** ❻ (open Tues–Sun; Thur and Sun pm only; entrance fee; tel: (305) 284-3535), on UM's campus at 1301 Stanford Drive, is one of the area's best museums. Its permanent collection of 8,000 works

In the 1980s and early 90s, UM's football team, the Hurricanes, were virtually unstoppable and were national champions no less than four times. Home games are played at the Orange Bowl Stadium. Call (800) 462-2637 for tickets.

BELOW:
Spanish-style Coral Gables residence.

includes Egyptian, Greek and Roman antiquities, Renaissance and baroque art, 19th- and 20th-century European and American pieces, ancient art from Latin America and an impressive Asian collection. Highlights to look out for are the Alfred I. Barton Collection of Native American art – one of the finest in the country – which includes Pueblo and Navajo weavings, and the Samuel H. Kress Collection, which has works by European masters such as Cranach the Elder and Tintoretto. The museum also hosts a number of excellent temporary exhibitions each year.

Map on page 178

Villages of the world

Scattered around Coral Gables are small village-like enclaves created by Merrick's architects to include more eclectic influences than the predominant Mediterranean Revival style. A drive around **Merrick's Villages** ❼ will reward you with a dizzying range of styles: **Chinese Village** (on Riviera Drive at Menendez Avenue) with its sloping tiled roofs; the **Dutch South African Village** (Le Jeune Road at Maya Street), modeled on the farmhouses of 17th-century Dutch colonialists; the **French City Village** (Hardee Road at Cellini Street); the **French Country Village** (Hardee at Maggiore Street); the **French Normandy Village** (Le Jeune at Viscaya Avenue); the **Italian Village** (Altara Avenue at Monserrate Street); and the **Colonial Village** (Santa Maria Street), which was designed to evoke the image of New England homes.

This colorful facade is characteristic of houses in the French City Village.

The Gables is also blessed with fine restaurants, most of them on, or just off, Ponce de Leon Boulevard. **Restaurant St Michel** is a favorite place with Gableites for continental dining and leisurely Sunday brunches. The restaurant is contained in the exquisite little **Hotel Place St Michel**, at 162 Alcazar Avenue,

BELOW: graduation day at the University of Miami.

Map on page 178

also built during the Merrick era, with high ceilings and individually furnished rooms filled with antiques. Elsewhere, the continental cuisine served up at **La Palma** (116 Alhambra Circle) has picked up accolades from notable food critics, and another popular choice is **Christy's**, at 3101 Ponce de Leon.

Ponce is also one of the starting points of Gables Gallery Night, a once-a-month tour that takes art-lovers and lookers to 18 Coral Gables galleries. Free, open-air trolley cars move from gallery to gallery and allow visitors to come and go as they please, to peruse the art, fine photography and antiques, and to sample a little complementary wine and cheese along the way.

South of Sunset Drive

Another side of Coral Gables is its pricy neighborhoods in the southeast. To see them, go south on Le Jeune Road, across US 1, and over a waterway to **Cartagena Plaza**, where Le Jeune, Sunset, Cocoplum and Old Cutler roads converge. There is a giant sculpture of a shoe in the center of the traffic circle. Continue southwest on Old Cutler. If the neat homes on the west side of the road fit quite well into the Gables' average $275,000 value, the Cocoplum mansions lining the waterways leading out to Biscayne Bay are in a world by themselves.

BELOW: tranquil scene at Fairchild Tropical Garden.
RIGHT: Classical statues line the Biltmore Hotel's large pool.

Local authorities insist that these $1 million-plus houses on roads with names like Mira Flores and Vistamar must conform to strict zoning laws in their color and roof styles. New homes have to fit the pattern of those already here.

There are two other luxury home divisions, on Casuarina Concourse and Arvida Parkway, before you come to the 100-acre (40-hectare) **Matheson Hammock Park ❽** (9610 Old Cutler Road; open daily; free), which was developed in the 1930s on land donated by pioneer Commodore J. W. Matheson.

The park, a popular weekend spot for residents, has a marina and a small beach. A man-made tidal pool – once a coconut grove – is separated from the bay by a walkway and allows small children a calm place to play in the water. There are picnic facilities, walking trails through the mangrove swamp, sailboat rentals for day-time fun and the **Red Fish Grill** for fine dining in the evening.

Next door to Matheson Hammock Park is the end of the Coral Gables experience – the 83-acre (34-hectare) **Fairchild Tropical Garden ❾** (10901 Old Cutler Road; open daily; entrance fee; tel: (305) 667-1651), the largest of its kind in the continental United States. The garden, which has been open to the public since 1938, is supported by membership fees, grants, donations, admissions and a small endowment. It was named in honor of the distinguished botanist Dr David Fairchild.

Here, beside lakes and winding paths, is an outstanding collection of tropical flowering trees, and some 5,000 ferns, plants and orchids, with exotic names like the fire tree from Australia, the talipot palm from Sri Lanka and the ponytail tree from Mexico. Many of the species found here are rare and endangered. Tram tours of the garden leave every hour, but walking tour guides give visitors a closer look at the labeled flora. The City Beautiful is that indeed, right to the end. ❏

COCONUT GROVE

*Once the haunt of freethinkers, hippies and poets, Coconut Grove
has evolved into an upscale neighborhood with swanky shops
and a night-time buzz second only to South Beach*

Map
on page
178

A ll that has remained of Coconut Grove as a freewheeling, Bohemian village is the reputation. Indeed, it was once home to writers and artists and
was likened to New York's Greenwich Village and London's Chelsea. It
was home to off-the-wall types like the huge, leonine Eugene Massin, an award-
winning sculptor and painter with a booming laugh that could shatter glass, or
the nomadic Bill Hutton, New York advertising man-turned-painter, who would
record his scenes of Grove life on pieces of wood and hawk them on the street
to buy food and wine.

These people are still here, but their numbers are dwindling. These days,
Coconut Grove is a place of chic, trendy shops, restaurants and lots of bars. It
is a favorite destination for Miami's young crowd. It's a nice place to hang out,
but people like Massin and Hutton who brought the artistic edge to the Grove
probably cannot afford to live here anymore.

An influx of people wanting to purchase that Grove groove has created a real
estate boom in the area. New Mediterranean-style townhouses have gone up
alongside early 20th-century, bougainvillea-draped homes built by pioneers.
The Grove has been gentrified.

The Bohemian soul still comes out once in a while, though. In December, for
example, there is the totally irreverent King Mango
Strut, a spoof of the buttoned-down Orange Bowl
Parade that takes place in Downtown Miami. The
King Mango pokes fun at just about everything,
including local politicians and national figures.

Every February, like swallows to Capistrano, hundreds of artists from around the country flock to the
Grove for the three-day Coconut Grove Arts Festival
to display their skill in watercolors, oils, graphics,
ceramics, photography and sculpture to more than a
million visiting spectators.

Coconut Grove has managed to survive the changes
beautifully, blending the long-established and the
ever-changing, the constant and the capricious. The
well-heeled who have just parked their Porsches and
Jaguars on their way to dine on **Commodore Plaza**
rub shoulders with the tattered-jeans set whose hairdos
stick up sharply like stalagmites. The fads come and
go. For a time, teenagers wearing tight shorts and hal-
ters will weave in between the cars on **Main Highway**
on rollerblades; then, that thrill gone, they switch to
skateboards and bicycles.

Still, in the Grove the old do not frown on the new;
they have learned to drift with the winds of change,
even when those winds introduced clouds of marijuana in the late 1960s and the village was suddenly
invaded by runaway long-haired "hippies" protesting
the Vietnam War. Long-term residents' only linger-

PRECEDING PAGES:
outdoor cafes on
Commodore Plaza.
LEFT: a quirky
Grove boutique.
BELOW: customized
mailbox.

ing regret about the Grove is that the community lost its independent status as the area's original settlement, when it was annexed (surreptitiously, they will tell you) by the City of Miami in 1925. Many of them still staunchly have their mail addressed to Coconut Grove, zip code 33133.

At midnight, only the South Beach streets are more alive than those of the Grove. Here diners linger over coffee at one of the village's many outdoor cafes after an evening at the theater, and couples stroll the red-bricked sidewalks lined with trees and streetlamps. This is where they come to plan and dream. If, in other, darker parts of the Grove, nefarious deeds are being committed, here in the village at least the mood is carefree and festive.

Historic highlights

As you leave Coral Gables and enter the Grove from the south, along Main Highway, you'll drive under a canopy of long-rooted trees. Keep your eyes open and you'll be treated to a peek at one of Florida's most beautiful churches. Although it looks like a venerable Spanish monastery, with bell towers and a niche containing a small sculpture of a saint carved out of coral, **Plymouth Congregational Church** ⑩, situated at 3400 Devon Road, only dates back to 1916. True to style, though, its iron-framed black wooden door did come from a 17th-century monastery in the Pyrenees. The facade makes an imposing backdrop for wedding photographs.

The Memorial Gardens behind the church, with borders of impatiens flowers, a huge poinciana tree and a variety of palms, is an oasis of peace. Now and again, the church and its environs receive some unusually exotic and colorful visitors: South American macaws and cockatoos of brilliant reds and greens like to spread their wings and visit the neighborhood.

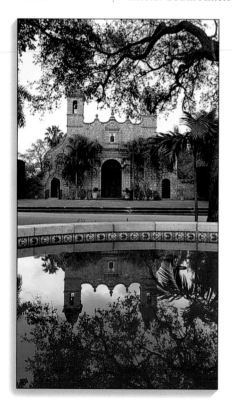

Farther along Main Highway, head off to the west, along Charles Avenue. Charles and the neighboring streets are the remnants of Coconut Grove when it was Miami's first black settlement. Most of its residents were Bahamian pioneers, immigrant "conchs" who came to work at the nearby Peacock Inn. Their first-hand experience with tropical plants and building materials proved invaluable to the development of Cocoanut Grove (as it was spelled then). Some of the small, shotgun-style wooden houses here date from the 1890s.

Grove streets such as Charles, Mary and Frow are named after Bahamians. In the summer of 1896, when the vote was taken on whether to incorporate the new city of Miami, 5 miles (8 km) to the north, 43 percent of the 368 men who voted were black, mostly of Bahamian ancestry.

At the junction of Charles and SW 37th avenues is the **Macedonia Baptist Church**, which served the first black congregation here. The AME Methodist Church, which housed the community's first school, once stood nearby. Also here is the **Coconut Grove Cemetery**, one of Miami's oldest, first used in 1906. Some of the tombstones are shaped like torsos and gumbo limbo trees, an ancient symbol of regeneration. The style can be traced back to the Bahamas. Those too poor to buy grave markers would break off a tree branch and plant it over the grave.

Marjory Stoneman Douglas, leading campaigner for the preservation of the Everglades, lived in Coconut Grove from 1926 until her death in 1998. Her tiny cottage is at 3744 Stewart Avenue, south of the village center.

BELOW: Plymouth Congregational Church.

Map on page 178

Back on Main Highway, the **Taurus Chops**, at No. 3540, really marks the southern end of the village. A one-story cypress restaurant built in 1922, with oak beams and tables fashioned from ships' doors, it is a popular stopping-off place for commuters heading toward South Miami.

Just up the street is the **Coconut Grove Playhouse** ⓫, 3500 Main Highway, another aspect of the village's culture. The building, with its red Mediterranean-style roof and white curlicued pillars, was the brainchild of industrialist George Engle, who opened it as a cinema in 1926. It became a legitimate theater in 1956, attracting stage luminaries like the maverick Tallulah Bankhead, who once conducted a press interview while seated on a toilet. It was a gesture that left Groveites, long since inured to such drollery, unfazed. The 1,100-seat theater was taken over by the state of Florida and now stages mostly Broadway-bound musicals and bedroom farces imported from London.

Shielded from bustling Main Highway by a forest of trees, the **Barnacle State Historic Site** ⓬, at No. 3485 (open Fri–Sun; entrance fee; tel: (305) 448-9445), is a welcome sanctuary from the Grove's flamboyance. This is the home Commodore Ralph Munroe constructed in 1891 on a coral ridge overlooking Biscayne Bay. It was just a bungalow until 1908, when more space was needed. Most people, when adding on to a house, would place a second story over the first. Munroe did just the opposite. He raised the original bungalow up to become the second floor, and built a whole new first floor underneath. He obviously knew what he was doing: the Barnacle survived both the devastating hurricane of 1926 and Hurricane Andrew in 1992, with very little damage. Inside the house you will see Munroe family heirlooms, period appliances such as an early refrigerator and many of the original furnishings.

Coconut Grove Playhouse established its cultural credentials at its theatrical debut in 1956, when it put on the US premiere of Samuel Beckett's Waiting for Godot.

BELOW: the Grove's Bahamian neighborhood.

Ralph Munroe was the single most significant force in the development of the character and prosperity of Coconut Grove. When he purchased the Barnacle property, he left the hardwood hammock in its natural state. He was a builder of sailboats, and the last one in existence, the ketch *Micco*, was displayed here until Hurricane Andrew reduced the 101-year-old boat to splinters. *Egret*, a replica of one of his boats, is now anchored offshore.

Shop 'til you drop

Main Highway's first major intersection is with Commodore Plaza, a short street full of shops, restaurants and bars. On the corner is the **Coconut Grove Realty** building, its design all circles and swirls, a sort of updated, pseudo-Art Deco. The **This 'n That** thrift store at 3155 Commodore Plaza, run by the Plymouth Congregational Church's women's fellowship, sells various items of clothing, books and kitchenware. For a relaxing meal try **Franz and Joseph's** at No. 3145. It still has a bit of the old Grove, with an offbeat charm, gentility and a friendly atmosphere.

Commodore, just a block long, ends at Grand Avenue. To the west, at 3216 Grand, is **Grove Cycle**. One of the friendliest bicycle shops in the city, it offers a huge selection of rental bikes ideal for a cruise through the Grove. Farther west Grand Avenue leads into the "Black Grove," a vast contrast to the omnipresent wealth in the village. Grand Avenue comes into its own during the first weekend in June with the Goombay Festival, when residents celebrate their Bahamian roots with music, dancing and a splurge of ethnic food. To the east, at 3067 Grand is perhaps the Grove's most anachronistic store: the **Krest Five & Ten**, which continues to stock the little necessities of life.

TIP

If you want to watch a movie in the Grove, but you're not in the mood for a Hollywood blockbuster, head for the 16 screens at CocoWalk. They have a policy of screening independent and art-house films alongside the big new releases.

BELOW: indigenous foliage at the Barnacle
RIGHT: kids' shop.

Along with Commodore Plaza, another short street of shops – Fuller Street – joins Grand Avenue with Main Highway. The **Old Bank Building**, at the corner on Main, was where the local bank did business until 1960 when it moved into a spanking new building on South Bayshore Drive. Here, too, are the **Florentino Shops**, 22 of them, the majority being boutiques and sportswear outlets. Upstairs is **Fuddrucker's**, a self-service restaurant, whose balcony chairs overlook Main Highway.

At the same corner of Fuller and Main is **Joffrey's Coffee Company**, one of those oh-so-trendy coffee houses that seem to have popped up on every street corner in America. Joffrey's has a loyal clientele who manage to sit at the outdoor tables for hours on end, sipping their exotic coffee concoctions and watching the colorful parade of locals go by.

Heading northeast along Main Highway will bring you to the nerve center of the Grove – the intersection of McFarlane, Main and Grand. It is dominated by **CocoWalk ⓭**, at 3015 Grand Avenue, a big, pink, Mediterranean-style open-air mall with towering palms and three levels of terraces and balconies. Ultra-modern and in some ways a bit too commercial-looking for this old Miami neighborhood, CocoWalk has nevertheless brought new life to the Grove in recent years. It houses several restaurants, dozens of boutiques, and its own 16-screen movie theater. The mall also features free, live concerts on weekends and, some week nights, artists who sketch caricature portraits or sensual flamenco dancers who really work up a sweat.

Down the street is the **Oak Feed Store**, at 2911 Grand Avenue, where the health-conscious seek out nutritional candies, drinks, vegetables, bread and vitamins; its presence is registered by a huge carrot sign on the front. And, farther

Map on page 178

Café Tu Tu Tango, on the second level of CocoWalk, does tasty tapas and is great for people-watching.

BELOW:
CocoWalk mall, the local hub of activity.

BELOW: fancy dress for the Grove's annual King Mango Strut.

along, between here and Mary Street, are the Grove's two most ornate expressions of the sumptuous life: Mayfair House and the Streets of Mayfair.

Mayfair House, at 3000 Florida Avenue, is a grand, 180-room hotel with Japanese tubs in its suites. Its semi-circular entrance contains a mosaic pool and fountains with statues of anhinga birds standing on one leg. The front door, guarded by a liveried doorman, is of carved mahogany, as are the walls in the small marbled reception area inside. Its rooms, with balconies spilling over with ferns, take up the top three floors of the five-story mall **Streets of Mayfair** ⓭. In the mall you can shop or take in a movie in the flamboyant atmosphere of mosaic-tiled floors and stairways, copper sculptures, noisy fountains and a profusion of greenery. It is the work of Miami architect Kenneth Treister, who was once a student of Frank Lloyd Wright.

Toward the bay

Heading down McFarlane Avenue you reach **Peacock Park**, at the southern end of South Bayshore Drive. It was here that the Peacock Inn, the area's first hotel, was built in 1882 by Charles and Isabella Peacock. At that time, it was the only hotel in the 230-mile (370-km) stretch between Lake Worth and Key West. Now the park is mostly taken up by a baseball field and the woodsy **Chamber of Commerce** building.

Across from Peacock Park, where South Bayshore Drive meets McFarlane Avenue, is the **Public Library**, a coral-rock building with a sloping tiled roof and veranda that would not look out of place as a luxury jungle safari lodge. The land was donated by Commodore Munroe – his first wife is buried in the grounds – and the library was started in 1895 by writer Kirk Munroe (no rela-

tion) and his wife as a reading group called the Pine Needles Club. After the original building opened in 1901, the group used to send books by boat to the new Miami settlement that was growing just up the coast. In 1957 it became a branch of the Miami library. The present building opened in 1963.

Next door is the clubhouse of the **Woman's Club of Miami**, another example of coral-rock construction. It was built in 1921 and is on the National Register of Historic Places.

Take South Bayshore Drive as it heads toward downtown Miami. You'll first pass the renovated **Coconut Grove Exhibition Center**, which hosts numerous exhibitions and conferences every year. Beyond that, the bougainvillea-draped balconies at No. 2669 belong to one of Florida's classiest hostelries, the 13-story, 181-room **Grand Bay Hotel**, which even ascribes to itself in the telephone directory the accolade of the Mobil Five-Star Rating for Excellence. Shaped like a Mayan temple, its entrance is dominated by a bright red steel funnel-shaped sculpture tied with what looks like a convoluted bow, an untitled work by Alexander Liberman.

The view to the east now is of hundreds of masts bobbing in Biscayne Bay. These yachts are tied up at the **Dinner Key Marina ⑮**, the city's largest, with 575 moorings. Here, too, at the end of Pan American Drive, is **Miami City Hall**, where the local commission has its weekly meetings. The Art Deco structure was built in 1934 by Pan American Airways, as the terminus for its flying boats, and was immediately declared the "most beautiful air transport base in the world." From 1930 to 1945, in the heyday of romantic air travel, Pan Am took passengers in luxury seaplanes known as "clippers" from Biscayne Bay to far-away destinations like China and Brazil. Some of the earliest flights were under-

Map on page 178

TIP

A fun way to explore the waters off Coconut Grove is to rent a kayak. Shake-A-Leg Miami (tel: (305) 858-5550) has a range of craft available. They operate from a trailer at 2600 South Bayshore.

BELOW:
Deco details on Miami City Hall.

Map
on page
178

*There are astronomy
shows daily inside
the 65-ft (20-meter)
dome of the Space
Transit Planetarium.*

BELOW:
fishing craft, Dinner
Key Marina.
RIGHT: flamingo
singles bar.

taken without radios, and carrier pigeons were brought along – to be released to summon help if the plane ditched into the sea. A display case inside the building contains models of the various clippers.

If you feel like dining with a view of the bay as a backdrop just take your pick. Next to the City Hall is the casual outdoor setting of **Scotty's Landing** or the classier dining room of the **Chart House**. Back on South Bayshore, at No. 2550, is a colorful restaurant named **Monty's**, which can serve its special fish and seafood dishes to up to 700 people at a time.

Up the coast

As you head north, South Bayshore Drive becomes South Miami Avenue but the ambiance of the Grove can still be felt at **Kennedy Park**, where Groveites jog or cycle in the early morning, pausing only to turn toward the bay and watch the sun come up from behind Key Biscayne. Between here and Peacock Park to the south lie no fewer than three sailing clubs: **Coral Reef Yacht Club** (established in 1955), the **Coconut Grove Sailing Club** (1946) and, between them, the granddaddy of them all, the **Biscayne Bay Yacht Club**, founded in 1887 by pioneer Commodore Ralph Munroe, but occupying its present site since 1932. If one wishes to join the prestigious Biscayne Bay Yacht Club, one must be recommended by three of its 250 members, then, once accepted, sit back and wait for one of them to die.

Farther north, take the first right after Mercy Hospital and you will come to an unusual conical church built in 1966 in a serene spot on the edge of Biscayne Bay. Held sacred by the city's Cuban population, the **Ermita de la Caridad** ⓰ is actually a shrine to the Virgin of Charity, Cuba's patron saint. A mural inside the church depicts the history of Catholicism in Cuba and shows the Virgin and her shrine on the island. The altar is oriented toward Cuba (rather than the usual eastward), reminding parishioners about their "lost" homeland across the waves.

Next up the coast, at 3251 S Miami Avenue, is one of the area's most intriguing attractions – **Vizcaya** ⓱ (open daily; entrance fee; tel: (305) 250-9133). This grand, Italian Renaissance-style mansion is filled with a superb collection of 15th through 19th-century art and European furniture, and is surrounded by manicured gardens and nature trails. Built as a winter residence, it was completed in 1916 by James Deering, the International Harvester millionaire. There are daily guided tours. *(See pages 198–9 for a full description of the house and gardens.)*

Across the road, at No. 3280, is the **Miami Museum of Science and Space Transit Planetarium** ⓲ (open daily; entrance fee; tel: (305) 854-4247). The museum explores the mysteries of science with more than 150 exhibits, live demonstrations of scientific phenomena and unusual natural history specimens. Hands-on exhibits let children touch as they learn about physics, electricity, health, light and sound. An outdoor wildlife center, which rehabilitates injured birds of prey and reptiles, features live hawks, snakes, insects and more. The Planetarium has astronomy and laser shows, as well as lectures and telescope viewings. ❏

VIZCAYA: PALAZZO LUXURY ON THE BAY

A bayfront villa surrounded by formal gardens, Vizcaya recalls Renaissance Italy and offers a glimpse into the South Florida of days gone by

Inspired by the country houses of the Italian Veneto, International Harvester tycoon James Deering built this bayside winter retreat for himself in 1916. The estate was named after the Basque word for "elevated place," which is also the name of one of the Basque provinces on the Bay of Biscay, itself the namesake of Miami's Biscayne Bay. Built on 180 acres (73 hectares) of shoreline, pineland and hammock, the house was designed to resemble an Italian Renaissance villa, but also has baroque, rococo and neoclassical features. Deering, his architect Burrall Hoffman Jr and painter Paul Chafin traveled to Italy to study architectural details that could be used in the villa. Along with the doors, ceilings and fireplaces they brought back, native Florida materials such as limestone were used to give Vizcaya a local feel.

VILLA OF DREAMS

The house has 70 rooms and required a staff of 30 during the four winter months the Deerings stayed here. Today you can tour half of the opulently decorated rooms. Every detail, from the black-and-white marble tub to the gold-leaf cornices, is exquisite. A swimming pool extends from the sun-lit exterior to an imaginative grotto beneath the house, its ceiling decorated with shells and carved stone. Outside, you can stroll through 10 acres (4 hectares) of formal gardens, dotted with fountains, pools and sculptures, and then sit beside the bay and take in the view.

▷ **GARDEN GUARDIANS**
The 17th-century statuary decorating the gardens includes busts and mythological figures such as Neptune, Minerva and Apollo.

▷ **FORMAL GARDENS**
The villa's south side faces Italian Renaissance-style gardens. Unlike flower gardens, they are characterized by stone, water and greenery.

△ **MARBLE FLOORS**
The floors in the house are laid out in geometric patterns of richly colored marble, reminiscent of Italian *palazzi*.

△ **MUSIC ROOM**
Decorated in the lively spirit of Italian Rococo, this room is home to an 18th-century harpsichord and a Louis XVI harp.

▷ **TEA HOUSE**
At one end of the sea wall, a bridge leads to the delightful Tea House, inspired by French architecture.

RENAISSANCE-INSPIRED FUN

Every March the four-day Italian Renaissance Festival takes over the highly appropriate venue of Vizcaya's gardens. With jousting and juggling, chain mail and chess matches, kings and costumes, it is the only event like it in the Americas.

There's something at the festival for everyone. Music lovers can listen to tavern wenches and minstrels singing ballads, or musicians with lutes, horns and dulcimers recreating the sounds of a quieter time. Theater lovers can watch performances put on by the Commedia del Arte Players. A living chess match has men and women moving across a giant chess board, with sword fights often deciding who remains standing and who is captured. Flag throwers and jesters entertain you as you wander through the gardens. Food stalls provide plenty to eat, and craftspeople sell jewelry, swords, crystals and much more.

The event is run by hundreds of volunteers who are coached to act in the manner of the period. They spend the entire year making elaborate costumes and dress as courtiers or peasants. To be true to the time, no zippers are allowed. For more information call Vizcaya, (305) 250-9133.

△ EAST FACADE
The three arches of the east facade, situated between the fortress-like corner towers, lead you out to the sea-wall promenade and stone barge.

▷ SWEET DREAMS
Deering named each guest room after its design style. The Cathay Bedroom is decorated with chinoiserie, popular in the 18th century.

KEY BISCAYNE

*Connected to the mainland by a single causeway over the bay,
Key Biscayne and its partner island Virginia Key offer some of
the best beaches and oceanfront parks in Greater Miami*

Map
on page
204

En route to **Key Biscayne**, passing the tollgate and crossing the causeway, you will drive smack into blue sky and bluer water. You might begin to think, much like other Key Biscayners: "I'm home." That peek back at the Miami skyline, so intense in white light, is just enough to confirm it for you: this is the perfect distance from the bustle and busyness.

"Home" is a 5-mile (8-km) by 1-mile (1.5-km) sliver of land off Miami proper, only 15 minutes' drive from downtown Miami and a secret so convenient and comfortable that Key Biscayners, in their laid-back way, will not rush to tell. Despite their "Island Paradise" boast on their welcome, Key Biscayners will insist, out of small-town courtesy, "there's nothing special here."

Part truth, part conspiracy, the secret of Key Biscayne is the mesh of ordinary life and extraordinary setting. Without much ado, Key Biscayne envelops visitors in small surprises, unfolding quietly, even slyly, its history and its heart.

Two of hundreds of islands that surround the tip of Florida, Key Biscayne and its neighbor, **Virginia Key**, are sedimentary barrier islands, strung north-south, parallel to the South Florida coast. They began as sandbars, millions of years ago. As waves and wind piled limestone and quartz on top of hard coral rock, islands emerged, a barrier between the Atlantic Ocean and the mainland.

Even when trees and shrubs arrived, the island was not appealing – a tangle of mangrove swamps, jungle, coral rock and sand dunes infested with snakes, monkeys and mosquitoes. Nevertheless, this place captured attention. English explorer John Cabot spotted the southern tip in 1497, calling it Cape of the End of April. Juan Ponce de León claimed it for Spain in 1513.

Its name changed, depending on the mapmaker: Promentorium Floridae, Cape Florida, even Sandwich Gulf. "Biscayne," appearing on Spanish maps as early as 1765, may honor a merchant-mariner, the Keeper of Swans at the Spanish Court, or a ship owned by El Biscaino and wrecked in the mid-1500s. Is the confusion artful? Perhaps even the earliest islanders thought: If they don't know, they won't find us. But surveyors left a marker in 1655. (Look between the 10th and 18th fairways at the Key Biscayne Golf Course.)

Developers arrived in the early 1900s to clear land, dredge shallow Biscayne Bay, fill the swamps and – presto! – create a synthetic island and shore. Under the supervision of Dr. William "Commodore" Matheson, Key Biscayne was transformed from a wasteland.

Matheson opened yacht basins, 18 miles (29 km) of roadway, and then planted, planted, planted: 100,000 Nucifera coconuts, Australian pines, sea grapes, tropical almonds, mangos, bougainvilleas and date palms. From his bayside mansion, he set the early tones of exclusivity.

PRECEDING PAGES:
secluded cove on
Key Biscayne.
LEFT: cycling over
the causeway.
BELOW:
flower power.

The modern Key Biscayne community began when the Rickenbacker Causeway was opened in 1947, with a daunting 25-cent toll. Named after, and built by, a World War I flying ace, it loped over Biscayne Bay, a waterway shared with the rest of Miami. With the bridge came "mainlanders," out to exploit, according to local Key Biscayners.

Until then, unlike other resorts, Key Biscayne had successfully avoided overcrowding. In the early 1950s, the Mackle Brothers developers built modest track housing in order to lure World War II veterans with GI loans to the desolate island. Working-class neighborhoods emerged. Then, like other points in Miami, Key Biscayne caught construction fever, and zoning went awry. Apartments turned into condominiums.

As President Richard Nixon brought the winter White House to the island in the 1970s, homeowners watched as the world discovered Key Biscayne. Amid gentrification, a Mackle home, bought for $15,000 in 1955, sold for $200,000 in 1985 and would now fetch double that. Today, real estate advertisements fatten *The Islander News*, the island's weekly paper, and many who work on the island cannot afford to live there. In the push, developers have also claimed famous sites, such as the Key Biscayne Hotel, demolished to make way for a massive condominium complex.

Sailboarders gather at Windsurfer Beach and then head out into the steady winds of Biscayne Bay.

Virginia Key

To reach Key Biscayne and Virginia Key, take the **Rickenbacker Causeway** across Biscayne Bay, from the mainland at Brickell Avenue and SW 26th Road, about 2 miles (3 km) south of downtown Miami. Before you cross the main span over the bay, about 200 ft (60 meters) east of the tollgate is **Hobie Beach**, one of the most popular places, nationwide, for owners or renters of catamarans. Ribbons of cement, pebbles and sand edge the bay, with parking and picnicking sites tucked under a canopy of Australian pines.

Adjacent **Windsurfer Beach** (first past the tollbooth) captivates windsurfing *aficionados*. Averaging 18 knots in March through April, winds from the east and southeast move sailboards along at an easy pace. Flat, shallow, waveless water makes surfing ideal for beginners. Late summer hurricane winds thrill daredevil pros. Equipment rentals and lessons are negotiable on the spot. Stretching parallel, north of the causeway, is **Jet Ski Beach**, where motorized skiers roar free – jet skis are actually banned from many other areas around Miami because of their danger to manatees and other marine life. Stands along this stretch offer windsurfing classes and board rentals as well as jet skis, bicycles and scooters for hire. You can even try an ultralite flight over the bay.

On the far side of the bridge, the Rickenbacker Causeway alights on **Virginia Key ❶**, which has one of the most pristine beaches on these relatively untouched islands, though developers and preservationists are still arguing. **Virginia Key Beach** offers a 2-mile (3-km) stretch of sand, and water deep enough to truly indulge swimmers. Families, hammocks swaying, move in for the day. Be aware that the undertow can be strong in these waters.

Key Biscayne

Rickenbacker Causeway
VIRGINIA KEY PARK
❷ Miami Seaquarium
National Oceanographic & Atmospheric Administration
Bear Cut
North West Point
❶ Virginia Key
Biscayne Nature Center
Crandon Park Marina
Biscayne Bay
KEY BISCAYNE GOLF COURSE
Crandon Boulevard
Crandon Beach
West Point
International Tennis Center
CRANDON PARK ❸
ATLANTIC OCEAN
Key Biscayne
East Dr.
Harbor Drive
Hampton Ln.
Fernwood Rd.
Crandon Boulevard
Glenco Ave.
Heather Dr.
Galen Dr.
Harbor Point
Wood Drive
Mashta Dr.
South West Point
S. Mashta Drive
Island Drive
C. Florida Dr.
Crandon Blvd.
N
❹ Bill Baggs Cape Florida State Recreation Area
0   1 mile
0   1 km
Cape Florida
❺ Cape Florida Lighthouse

As a break from the sun, follow the dirt roads to the northeastern part of the island, which offers magnificent views of the rest of Miami. Also here is **Jimbo's Shrimp**, a fish smokehouse and bar, guarded by old-timers playing an Italian version of bowls called *bocce* and chewing tobacco on the veranda.

Also on Virginia Key is the 35-acre (14-hectare) **Miami Seaquarium** ❷ (4400 Rickenbacker Causeway; open daily; entrance fee; tel: (305) 361-5705), where visitors can meet, pet and feed sea lions and dolphins, plus view sharks feeding at exhibition halls. Flipper, the world's most televised dolphin, and Lolita, a 5-ton killer whale, perform daily. Endangered birds and reptiles nest in the Lost Islands, a wildlife sanctuary where official efforts to rescue, rehabilitate and reproduce threatened species have been under way since 1955.

Not far from the Seaquarium, the southern tip of the island houses a mecca for marine scientists. Environmental research, especially into the ocean and atmosphere, is under way at the National Oceanographic and Atmospheric Administration and the Rosenstiel School of Marine and Atmospheric Science.

Key Biscayne

Beyond Virginia Key, the causeway crosses narrow **Bear Cut** to reach Key Biscayne itself. East along its sandy northern shore, Key Biscayne has its own petrified forest – a black mangrove reef of fossilized wood and roots, the only such site reported in the world. Wearing sneakers you can hike in the waters to explore this unique environment, which stretches along the shore for about 1,300 ft (400 meters), and juts seaward 350 ft (100 meters). The **Marjory Stoneman Douglas Biscayne Nature Center**, at 4000 Crandon Boulevard (tel: (305) 642-9600), offers guided walks along this fascinating shore.

Map on page 204

TIP

Don't let the insalubrious address (Sewerline Road) or scruffy look of Jimbo's Shrimp put you off. The home-smoked salmon is legendary and goes down well with a cold beer.

LEFT: dinner time at Miami Seaquarium.
BELOW: bucolic scene at Jimbo's Shrimp.

The northern part of Key Biscayne is occupied by **Crandon Park** ❸. Donated by the Matheson family, its 1,400 acres (570 hectares) carry a few reminders – royal palms, mangroves – of its heyday as a coconut plantation. Slogs through the seagrass and coastal hammocks in the northeast wilderness take visitors back even earlier.

At the northern end of the park is the **Crandon Park Marina**. Here, captains of charter boats – from as far afield as Hatteras, Bertram or Monterrey – dock to clean and sell a catch. Half-day and full-day excursions can search for sailfish and dolphin year-round. Anchor at **Sundays on the Bay** (5420 Crandon Boulevard) for a spot of brunch or night-time reggae. Alternatively, watch the sunset hues tinge Miami's skyline from **The Rusty Pelican**'s prime vantage point at 3201 Rickenbacker Causeway.

On the Atlantic side is Crandon Park's 3-mile (5-km) swatch of beachfront, consistently rated one of the US's top 10 beaches. The beach and nearby parkland include several soccer and softball fields, an 18-hole public golf course and 75 barbecue grills. Considered by many to be the very best "party beach" in Miami, it can turn into pandemonium when fun-seeking visitors fill the four parking lots in midsummer. A carousel dating from 1949 has been renovated and is open to the public. The nearby Quiet Gardens, inhabited by exotic birds and iguanas, are a reminder of the long-gone days of Crandon Park Zoo.

Also in Crandon Park is the **International Tennis Center**. Here, nearly 300 top-ranked tennis players compete in the Ericsson Championship for two weeks every March. As many as 200,000 visitors watch top players like Andre Agassi, Pete Sampras and Venus and Serena Williams compete for a $2 million purse. When the tournament is not running, the courts are open to the public.

BELOW: the Rusty
Pelican marina with
the downtown
skyline behind.

Despite the occasional onslaught in the summer or for the tennis, a quiet tempo still clings on the island. Life in "the village" beyond Crandon Park makes this clear. There are few traffic lights and few traffic jams. Tourist season often means only a few seconds' wait before a left turn or a few minutes' longer search for parking near the grocery. Visitors get the same treatment as locals, with no routes designated scenic, few tourist brochures, no crucial road signs.

Shops are more retro than trendy, delivering the basics with an old-fashioned service. Most are clustered along **Crandon Boulevard**, which bisects the island north to south. With the Atlantic as a backdrop, hotels such as the Sonesta Beach, Grand Bay and Silver Sands provide private beachfronts away from the public parks for those not blessed with their own accommodation, which often comes with beach club membership.

Year-round, residents cycle, walk or jog along the beach, causeway or park tracks. For no-sweat cycling on terrain that is almost completely flat, enquire for rentals at **Mangrove Cycles** in the Square Shopping Center at 260 Crandon Boulevard (closed Mon; tel: (305) 361-5555).

Map on page 204

Cape Florida

For the real Key Biscayne experience, join beachcombers for a walk into **Bill Baggs Cape Florida State Recreation Area ❹**, (open daily; entrance fee; tel: (305) 361-5811). Here, in the 494-acre (200-hectare) preserve, a dense canopy of Australian pine and sea-grape trees was once the main attraction, but Hurricane Andrew changed all that. Situated at the southernmost tip of Key Biscayne, with nothing nearby to break the winds, **Cape Florida** suffered a major hit in the 1992 storm and was one of the most devastated areas in Miami proper.

BELOW: a boardwalk at Bill Baggs State Recreation Area.

Map
on page
204

*One of the few lonely
structures still fending
off the wind and
waves in Stiltsville.*

BELOW: Cape
Florida Lighthouse.
RIGHT: Crandon
Park Beach.

Park rangers began an industrious re-greening effort in the mid-1990s, planting millions of tiny native seedlings. With Mother Nature's help, and no direct hurricanes since Andrew, the park is on the road to full botanical recovery. Cape Florida attracts nature lovers and sun worshippers in both the winter and summer months, and it is now the state's fourth busiest park – in a state park system rated number one in the country – with annual attendance edging near three-quarters of a million.

The litany of outdoor fun is well-known to all the hedonists: you can swim, sunbathe, picnic, fish, cycle, jog, hike or, in the words of Baggs himself, the *Miami News* editor whose crusade preserved the park, "listen to the drawl of the sea."

On the beach, also regularly listed in the country's top ten, white sand, albeit dingy, and often studded with seaweed and stinging man-o'-wars, reaches along the oceanfront. On-the-spot treats include tropical fruit drinks and Key lime pie at the island's most eclectic concession stand.

A bayside seawall hosts anglers in search of bonefish, grouper, jack, snapper and snook. Fishing here is just as scenic as it is from the pier of the old Rickenbacker Causeway bridge.

History buffs can visit the 95-ft (29-meter) **Cape Florida Lighthouse** ❺ and take the 109 steps to the top of the oldest structure in South Florida. Perched on a sand dune, the lighthouse has been restored to its former glory, and given a new coat of paint. Tours are given at 10am and 1pm Thursday through Monday. Get there early as places on the tour are limited to ten people.

The lighthouse, completed in 1825, beckoned travelers. Keeping ships afloat despite storms, uncharted waters, sandbars and submerged reefs, it promised newcomers a smooth landing and an easy life. Hardly. In 1836, during the Second Seminole War, the lighthouse was attacked by Seminoles, angry that their land was being appropriated by settlers. Barely escaping a roasting, the lightkeeper clung to the lighthouse platform until he was rescued by a Navy schooner. Damaged by Confederate sympathizers during the Civil War – to ensure that Union sailors could not use it as a navigational aid – the lantern was eventually extinguished in 1878. It was not "lit" again until 1978.

The nearby surf is classic. It was here that John Wayne waded, Hollywood-style, escaping from a smoking PT boat in the 1945 movie *They Were Expendable.*

Just offshore is a piece of hidden Miami. Near the Key's southern tip, where the Atlantic Ocean meets Biscayne Bay, is **Stiltsville**, a collection of now-dilapidated bungalows perched on stilts in the ocean. Built as weekend getaways, only a few of the 14 structures remain, planted in the water like concrete-and-wood flamingos. The future of these architectural oddities is threatened, since they lie within the Biscayne National Park and their lease ran out in 1999. Politicians, owners and historians have joined to plead for their salvation.

In these waters, charter boats pass by without stopping, en route to deep-sea fishing in the Gulf Stream. Their wakes rock bonefishers, upright on flat-bottomed boats. Then, it's quiet again, only interrupted by the occasional curious cormorant. ❏

HEADING SOUTH

The southern tip of Miami extends into an area renowned for its rich soil and bountiful produce. In among the strawberry fields, there is plenty to see and do, especially for families with kids

Map on page 214

South Miami-Dade County, situated around the community of **Homestead** and a disappearing agricultural area from the early 1900s known as the **Redland**, is 25 miles (40 km) from downtown Miami but years away in time. This is what Miami once was: rural, small town, Southern, a place for a barbecue rather than a *boulangerie*.

In 1992, Hurricane Andrew charged right through this district, the hardest-hit section of the Miami area. Hundreds of businesses and homes were totally destroyed, and many tourist attractions took years to rebuild. Rational-minded scientists and botanists insist that South Miami-Dade – specifically the Everglades and the rich farmlands – got a much-needed pruning by Mother Nature, and in fact will be better off in the future because of the storm. The foliage may indeed have grown back thicker than before, but the emotional scars on residents and shopkeepers have taken longer to heal.

The hurricane notwithstanding, Homestead and its surrounding area are still "old Florida." This is a place with the smell of the earth, with pick-up trucks, turnip greens, two-lane streets lined with tunnels of majestic Royal Palms, and a hardware store on the main street. Drive through farmland in the Redland in winter and you'll smell the lime trees in blossom. There is an annual rodeo, and cowboy boots are worn not as a fashion accessory but as everyday dress. But change, like the lime blossoms, is in the air. Once as corny as Kansas, South Miami-Dade is suddenly a new frontier of yuppification. The Volvos are heading south.

Once heartland, the area is now the gateway to the Keys, the Everglades and the water wonderland of Biscayne National Park. Homes from the 1920s are being "saved" by yuppies. Organic farms are cropping up all over, home to folk escaping the urban sprawl for a more relaxed, rural lifestyle.

Attractions en route

To reach Homestead from downtown Miami take US 1, but before you head too far south turn east on 112th Street and listen for the squawking. **Parrot Jungle** ❶ (11000 SW 57th Avenue; open daily; entrance fee; tel: (305) 666-7834) is a bird sanctuary where the free-flying parrots are tame enough to pose for a picture sitting on your head, arms and shoulders. There's a petting zoo, trained animal shows and a botanical garden, along with lots of exotic wildlife. The Jungle is moving to a new location – Watson Island on Biscayne Bay – in 2001.

Farther south, just off Old Cutler Road, at 16701 SW 72nd Avenue, is the **Deering Estate** ❷ (open daily; entrance fee; tel: (305) 235-1668). Here you can experience the elegance of a lost era in the renovated

PRECEDING PAGES: gibbons at Miami Metrozoo. **LEFT:** blooming orchids. **BELOW:** the pride of Parrot Jungle.

historic home of industrialist Charles Deering, brother of James Deering, who built Vizcaya. In 1913 Charles bought the 420-acre (170-hectare) estate to build a winter residence for his family, and to store his yacht, furnishings, fine paintings and tapestries. It had been the site of Richmond Cottage, the first hotel between Coconut Grove and Key West, opened in 1900. Deering had his winter home built in the Mediterranean-Revival style, to remind him of the castles he owned in Spain. Visitors can tour the house and take nature trails among rare native plants in the hardwood hammock.

A western detour

Another possible detour even before you head south is the Tamiami campus of Florida International University (FIU), which lies between Southwest Eighth Street, Coral Way and SW 107th and 117th avenues. The **FIU Art Museum** ❸ (open daily; Sat and Sun pm only; free; tel: (305) 348-2890) has an extensive collection of contemporary sculpture on display throughout the grounds of its 26-acre (11-hectare) Art Park. The collection emphasizes Latin American and 20th-century American art and includes pieces by Alexander Calder, Willem de Kooning and Richard Serra.

Head southwest from FIU and you reach **Weeks Air Museum** ❹ (open daily; entrance fee; tel: (305) 233-5197), a collection of 35 antique aircraft based at Tamiami Airport, 14710 SW 128th Street. Exhibits include an all-plywood DeHavilland, a TP40 Warhawk, a B-29 cockpit and a South Pacific display. The countryside here is like Orange, California, a 1920s center for orange and lemon groves where one-time farmhouses have been swallowed by Los Angeles' growth. Miami has not yet swallowed Dade's deep south. But hurry while it lasts.

TIP

The coastal wetlands that fringe the Deering Estate include 130 acres (53 hectares) of mangroves and salt marsh, plus the island of Chicken Key. These can be explored on a canoe tour; call ahead for reservations on (305) 235-1668.

BELOW:
tropical foliage, a common sight in South Miami.

Southern Miami

Talk to the animals

South Miami-Dade, known for its farms and flora is also a place for fauna. **Miami Metrozoo** ❺ (12400 SW 152nd Street; open daily; entrance fee; tel: (305) 251-0400) is one of the best zoos in the country, a cageless sprawl over 290 acres (115 hectares) that has wisely specialized instead of trying to be a Noah's Ark of every animal. Opened in 1981, the zoo is dedicated to tropical life; there are no polar bears here.

The zoo has more than 225 species living in "natural" island sites surrounded by moats. Animals come from the African and Asian plains and jungles, Asian forests, Eurasian steppes and Australia. An elevated monorail travels through the park, which features a lake and various meadows.

There are first-rate exhibits: a koala park, Komodo dragons, a petting zoo that features elephant rides, plus an ecology theater and the white Bengal tigers, two of only 150 left in the world.

Adjacent to Metrozoo on SW 152nd Street is the **Gold Coast Railroad Museum** ❻ (open daily; entrance fee; tel: (305) 253-0063), featuring 50 pieces of railroad equipment from different eras. The 1942 *Ferdinand Magellan* was the presidential car for Franklin D. Roosevelt, Harry S. Truman, Dwight D. Eisenhower and Ronald Reagan. Walk through the narrow confines of a working dining car, see steam and diesel engines and peer out of a 1948 stainless-steel, domed passenger car used by the *California Zephyr*. On the weekends the museum fires up a train, and it chuffs up and down a 1.3-mile (2.1-km) track.

Almost directly south of Metrozoo is **Cauley Square**, a former railroad town that still faces the old tracks and highway US 1 at 224th Street. It is 10 acres (4 hectares) of nostalgia, featuring several shops selling crafts and antiques, all

Map on page 214

The koalas at Metrozoo arrived in 1988, the first of their kind to have a permanent home on the East Coast. They acclimatized so well that in 1989 they produced an heir, the first koala birth in the country outside California.

BELOW: deep-pink flamingos, Miami Metrozoo.

Map on page 214

Built in the 1920s and '30s, Coral Castle includes symbolic sculptures such as this crescent moon.

BELOW: antiquarian bookstore at Cauley Square.

of which are linked by paths. There is a quaint tea room for lunch. This is not Disneyland, not a mall, but the way things used to be, insists the owner.

The nearby flatland is ideal for bike rides and a 20-mile (32-km) loop can be wound through the Redland. Or pop the top down for a drive in a convertible, poking around country lanes looking out for homes and farmsteads, many of which are officially designated by the county's historic preservation division. A quarter of the county's historic homes and buildings are found here. Because the area is still zoned for agriculture, most homes sit on a minimum of 5 acres (2 hectares). It is the size of properties that attracts potential buyers, particularly to old farmhouses with established tropical vegetation.

About 3 miles (5 km) west of Cauley Square is **Monkey Jungle** ❼ (14805 SW 216th Street; open daily; entrance fee; tel: (305) 235-1611), a roadside attraction dating from 1935 that features walking tours of shaded grounds full of primates. These passive exhibits may be out of style but at Monkey Jungle the residents roam free in the trees while you watch from fenced-in enclosures. There's a tropical rainforest filled with monkeys and rare parrots.

Blushing berries

From Christmas to April, South Miami-Dade fills with rows of vivid strawberry plants stretching to the horizon. One of the oldest properties is **Knauss Berry Farm**, at 15980 SW 248th Street. Run by a religious order that hails from Indiana, it offers fresh berries, other fresh-picked produce, thick milk shakes and home-baked pies and rolls.

For those who prefer to do it themselves, several fields offer U-pick berries plus tomatoes, onions, squash and other winter produce. Prices are about half of what you pay at retail. Drive north or south on **Krome Avenue** and watch for signs.

The **Preston B. and Mary Heinlein Fruit and Spice Park** ❽ on 187th Avenue and SW 248th Street (open daily; entrance fee; tel: (305) 247-5727) is a 35-acre (14-hectare) tropical botanical garden. Here you can travel the world by taking in over 500 varieties of fruits, herbs, spices and nuts from Asia, Africa, South America and the Mediterranean. Depending on the season, you will stroll the grounds among trees and shrubs in bloom or in fruit. Sampling the fallen fruit is allowed but picking or harvesting anything is forbidden. A gourmet store sells dried exotics, jellies, jams and cookbooks.

On the outskirts of Homestead, at 28655 S Dixie Highway, is a spooky attraction. **Coral Castle** ❾ (open daily; entrance fee; tel: (305) 248-6344) is a coral-rock mansion built by a Latvian immigrant to his unrequited love. The house has a 9-ton gate that swings open to the lightest touch and a 2-ton Valentine heart.

Homestead itself is coming back strong after Hurricane Andrew. It's known for its good home cooking, especially at the many authentic Mexican restaurants that serve the large number of Mexican farm workers. One successful project is the **Metro-Dade/Homestead Motor Sports Complex**, site of the Miami Grand Prix. Located near Palm Drive, the complex hosts motor races and test runs throughout the year. ❏

Hurricane Andrew

I t was South Florida's worst nightmare. Just before dawn on August 24, 1992, a storm packing 160-mph (260-kph) winds and a 12-ft (4-meter) tidal wave slammed into the southern part of the state, leaving in its wake a surreal scene of devastation.

Hurricane Andrew, the worst natural disaster ever to hit the US, destroyed over 60,000 homes and left 150,000 people – 10 percent of Miami-Dade County – homeless. The category 4 hurricane left a 30-mile (48-km) wide swath of damage worth an estimated $25 billion. In Miami-Dade County 40 people lost their lives.

Hardest hit were the rural and suburban areas about 20 miles (32 km) south of downtown Miami – Homestead, Kendall, Florida City – most of which were totally destroyed. Parts of Coconut Grove and Coral Gables were also badly damaged. Cape Florida, at the tip of Key Biscayne, suffered a direct hit.

Along with piles of debris around the city, Andrew left a battlefield of wounds: houses, high schools, gas stations, shopping centers and churches were demolished; cars smashed and overturned; boats damaged and blown ashore; airplanes crumpled; all leaving a severely scarred landscape of uprooted trees.

In the days and weeks that followed, thousands of civilian volunteers from around the country, along with the American Red Cross, poured in to help. The president deployed 20,000 US troops to the area to help deter looting, clean up debris, and build temporary tent cities. But locals complained that officials, caught in a bureaucratic confusion with no one in charge, took too long before mobilizing assistance – tens of thousands of people went for days in the summer heat without food, water, medical care or shelter. So desperate was the situation that Florida City police officials hijacked a water truck that was headed for nearby Homestead.

Along with the human suffering, animals also fell victim to the storm. Thousands of dogs and cats, not allowed into the shelters, were left on the streets to fend for themselves. One homeowner woke to find a shark floating in his swimming pool; others found fish in their television sets.

When the images of the hurricane hit the news, foreign aid flowed in from around the world as if Dade County – one of the most cosmopolitan counties in the US – were suddenly a Third World country. Canada, Japan and Taiwan all sent relief. Even President Yeltsin offered to send Russian workers and machinery to help with the clean-up. Thanks to these offers of help and massive rebuilding projects, the area has now fully recovered.

One positive outcome was that the county, often beleagured by racial conflicts, was left a more cohesive community. Residents, white, black, Cuban and Haitian, worked together. "As one we will rebuild" was the spirit.

And, fortunately for the vital tourism industry, the damage wreaked by Andrew to most busy tourist areas was minimal. Had the hurricane's eye hit just a few miles to the north, the city would likely have been wiped out. Hurricane Andrew, the awesome force of nature, could have been much worse. ❑

RIGHT: Hurricane Andrew showed no mercy on its rampage through South Miami.

NORTHERN MIAMI

Map on page 222

Whether it's a string of historic neighborhoods along Biscayne Bay, a private art collection or a run-down part of the city transformed by immigrants, Northern Miami holds many hidden treasures.

A good place to start is a nondescript structure in Wynwood, a run-down neighborhood about 2 miles (3 km) north of the downtown skyscrapers. The 40,000-sq-ft (3,700-sq-meter) building at 95 NW 29th Street, a former warehouse for the US Drug Enforcement Administration, has been renovated as a private museum and houses the **Don and Mera Rubell Collection ❶** (open Thur–Sat or by appointment; free; tel: (305) 573-6090). The Rubell family, who own several hotels in South Beach and were involved in the New York art world and the redevelopment of SoHo, claim one of the world's finest collections of contemporary art.

The collection numbers about 1,000 pieces, dating from the 1970s to the present day. Almost every important artist of that period is represented, including Keith Haring, Francesco Clemente, Jeff Koons, Jean-Michel Basquiat, Paul McCarthy and Cindy Sherman. Together the works underline the Rubells' taste for risk, provocation – and size. Two of the biggest pieces here are Beverly Semmes' *Blue Gowns*, an overwhelming installation of three giant gowns cascading from a 22-ft (7-meter) wall, and Jose Bedia's untitled 1995 installation, commissioned by the Rubells, which incorporates a Cuban raft, found objects, drawings and aspects of Afro-Cuban religion.

PRECEDING PAGES: Easter Sunday Mass, Little Haiti. **LEFT:** Haitian woman. **BELOW:** Caribbean colors.

To the northeast, on the corner of Biscayne Boulevard and 38th Street, it would be hard to miss the **American Police Hall of Fame and Museum ❷** (open daily; entrance fee; tel: (305) 573-0070). This is because a police car is climbing the western facade of the building. It is the US's only memorial and museum honoring all police in federal, state, county and local departments.

The museum contains about 10,000 artifacts collected over more than 30 years, illustrating the history of law enforcement. Exhibits feature officers and notorious criminals, prisons, stocks and pillories. There are also more gruesome displays that include a real electric chair and gas chamber.

From here, head west across the railroad tracks into the **Design District ❸**, one of the oldest neighborhoods of Miami and undergoing its own brand of yuppification. It was practically abandoned by interior designers in the 1980s who feared crime and the area's proximity to Little Haiti. But in the late 1990s, artists who could no longer afford South Beach's prices crossed the bay. Falling in love with the large spaces for their studios and the gorgeous 1920s architecture, they're reinventing the district as a hip neighborhood with galleries, furniture stores, restaurants and clubs. **Power Studios**, at 3701 NE Second Avenue, offers music on three stages, dining and dancing, along with production facilities.

A Caribbean community

Continuing north, the music will pull you into **Little Haiti ❹**, an enclave of Caribbean culture that began to take shape in ways that were both dramatic and subtle in the late 1980s. Here the storefronts leap out at passers-by, seeming to vibrate to the Haitian music blaring from sidewalk speakers. The multilingual signs advertise peculiarly Haitian products – the latest *compas* records, custom-tailored "French-Styled" fashions and culinary delights such as *lambi* (conch) and *griot* (fried pork). And, unlike so many neighborhoods in the age of the automobile, Little Haiti's streets are filled with pedestrians.

Houses wear coats of pink, blue, red and yellow, the colors found in the Caribbean countryside and far from the subtle Art Deco pastels of Miami Beach. These colors, the vivid hues of the sunlit tropics, are most evident in the folk-art murals on the storefronts, walls and billboards scattered throughout the community. Many murals are painted by local artists, their subjects ranging from store names to political demonstrations, floral collages and Haitian people. While widely scattered throughout the neighborhood, they are especially prevalent along **NE Second Avenue** and **54th Street**.

Along NE Second Avenue, all the way from **45th** to **84th Street**, Haitian stores predominate. At the corner of NE First Avenue and 54th Street, stop for a tropical taste treat at **Lakay** ice cream shop. Exotic flavors include *cachiman* (sweetsop), *corosol* (soursop), mango, tamarind and many more. A few blocks north, pop into **Libreri Mapou** at 5919 NE Second Avenue. This bookstore stocks a large selection of Creole and French publications, as well as Haitian paintings and crafts. Owner Jan Mapou, a staunch promoter of Haitian culture, holds readings and other cultural events above the store.

Contrary to negative images in the media, Miami's Haitian immigrants are rarely illiterate or unskilled and are generally better qualified than countrymen who stay behind. Many arrive college-educated and fluent in English from elsewhere in the US and become Little Haiti's leaders.

BELOW: Haitian restaurant on 59th Street.

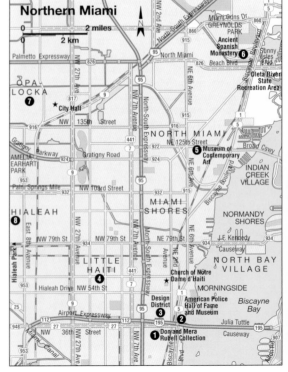

Just around the corner, at 120 NE 59th Street, is **Toussaint Louverture Elementary School**, the only Miami-Dade County school named after a Haitian hero. Toussaint Louverture was a freed slave who led the uprising against the French in Haiti that produced the first emancipation of slaves and the first modern free black republic. The school contains a statue of the hero, donated by the city's Haitian community, and its stucco walls reflect Caribbean colors all boldly applied, in broad sweeps.

Back on NE Second Avenue, at the junction with NE 60th Street, is Little Haiti's spiritual center, the **Church of Notre Dame d'Haiti** and the **Pierre Toussaint Haitian Catholic Center**, which occupy the buildings and grounds of a former Catholic girls' high school. The chapel's splendid stained-glass windows depict the family of the freed Haitian-born slave Pierre Toussaint, who became a tireless charity worker in New York in the late 18th century and is currently being considered by the Vatican for sainthood. Another wall is covered with a mural that depicts the journey of Haitians to South Florida.

Mass is held daily, but every effort should be made to attend a Sunday service. Then, the chapel overflows with worshippers, immaculately attired. A Haitian band and choir provides music, a blend of French melodies and African rhythms that is much more mellow and mellifluous than most Afro-Caribbean music.

Alongside the bay

A stone's throw from Little Haiti are some of Miami's most picturesque historic districts. Like pearls strung on a necklace, these neighborhoods line the western rim of the bay, east of Biscayne Boulevard. One of the most established is **Morningside**, just north of 55th Street. Here, one finds a fantastic collection of

Map on page 222

The neighborhood of El Portal, just north of Little Haiti, is the site of a Tequesta village dating from AD 500. Pottery and arrowheads have been unearthed, but all you can see above ground is a burial mound at 500 NE 87th Street.

BELOW: the streets of Little Haiti are seldom silent.

Map on page 222

Until 1999, horse races were held every spring at the Hialeah Park racetrack, which was built in 1925.

BELOW: Moorish arches and minaret in Opa-Locka.

Mediterrranean-Revival and Art Deco homes that look onto wide tree-lined avenues. Farther north are Upper Eastside, Belle Meade and Shorecrest.

Beyond them, in the City of North Miami, is the **Museum of Contemporary Art ❺**, at 770 NE 125th Street (open Tues–Sun; Sun pm only; entrance fee; tel: (305) 893-6211). It's the Miami area's newest art museum, known for its provocative and innovative exhibitions and fresh approach to contemporary art.

Continuing north to the City of North Miami Beach, there is another hidden jewel – the **Ancient Spanish Monastery ❻** (16711 W Dixie Highway; open daily; entrance fee; tel: (305) 945-1461). This 12th-century monastery was brought from Spain in 1925 by newspaper magnate William Randolph Hearst. The dismantled building was eventually rebuilt in its current location in 1952.

Northwest suburbs

Northwest of downtown Miami are the cities of Opa-Locka, Hialeah and Miami Springs, which provide a totally different perspective on the Greater Miami area than that of the dynamic metropolis to the south. These three cities are middle-class suburbs that were created during the real estate boom of the 1920s, using exotic architectural themes as marketing schemes to attract buyers.

In 1921, Glenn Curtiss, an early aviation pioneer, teamed up with cattle rancher James Bright and began the development of Hialeah. The architecture of the new city was based on the Spanish churches of the California missions. Three years later, Country Club Estates, later renamed Miami Springs, came to life as an affluent, planned community in the Pueblo-Revival architectural style. In 1925, Curtiss embarked on the city of **Opa-Locka ❼**. This time the outrageous Moorish-Revival theme was used, inspired by the *Arabian Nights* stories.

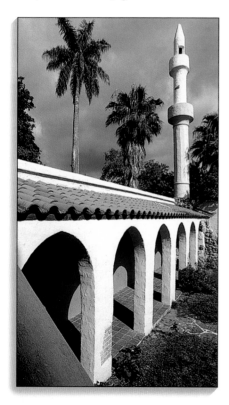

Buildings sported horseshoe arches, domes and minarets, while streets were given names like Ali Baba and Sharazad.

The Opa-Locka Company Administration Building, currently the **City Hall**, is the city's most impressive building, located on Sharazad Boulevard. The building has been fully restored to its former splendor, with embellished domes and crenelated parapets.

The **train station** is probably the finest example of the fantasy Moorish-Revival style. The structure was built in 1927 and is most noted for the use of multicolored, glazed ceramic tiles in a variety of patterns. Twin domes facing the direction of southbound trains herald the arrival of visitors to this Arabian wonderland. But visitors are scarce these days. Trains no longer stop, and the station, like much of Opa-Locka, awaits the awakening of a new and brighter day.

Hialeah ❽ is south of Opa-Locka. Its major attraction has always been **Hialeah Park** (open Mon–Sat; free; tel: (305) 885-8000), one of the most beautiful horse-racing venues in the country, and home to what is said to be America's best library on thoroughbred racing. The park features a grandstand and clubhouse more reminiscent of an opera house than a racetrack, and manicured gardens with fountains and statues. Hundreds of pink flamingos, originally imported from Cuba, live in the park, which has been designated a bird sanctuary by the National Audubon Society. ❑

Voodoo Boutiques

The first thing you notice as you enter the door is the smell – sweet, pungent and intoxicating. Listed in the Miami telephone book under religious goods, *botanicas* (shops that sell magical herbs and religious paraphernalia) are living testimony to the controversial fact that African mysticism is alive and well in modern Miami. Usually tucked away in neighborhood shopping centers, *botánicas* cater to practitioners of the Afro-Caribbean religions of Santería and Vodou (voodoo).

Stocked on the shelves is a supernatural potpourri: aromatic roots, tranquility balm, serenity salve, virility pills, black cat repellent, dried alligator flesh, floor polish to ward off greed, rosary beads, statues of saints, black candles, bile of bullock, bones arranged as crosses, numerology books, stuffed monkey heads and voodoo dolls equipped with pins.

While *botánicas* are most popular in the neighborhoods of Little Haiti and Little Havana, they are found throughout the city and all have a combination Jesus Christ, Black Magic, Alice in Wonderland persona.

Both Vodou and Santería have their roots in the religion of the Yoruba tribes of West Africa. They were carried to the Caribbean by slaves and took on a Christian character when the slaves were forced to adopt Christianity. Secrecy over the religion was common because the slaves knew the colonizers feared it might unite them and foment rebellion. In Haiti, it became Vodou. In Cuba and other areas, it became Santería. Both were brought to Miami by Caribbean immigrants.

While there are differences between the two, both are animistic and pantheistic and utilize drum-beating, chanting and the offering of animal sacrifices to influence the gods. Followers communicate with spirits who are found in nature, occasionally beat themselves with twigs to ward off evil spirits, and cast magic spells to change the future. Local sociologists say that the practice of both religions among Miami's Caribbean immigrants is a remedy for the pressures they feel to assimilate to American life.

Botánicas, which never existed in the Caribbean, where medicinal herbs were commonly sold at marketplaces, are a relatively modern phenomenon in Miami. While the *botánicas* themselves are a peculiar yet peaceful addition to Miami, the eccentric and exotic ceremonies of Santería and Vodou have provoked some controversy. In some neighborhoods, locals have complained about the disappearance of dogs and cats, and animal rights groups have protested against the killing of chickens and goats in sacrifices. Practitioners have also been accused of breaking into coffins in city cemeteries and stealing human remains for ritual use.

In defense, the practitioners have complained of persecution and petitioned the US Supreme Court for their practices to be considered legitimate religions.

It is difficult to determine how many people take part in these religions in Miami, because they are mostly practiced at home, under a veil of secrecy. But the large number of prospering *botánicas* suggests a figure well into the tens of thousands. ❑

RIGHT: ceramic "saint" on sale in a *botánica*, showing the influence of Christian iconography.

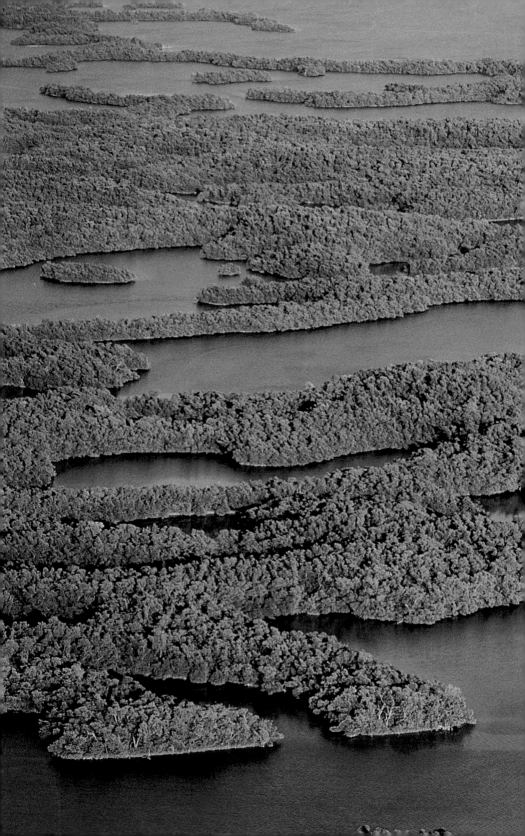

EXCURSIONS

Beyond Miami are treasures galore, from the material wealth of Palm Beach to the natural riches of the Everglades

E scape from hot-headed Miami is easy. The road north takes you along the Gold Coast – a nickname given to the oceanfront stretches of Broward and Palm Beach counties and justified by the discovery of Spanish treasure in nearby waters. This pleasure trek retraces the tourist migration routes that fed the rush south in the early 20th century. Tens of thousands of Florida's first tourists poured in a steady flow down this coast, leaving small oases every dozen miles or so. Fort Lauderdale, with its busy canals and buzzing seafront, and upper-crust Palm Beach are the cream of the resorts.

Florida's west coast is also accessible on a day-trip. Here, the Gulf of Mexico caresses fine, bleached sand; its warm waters undulate gently, or not at all; and shells of every color and shape are washed up on the sands, to the endless delight of beach-combing vacationers. However, developers have laid siege to this once placid part of Florida. Naples and Fort Myers are rapidly growing towns, and parts of the west coast have begun to resemble the waterfront wall of windows characteristic of the Miami to Palm Beach strip. But the old west coast lingers in places south of Naples, and protected stretches of coastline can be seen on the islands of Sanibel and Captiva.

En route to the west coast you pass through the swamplands of the Everglades – an alligator-filled area that covers most of Florida's southern tip. The Everglades' somewhat unglamorous waters hide a fascinating blend of fauna and flora, which inhabit a unique natural environment of huge ecological importance. Here, visitors can park the car and hike off into the watery wilds of sawgrass and hardwood hammocks to see how most of southern Florida once looked.

Finally, south of Miami, Florida doesn't just come to an abrupt end, but trickles gently away in a splash of coral and limestone islands known as the Keys ("key" being an anglicization of *cayo*, the Spanish word for "little island"). They stretch from Miami's Biscayne Bay to the Dry Tortugas, just 86 miles (140 km) north of Cuba. From the scuba culture of Key Largo to the Bohemian counterculture of Key West, each island maintains its own identity. Mañanaland, Margaritaville, the American Riviera – the Keys have been called many things. Whatever you call them, they are a place to throw off your shoes, kick back and leave the hustle and bustle behind. ❏

PRECEDING PAGES: sailing off the Gold Coast; some of the so-called Ten Thousand Islands near Everglades City. **LEFT:** fisherman's dream, Key West.

Gasparilla Island S.R.A.
Boca Grande
Point Boca Grande
Cayo Costa S.P.
Cayo Costa
Captiva
Captiva Island
J.N. Darling National Wildlife Refuge
Sanibel Island

Pirate Harbor
North Fort Myers
Bokeelia
Pine Island
Matlacha
Cape Coral
Flamingo Bay
Punta Rosa
St. James City
Sanibel
Caloosahatchee River
75
80
765
78
80
767

Alva
La Belle
Lehigh Acres
Tice
Fort Myers
Fort Myers Villas
San Carlos Park
Corkscrew
Corkscrew Swamp
867
Sanibel
Fort Myers Beach
Estero Bay

Felda
Corkscrew
Immokalee
Bunker Hill
Okaloacoochee
Harker
Slough
Sunniland
Corkscrew Swamp Sanctuary
Everglades Wonder Garden
Bonita Beach
Bonita Shores
Wiggins Pass S.R.A.
Naples Park
Vanderbilt Beach
North Naples
Naples
East Naples
Bonita Springs
846
858
951
Big Cypress
Golden Gate
856
84
41
951
Fakahatchee
Swamp
Miles City
Strand
Deep Lake
Fakahatchee Strand State Preserve
Jerome
29
29
832

GULF
OF
MEXICO

Collier Seminole S.P.
Marco
Marco Island
Collier City
92
Goodland
Gullivan Bay
Cape Romano
Ten Thousand Islands
Everglades City
29
Ochopee
Tamiami T
Chokoloskee
Chevelier Bay
Alligato
Ba

Highland Point

Ponce
Leon B

North We
Cap

Dry
Tortugas

Key Deer National Wildlife Refuge
Great Wh
Heron
N.W.R
Seven M
Bridge
Summerland Key
Big Pine
Key
Big Pine
27
Great White Heron National Wildlife Refuge
Perky
Marquesas
Keys
Key West National Wildlife Refuge
Boca Grande Channel
Key West
Stock Island
El Chico
Ramrod Key
Sugarloaf Key
Looe Key National Marine Sanctuary
Bahia Hon
State Park
28
Key West
29
Big Coppit Key

F   l   o

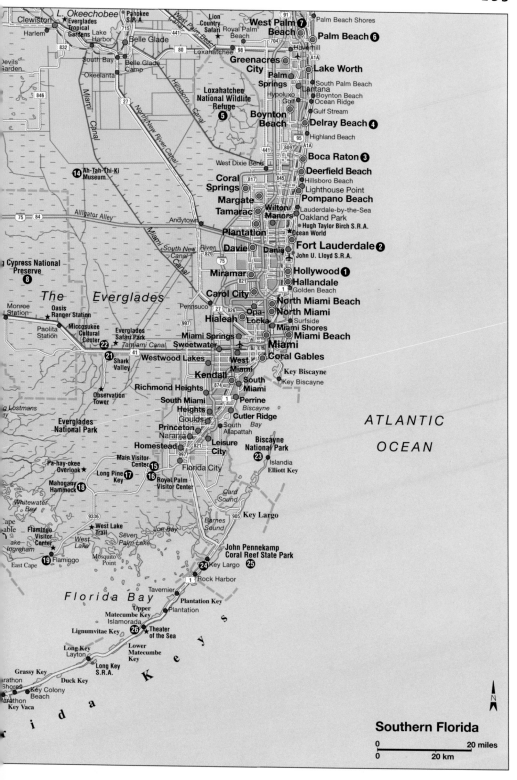

Southern Florida

0   20 miles

0   20 km

THE GOLD COAST

Sun and sea are the main reasons to head north. The coast is one long chain of beachfront resorts, from the boaters' paradise around Fort Lauderdale to the millionaires' playground of Palm Beach

Map on pages 232–3

W hen driving north up the coast from Miami, there is no excuse for sticking to I-95 or Florida's Turnpike, especially if you have a bit of time on your hands. Although they are the quickest way to access many of the towns along the coast, neither of these superhighways makes for an interesting drive. On the other hand, Highway Alternate 1 Atlantic, or, as it's commonly known, A1A, is the route of choice. Following the coast as closely as possible, it is occasionally scenic, occasionally overwhelmed by the condos and hotels which blot out the ocean, and often crowded. But it's rarely boring. The reward for enduring the traffic lights and detours will be some memorable rides through seaside resorts that beg for long stops. Here and there, mom and pop motels hang on, and garden apartments with names like Betsy-Marv or Blue Sea Kitchenettes sit behind white board fences. Interspersed are strips of fast-food restaurants and tee-shirt shops.

Morning and evening, joggers pack the A1A roadsides. On weekend mornings, skin-suited cyclists whirr colorfully close to the curbs. Docks and marinas shelter boats along baysides. As the road extends north, counties and towns more generously preserve beachfront for parks. Finally, 70 miles (110 km) north of Miami, you come to Palm Beach, where the legacy of Henry Flagler, south Florida's railroad and tourism pioneer, endures most authentically.

LEFT: conspicuous wealth in Palm Beach.
BELOW: staying cool on the coast.

Broward County

The transition from Golden Beach in northernmost Miami-Dade County is from one of the last single-family beachfronts to the abruptly soaring canyon of **Hallandale**. Halland was a Swede from New York enlisted by Flagler in the late 1890s to farm tomatoes west of the railroad. However, times change. By the 1930s Hallandale had become a notorious gambling town controlled by the Lansky brothers. Hallandale today forms a vast "U" along the beach; at the bottom are the four boulevard lanes of a briefly impressive A1A between parallel high-rise walls of condominiums. The **Diplomat Country Club and Resort** has been the city's landmark leisure facility since 1957.

Next up is **Hollywood ❶**, now merely a shadow of its 1920s glory. Joseph W. Young, an Alaskan gold-miner and sometime newspaper publisher, rode the crest of the land boom until he crashed into the triple wall of the 1926 hurricane, the land bust and the Depression. The scale of his style, if not the grace, endures at the **Hollywood Beach Hotel**, now turned into a time-share and tarted up with two stories of shops and restaurants called **Oceanwalk**. Take a look at the display of colored photo blow-ups that recall the hotel's heyday – it was a Mediterranean classic:

solid, grand and dripping in grotto moss. Elaborate colonnades lifted ceilings heavenward for America's boom-time elite.

These days **Hollywood Boulevard**, dividing around wide circles on its way from town, dumps and collects its traffic along ramps that swerve daredevil-close to the front of the hotel, its elegance forever blighted. At the rear of the hotel, fronting the beach, is the **Broadwalk**, a pedestrian promenade lined with French-style restaurants, cafes and souvenir shops. Here, skaters, bikers and joggers weave in and out of retirees and tourists who are in no hurry. The French flavor is due to the tens of thousands of French Canadians who flock to Hollywood for winter vacations, transforming it into a bilingual community.

North beyond the Dania Beach Boulevard cut-off, the road extends to **John U. Lloyd State Recreation Area**, which encompasses one of the area's finest beaches. Footbridges cross a creek into pine forests that border the beach. In winter, old-timers gossip and sunbathe in webbed beach chairs behind their massive campers, living the retirement dream. At the far end of the park road, cruise liners dock across the channel at Port Everglades, the world's second largest cruise port and part of neighboring Fort Lauderdale.

Dania Beach Boulevard carries A1A briefly inland to highway US 1 between two sections of **West Lake Park**. Its 1,300 acres (525 hectares) make this the largest urban park in South Florida. Its entrance is to the south, on Sheridan Street. The town of **Dania Beach**, to the west, was settled by Danes and is known for its pretty antique shops that line US 1 through town.

If angling is your thing, head west to the **International Game Fish Association World Fishing Museum** (open daily; entrance fee; tel: (954) 922-4212), just off I-95 south of Griffin Road. Try your hand at virtual fishing and visit the

BELOW: one of Fort Lauderdale's many tranquil canals.

fishing hall of fame to see those big ones that didn't get away. Next door is Bass Outdoor World, one of the biggest sporting goods stores in existence.

Map on pages 232–3

Where the boys were

The skyscraper landscape of **Fort Lauderdale ②** pops up like the land of Oz from where US 1 lifts to accommodate the vast spaghetti of the I-595 airport interchange. Beyond the junction, A1A bears right toward Port Everglades and the beach, but US 1 carries you on to downtown Fort Lauderdale.

The city, especially an oceanfront area known as "**The Strip**," was for many years associated with youthful exuberance. The 1960 beach-party movie and song *Where the Boys Are* romanticized this beachfront stretch as the magnet for college students on Spring Break. Throughout the 1970s, The Strip became one big drunken beach party just like the movie. During the 1980s, however, local officials and residents grew intolerant of the noise and the brawls and began curtailing the students' behavior. New bars that were not part of hotels were banned, as was public consumption of alcohol. Arrests for violations were common. By 1990, many students had moved their antics north to Daytona Beach.

Stranahan House, overlooking the New River, is the city's oldest building.

Fort Lauderdale is grown-up now. And it deserves to be known for its outdoor dining and cultural attractions, many in the neighborhood along the north bank of the picturesque **New River**, which 1920s filmmaker Rex Beach used to call "the most beautiful stream in the world."

Downtown to the west are the **Old Fort Lauderdale Museum of History** (219 SW 2nd Avenue; open Tues–Fri; entrance fee; tel: (954) 463-4431) and the **Museum of Discovery and Science** (401 SW 2nd Street; open daily; Sun pm only; entrance fee; tel: (954) 467-6637). The latter is the largest science museum in South Florida and an ideal attraction for children,

BELOW:
Las Olas Boulevard connects downtown to the beach.

featuring hands-on educational exhibits such as video games and a bubble-making machine, as well as an indoor citrus grove and 300-seat IMAX theater. A few blocks east, at 1 E Las Olas Boulevard, is the **Fort Lauderdale Museum of Art** (open Tues–Sun; entrance fee; tel: (954) 525-5500). The museum boasts the country's most extensive collection of CoBrA paintings, sculptures and prints. Produced by artists in Copenhagen, Brussels and Amsterdam between the years 1948 and 1955, CoBrA artworks closely parallel those of the American abstract expressionist movement.

East along the **Riverwalk** (a series of mini parks and walkways beside the river) is **Stranahan House** (335 SE Sixth Avenue; open Sept–Jun Wed–Sun; July–Aug Wed–Fri; closed public holidays; entrance fee; tel: (954) 524-4736), restored to its 1913 look. Here, 20 years earlier, Frank Stranahan settled the pioneer trading post that was to become Fort Lauderdale. His house is now a museum and gift shop.

Florida's only vehicular tunnel separates Stranahan House from the **Riverside Hotel** and the shops along **Las Olas Boulevard**. Here visitors find quality boutiques, galleries and fine restaurants along a gas-lighted avenue of luxuriant landscaping. The hotel itself has been a town favorite since 1936, with tropical gardens that extend to the river.

On the waterfront

Head east to the other end of Las Olas and you can rejoin the beachside, palm-lined A1A. En route you'll see the striking canalfront subdivisions that front Fort Lauderdale's many miles of inland waterways. Here, water taxis shuttle visitors anywhere along a 7-mile (11-km) inland route.

Fort Lauderdale claims to berth more pleasure craft than any other Florida city. Many tie up at Bahia Mar Yacht Center off Seabreeze Boulevard. The real things sail from **Port Everglades**, in the southern part of the city. Once a land-locked lake, the port was opened to the Atlantic when a channel was blasted in 1928. "Cruises to nowhere," lasting a day or an evening, offer entertainment (plus the chance to gamble) aboard a cruise ship in the Atlantic, but you may prefer the more intimate *Jungle Queen*. This old-fashioned paddleboat navigates the New River, setting out from Bahia Mar on three-hour trips in the afternoon and longer dinner cruises. Guides will feed you tidbits about the millionaires who live in the fancy riverside homes.

North of Bahia Mar, and beyond Las Olas, is a new entertainment and dining complex, **Beach Place**, in the heart of the old "Strip". Farther north, hidden behind seagrape trees just before Birch Park, is **Bonnet House** (open for guided tours Wed–Sun; closed public holidays; entrance fee; tel: (954) 563-5393), perhaps the most curious sight in the city. Created by the late Evelyn and Frederick Bartlett, both artists, it is a lyrical mansion of artistic whimsy, decorated with unusual antiques and a bizarre collection of knick-knacks. The 35-acre (14-hectare) beachfront estate was given to Frederick by his father-in-law from an earlier marriage, Hugh Taylor Birch. In 1942, at the age of 93, Birch gave the state the 180 acres (73 hectares) that now constitute the park that bears his name.

The BBQ and Shrimp Dinner Cruise on the Jungle Queen is hugely popular. It lasts four hours and includes a vast meal and a vaudeville show.

BELOW: heading for the high seas.

Palm Beach County

The drive north from Fort Lauderdale is particularly rewarding. Each resort melts into the next until you hit **Pompano Beach**. Although it has grown rapidly as a resort, Pompano is still a major agricultural center, with a large wholesale vegetable market. Long before sunrise in the winter growing season, the market buzzes with growers and brokers bartering for the best prices.

Farther north, the light at **Hillsboro Inlet** is on private property, but its site is forever tied to the era of the barefoot mailman. From 1885 until just before Flagler built the railroad, when there was no land route to the settlements along this coast, letters were carried by contract mailmen who walked the beaches. They crossed inlets by boats that they tied to trees. When one day his boat was inexplicably on the wrong side of an inlet, carrier Ed Hamilton attempted to swim the channel and was never heard of again. He lost his life to duty at Hillsboro. At least one book, a resort and a lot of yarns have kept the legend of the barefoot mailman alive.

Beyond the inlet is **Hillsboro Beach**, a mere sand spit that has been built upon. The road curves between expensive oceanfront estates, buffered by heavy plantings, and the bayside, rimmed by private docks. Unfortunately, the town's zoning was broken in the 1980s and a large swath of beachside has since submitted to the zealous claws of commercialism.

But the worst is behind as A1A swings across Boca Raton Inlet into Palm Beach County and **Boca Raton ❸**. Boca was the creation of eccentric architect Addison Mizner (1872–1933), the darling of Palm Beach society in the 1920s and the aesthetic arbiter after Flagler. His graceful Mediterranean mansions still stand along the ocean road. About the time that George Merrick

Map on pages 232–3

BELOW: hanging out on the beach at Boca Raton.

was creating Coral Gables from tomato fields and Joseph Young was building Hollywood, Mizner dreamed up Boca Raton.

Indulged by the open wallets of his devotees, Mizner formed the substance of a dream resort, "the greatest in the world," he trumpeted. He even envisioned a fleet of gondolas romantically plying a man-made canal through town, but the waterway was never completed. The filled-in ditch instead became the Camino Real, whose tall palms grace the route to the **Boca Raton Resort**, considered one of Mizner's greatest achievements. The resort incorporates the original, pink **Cloister Inn**, whose loggias, archways, tiled patios and sculptured fountains convey the opulence of the 1920s.

More of Mizner's architecture can be seen in the homes he built in the Old Floresta district, about a mile (1.5 km) west of Boca Raton Town Hall.

After the boom burst, Boca limped along until after World War II but has since emerged as one of the best-managed communities along the Gold Coast. The town seashore is a varied series of excellent parks and open beachfront, and in one respect Boca still manages to eclipse its posh neighbor, Palm Beach: it fields a better polo team. Only Prince Philip's British group and the expert horsemen of Argentina are thought to be better. The action occurs every Sunday from January through April.

For an informative laugh in Boca, visit the **International Museum of Cartoon Art**, at 201 Plaza Real (open Tues–Sat; Sun pm only; entrance fee; tel: (561) 391-2200). The collection features comic books, cartoon strips and cells, and editorial and sports cartoons.

Like Boca Raton, **Delray Beach** ❹ is largely open to the sea, and it is a pleasant, inexpensive alternative to the plush resort cities to the north and south. On the seafront, a marker sites the **Orange Grove House of Refuge**, one of a series of primitive shelters that were spaced along the wilderness beaches between 1876 and 1896 from Cape Canaveral to Cape Florida. The purpose of these shelters was to offer protection to anyone who had the misfortune of being shipwrecked in these remote parts.

If visiting in winter, drive west a mile (1.5 km) along Atlantic Avenue and stop at the **Colony Hotel**. Its Moorish stucco facade, wicker lobby and small rooms have barely changed since the 1920s. Guests return year after year as long as they're able. They sit on the porch dressed in their finery, daring everything about the moment to deny their permanence. The hotel has hardly run down. True to the old style, it is open only November through April, only slightly longer than in Flagler's era.

Three miles (5 km) farther west along Atlantic Avenue and south on Carter Road is the **Morikami Museum and Japanese Gardens** (open Tues–Sun; closed public holidays; entrance fee; tel: (561) 495-0233), a 150-acre (60-hectare) park and museum of Japanese culture that marks the site of a thriving Japanese agricultural community from the early 1900s. It is also well worth making the trip 10 miles (16 km) inland to the **Loxahatchee National Wildlife Refuge** ❺ (open daily; entrance fee; tel: (561) 734-8303), which contains the most northerly part of the Everglades. The wildlife here is magnificent, ranging from alligators to a great variety of birds. An informative visitor center is also the starting point for two enchanting trails.

Map on pages 232–3

Seaside towns

Back at the coast and back on A1A, head north to **Gulf Stream**, a town so private it barely lets on that it's a town. No name appears on the ornate, Mizner-designed Gulf Stream Club. The Gulf Stream School is private, as is the St Andrew's Golf Club. But a beautiful concourse winds under a casuarina canopy that everyone can enjoy.

In **Manalapan** the scene is South Seas languid. Thatch roofs line the beach under swaying palms. Rows of drive-out mirrors are placed so that cars emerging from hidden mansions can avoid traffic otherwise obscured by privacy hedges and walls. Coppery sea grape leaves color-coordinate with barrel-tile roofs. No buildings obtrude along the waterway. Look instead for Rolls-Royces and Jaguars, and yachts marked Manalapan on their sterns tied to their home docks. Cyclists pedal by with surfboards under their arms.

High-rises reappear in **Lantana** but are better spaced apart on entering **South Palm Beach**. Across Lake Worth is the faintly pink Gulf Stream Hotel, a 1920s survivor and now an old-fashioned inn.

In exclusive Palm Beach, it's against the law to park almost anywhere, to own a kangaroo or any other exotic animal, or to hang a clothes line.

Palms and parties

You can leave Florida – and enter **Palm Beach ❻** – by continuing north on A1A. You can't miss it. The garish shopping centers and neon hotel signs vanish. Clean, uncluttered streets of class take over. The structures behind the high walls of concrete and ficus aren't museums, just second homes to Palm Beachers. Here even the fish swim in privileged waters, enjoying their own Rolls-Royce, added to the artificial reef some years ago. Signs warn that no stopping is allowed – Palm Beach likes to keep the people it doesn't know

BELOW: Nuestro Paradiso (1928) is one of Palm Beach's gorgeous homes.

moving, or concentrated in town where shopkeepers and custodians of civic institutions provide extra eyes.

There seem to be various stories as to the origins of the city's signature palm trees. The most popular relates how a boatload of Spanish sailors with 100 cases of wine aboard stumbled upon the barren strand in 1878. They sold their cargo, including 20,000 coconuts, to a shrewd islander for $20. The islander sold two coconuts for a nickel to his neighbors. They planted them in the sand and, *voilà*, the beach got its palms.

Henry Flagler fell in love with the palm-fringed island in 1892 and bought out the landholders who preceded him. His first Breakers Hotel burned down. So did the second. By the time the third one went up in 1926 – no less opulent today than ever – Palm Beach was the winter watering hole for American society.

Palm Beach wasn't merely wealthy. The rich were here at play. They dressed up and partied in the name of charity. Their benefit balls for every worthy cause ennobled their wealth. The Palm Beach way of life became the ultimate sanction for American ambition. For many it still is.

So, to appreciate Palm Beach in full swing – unless you prefer to gape at empty mansions undergoing beauty treatments and garden manicures – you must visit during the "social season," an indeterminate period of time that falls between Thanksgiving and Easter. That's when you'll see the pretty people who actually live in – or at least decorate – the palatial dwellings. The annual migration of money ignites a round of galas, charity balls and, in election years, political cocktail parties. People willing to pay up to $1,000 a plate can get invited to some of the prestigious, glittering balls. But it may take a larger donation to get into one of the political gatherings.

To find out who has partied where, people buy The Palm Beach Daily News. *It is printed on paper that is specially treated to prevent ink from smudging on expensive outfits.*

BELOW:
the world-renowned Breakers Hotel.

Opulence unlimited

As you approach Palm Beach from the south, Highway A1A leads to South Ocean Boulevard, which runs right past the Moorish estate of the late cereal heiress, Marjorie Merriweather Post, at No. 1100. It's called **Mar-a-Lago** and is now owned by entrepreneur Donald Trump. Its 17 acres (7 hectares), complete with golf course and 117 rooms, have been valued at over $20 million. At 702 South Ocean Boulevard is a home formerly owned by the late John Lennon. Next door stands a house that once belonged to Woolworth Donahue, heir to the dime-store fortune.

The next stop in Palm Beach is **Worth Avenue**, Addison Mizner's finest contribution to local charm. If Flagler gave Palm Beach stature, Mizner gave it grace – his Mediterranean-style mansions and shops, with their rich ornamentation and colorful shrubbery, were legendary in their time and can still be admired today. Worth Avenue was begun in the 1920s and has been one of the world's premier shopping streets since 1945, often compared to London's Bond Street and Paris's Faubourg St Honoré. Only three blocks long, the avenue compels because of its human scale. Buildings are mostly two or three stories. Shops are set among villa-like facades, extended by colorful canopies and graced by Palladian windows. Bougainvillea entwines wrought-iron gates that appear on top of ceramic staircases. Little *vias* (alleys) lead off to patios with fountains.

The Breakers, Flagler's famous hotel and the town's pre-eminent landmark, is farther north, at 1 South County Road. This Beaux Arts eminence dominates the oceanfront like a leviathan at sea. From its fountains and towers to its frescoed ceilings, it is the very articulation of order in a world of chaos, exactly how Flagler saw himself in the dog-eat-dog world of 19th-century capitalism.

Map on pages 232–3

TIP

There aren't many inexpensive places to eat in Palm Beach. Try the buzzing diner in Green's Pharmacy or Hamburger Heaven, both on South County Road.

BELOW: a serene arcade on Worth Avenue.

HENRY FLAGLER (1830–1913)

South Florida's standing as a vacation mecca for millions of yearly visitors is due in no small part to the efforts of Henry Flagler, railroad- and hotel-builder extraordinaire.

Born in Hopewell, New York, Flagler struggled in his early ventures but finally made his mark in the oil business, as a partner of John D. Rockefeller. Honeymooning in Florida in 1883, he saw the state's vast tourist potential and turned his attention to hotel construction, starting in St Augustine.

Realizing that Florida would never appeal to visitors without adequate transportation, Flagler then began work on the East Coast Railway, which linked his various resorts along the coast. In 1894, he brought the railroad to an end in Palm Beach, where it served his first hotel there, the Royal Poinciana – at the time the world's largest wooden structure and a playground of the rich and famous.

A year later Julia Tuttle convinced him to continue the tracks to Miami, and when the government announced the construction of the Panama Canal in 1905, the new possibilities for trade persuaded him to push all the way to Key West. This last project, linking island to island in a 100-mile (160-km) arc into the sea, involved awesome feats of engineering and cost the lives of 700 workers. Key West was finally reached in 1912, when Flagler was 82.

Map on pages 232–3

The Rambler,
*Flagler's railroad
car, dates from 1886.*

BELOW: old money.
RIGHT: relaxed local
on Via Mizner, a
pedestrian alleyway
off Worth Avenue.

Flagler's personal style is best expressed at Whitehall, on Whitehall Way. This was the $3-million palace he built in 1901 for his third wife, Mary Lily. Considered the "Taj Mahal of America," the house has marble interiors and fabrics of gold, as well as private collections of porcelain, paintings, silver, glass, dolls, lace and costumes. Flagler's private railroad car, *The Rambler*, has been restored alongside. Today, the house serves as the **Flagler Museum** (open Tues–Sun; Sun pm only; entrance fee; tel: (561) 655-2833).

Back towards Worth Avenue is the **Society of the Four Arts** (open daily; Sun pm only; closed public holidays; free; tel: (561) 655-7227), on Four Arts Plaza. This complex includes exhibition galleries (open Dec–Apr only), a formal garden and the stunning Four Arts Library building designed by Mizner's contemporary Maurice Fatio.

Whitehall, The Breakers and Worth Avenue are the crown jewels of Palm Beach opulence, but in this town each beautifully landscaped street is worth visiting. The best view is by bicycle. These can be rented at the **Palm Beach Bicycle Trail Shop** (223 Sunrise Avenue), close to a 3½-mile (6-km) lakefront trail untrammeled by automobiles.

The northern reaches of Palm Beach have more of the same. Just beyond 1075 North Ocean Boulevard is the former estate of the Kennedys. It became known as the "Winter White House" in the 1960s when John F. Kennedy first wintered here, but John Ney wrote of the local prejudice against this neighboring "royal family." It was here, in 1992, that Kennedy's nephew, William Kennedy Smith, was charged with raping a young woman he had met in a Palm Beach bar. After a televised trial, Smith was found not guilty.

The other Palm Beach

Across Lake Worth, the city of **West Palm Beach ❼** was conceived as an asterisk by Flagler. It was reserved for servants, gardeners and other peons who toiled to keep Palm Beach from crumbling, while their employers partied, shopped, played polo and made more money. In fact, Palm Beach still parks its garbage trucks around here. The drab downtown has no pretensions, but may prove a refreshing change from the rarefied air of Palm Beach. One very good reason to come here is to see the outstanding collection housed in the **Norton Museum of Art** (open daily; Sun pm only; closed Mon, Apr–Dec, and public holidays; entrance fee; tel: (561) 832-5196), at 1451 S Olive Avenue. Among its most vaunted possessions are works by French Impressionists and Post-Impressionists from Cézanne to Picasso, as well as some fine 20th-century American works – including pieces by Georgia O'Keeffe, Winslow Homer and Andy Warhol – plus a superb array of Chinese artifacts.

Fifteen miles (24 km) west of downtown West Palm Beach is **Lion Country Safari** (open daily; entrance fee; tel: (561) 793-1084), the area's top family attraction, where you can drive along miles of jungle trails past hundreds of roaming animals. The well-fed lions seem to have grown rather lazy, but it's thrilling to watch one lead a parade of cars or see a giraffe peering in at you; keep your windows closed, though. ❑

WEST OF MIAMI

Map on pages 232–3

The main reason to head west is for the gorgeous Gulf Coast beaches of Naples, Sanibel and Captiva, but don't ignore the intriguing swamplands and pockets of old Florida en route

In 1928, the wilds of Florida's southern tip were made accessible by the construction of a road known as the Tamiami Trail. Officially designated as highway US 41, it begins as Calle Ocho in Miami's Little Havana and heads west into the vast river of grass known as the Everglades *(see following chapter)*. Skirting the northern boundary of the Everglades National Park, it crosses Big Cypress Swamp before reaching Florida's west coast at the town of Naples, about two hours' drive from Miami. Apart from the fascinating natural habitats passed along the way, the best reasons to make the journey are the west coast's irresistible beaches, lapped by the calm, warm waters of the Gulf of Mexico and blessed with gorgeous sunsets.

Big Cypress Swamp

A ridge riddled with hammocks and cypress trees separates the Everglades proper from the **Big Cypress Swamp**, which is actually closer to the traditional image of a swamp than its more famous neighbor. It consists of marshes, sandy islands of slash pine and large stands of dwarf cypress sprouting from knee-deep water and muck. Giant bald cypress trees that once distinguished the area were nearly wiped out by loggers for use in the manufacture of boat hulls and coffins. The few that remain may be as much as 700 years old.

The swamp fills its own 2,400-sq-mile (6,200-sq-km) basin, of which about 40 percent is contained within the **Big Cypress National Preserve** ❽ (open daily; free; tel: (941) 695-4111). The main access point for the preserve is the **Oasis Visitor Center**, on the Tamiami Trail, about 60 miles (100 km) west of downtown Miami. There is scope for swamp-hiking here, but you'll need to obtain permission from the park rangers. Most people will probably be happy to drive along the "**Loop Road**" – a 23-mile (37-km) dirt road running south of US 41 between the Tamiami and Monroe ranger stations. On weekdays, very few cars use this road. That's because, in its worst sections, it is so pot-holed that anything over 20 mph (32 kph) requires a Jeep. The road narrows to one lane and enters a swamp of clear, fresh water, stunningly beautiful. A veritable amphitheater of wildlife hovers. Orchids and exotic red flowers that shoot from cypress-rooted bromeliads fire the imagination. The magic fades as the road improves.

If you do get a chance to hike in the swamp, you may see the paw marks of one of the few remaining Florida panthers in the wet marl. Watch also for the endangered Everglades swallow-tail kite. This area was once home to about 2 million wading birds, but plume hunters reduced their numbers to only a few hundred thousand by the late 19th century. Laws

LEFT: typical South Florida foliage.
BELOW: a strangler fig "strangling" a bald cypress.

*The Tamiami Trail,
which crosses the
Everglades, is the
most scenic route to
the west coast.*

BELOW:
hibiscus flowers
at Fakahatchee
Strand.

enacted to protect the fowl helped boost their numbers, but the flocks have diminished once more. The decline was particularly dramatic among wood storks – a population of 50,000 in the 1930s has dwindled to about 10,000. One of the best places to see them is at Corkscrew Swamp Sanctuary *(see below)*.

Farther west on the Tamiami Trail, and then south on SR 29, is **Everglades City**, the last outpost on the edge of a kingdom still ruled by wildlife. This town is the water gateway to a labyrinth of mangrove splotches known as the **Ten Thousand Islands**. Guided boat trips originate at the Gulf Coast Ranger Station here. During the summer season, sunset cruises take passengers into upper **Chokoloskee Bay** to observe the spectacle of as many as 20,000 birds returning to roost.

West again, and the Tamiami Trail brings you to the **Fakahatchee Strand State Preserve ❾** (open daily; free; tel: (941) 695-4593), the world's only known forest of royal palm and cypress combined. A short trail at Big Cypress Bend will introduce you to a whole array of flora, including magnificent orchids. In fact, the preserve boasts the largest concentration of native orchids in the United States, about 44 species of which have been identified, including the catopsis which grows nowhere else. Some of the cypress trees along the trail are more than 500 years old.

As the Tamiami Trail reaches the west coast, SR 951 branches south to **Marco Island**, once a gorgeous seascape that was fought over by environmentalists and developers. The latter won, but they made some concessions. Some consider that the new developments are among the state's better-planned communities. Developers have even erected artificial bald eagles' nests in the shadow of the condos in hopes of encouraging the birds to remain – evidence, they say, that

they will try to strike a balance between the needs of modern man and nature.

The quiet, old village of **Marco** at the north end of the island and **Goodland** on the southern tip still retain cottages and recall pleasant memories of an older Florida. Archeological digs have uncovered carvings, tools, masks and weapons used by the Calusa people, who lived here as long ago as 500 BC.

Naples: golfers' paradise

To the north is **Naples ⓾**, the most southerly town of any size on Florida's Gulf Coast and a sparkling place in the midst of a population explosion. It has been dissected into subdivisions filled with mobile homes, waterfront suburbs and condominium complexes. As the self-proclaimed "Golf Capital of the World" (it has the greatest concentration of golf courses in the state), this sedate and rather snobbish town does not appeal to everyone. Still, at the end of the scrubbed avenues are some excellent beaches, and there is an attractive pier where people like to fish.

There are interesting stores off US 41 at the **Old Marine Market Place**, a collection of old, tin fishing shacks that have miraculously been transformed into a trendy enclave of art galleries and boutiques. The Market's **Merriman's Wharf** is a casual waterfront bistro popular with Naples locals.

West of downtown, on Pine Ridge Road, is a spot sure to attract fluffy stuffed animal collectors. The **Teddy Bear Museum** (open Wed–Mon; entrance fee; tel: 941-598-2711), built by oil heiress and area resident Frances Pew Hayes, houses some 3,000 adorable bears from around the world. If you prefer living animals, however, you may want to visit **Jungle Larry's Zoological Park and Caribbean Gardens** (open daily; entrance fee), on

A few miles east of Everglades City is the village of Ochopee, famous as the site of the smallest post office in the US. It measures just 8 ft (2.4 meters) by 7 ft (2.1 meters).

BELOW: the beautiful expanse of Naples Beach.

Goodlette Road off US 41, where you can go on a self-guided tour to see tigers, elephants, snakes, birds and other wildlife.

A popular event that takes place on Radio Road west of Naples Airport has captured national attention. Here, the waist-deep **Mile-O-Mud Track** hosts the World Championship Swamp Buggy Races three times a year. The race course is flooded with water for two weeks before the races to ensure that it's in the worst possible shape.

Naples also forms the western edge of the Big Cypress Swamp. Northeast of town, on SR 846, is the fascinating **Corkscrew Swamp Sanctuary** (open daily; entrance fee; tel: (941) 348-9151), a haven for the rare wood stork. Here you can stand on the swamp boardwalk, look up at the awesome canopy of nests in the trees overhead and hear the giant birds squawking as they glide through the air in search of food for their young. To have any hope of seeing the wood storks you need to visit in winter.

Fort Myers, the home of a genius

From Naples you can take US 41 or I-75 to **Fort Myers ⓫**, which, with neighboring Cape Coral, was the fastest growing metropolis in the US during the 1970s. The population growth continues. The inventor Thomas Edison (1847–1931) managed to beat the rush when he built a home here in 1886, at the age of 39.

The **Edison Winter Home and Museum** (open daily; Sun pm only; entrance fee; tel: (941) 334-7419) sprawls across both sides of McGregor Boulevard (SR 867), beautified by the royal palms planted by Edison himself. The home and guest house, among the first prefabricated buildings in the US, were constructed in Maine and brought to Fort Myers by schooner. Tropical gardens engulf the homes.

Here, Edison invented the future and entertained famous friends like next-door neighbors Henry Ford and Harvey Firestone. He also offered to light up his new town with electrical installations, but the townspeople refused for fear the lights would keep their cattle awake at night.

Over the road, the museum contains photographs, personal items such as a gold watch, a collection of automobiles, and a treasure house of inventions, including 170 phonographs with huge, handpainted speakers and, of course, dozens of light bulbs.

Sanibel and Captiva islands

Fort Myers is the gateway to two islands where you can commune with nature within arm's length of modern amenities. In the 1960s and '70s, uncontrolled development threatened to turn **Sanibel Island ⓬** and neighboring **Captiva Island ⓭** into two more uninteresting specks heavy with high-rises. In 1974, however, Sanibel seceded from Lee County, set up its own city government and put a near halt to further growth. Thus, while you will find air-conditioned homes and hotels, restaurants, a few shopping centers, and, of course, popular beaches, Sanibel also has protected areas. The lovely **J.N. "Ding" Darling National Wildlife Refuge** (open daily; entrance fee) features a 5-mile (8-km) drive, the highlight of which

Guided tours of the Edison estate take in the adjacent home of car manufacturer Henry Ford. More in-depth historical and botanical tours are also available.

BELOW: an osprey with a fresh catch in J.N. Darling Wildlife Refuge.

is the sight of roseate spoonbills coming and going in groups as regimented as air force squadrons. Anhinga "snake" birds, sanderlings, herons and vultures are among the hundreds of other birds that make the refuge home. Fortunately for the peace of the wildlife, these preserves are usually of secondary importance to the tourists who descend on Sanibel. Captiva Island is more relaxed than chic Sanibel.

You can take boat trips to **Cayo Costa Island State Park**, north of Captiva. This is one of Florida's most unspoilt barrier islands, with superb bird life and 9 miles (14 km) of dune-backed beaches. For the full experience, stay overnight in one of the cabins on the island, but be prepared for only basic facilities (i.e. no hot water or electricity), and you'll need to take your own supplies.

Heading back

An alternative route back to Miami is to take "Alligator Alley" (I-75), which crosses from Naples toward Fort Lauderdale and then turns south to Miami. For a fascinating detour, leave the interstate at exit 14 and head north on County Road 833 for 17 miles (27 km). Here, in Big Cypress Seminole Indian Reservation, is the **Ah-Tah-Thi-Ki Museum** ⓮ (open Tues–Sun; entrance fee; tel: (941) 902-1113), dedicated to the culture and history of the Seminole Indians.

The Seminoles arrived in Florida in the 18th century, after being forced south by land-hungry Europeans. Later, their stiff resistance to attempts to evict them from the state resulted in the so-called Seminole Wars. The museum includes exhibits that show how they managed to survive in the inhospitable Everglades, and displays cultural artifacts such as moccasins, turtle-shell rattles, and weapons from the Seminole Wars. Also on site are a working Seminole village and Everglades nature trails. ❏

Map on pages 232–3

Seminole totem pole on display at Ah-Tah-Thi-Ki Museum.

BELOW: a "shunter" on the prowl.

SHELLING ON SANIBEL ISLAND

The renown of Sanibel is built on the shells that are tossed on to its beaches by the ton. Only Jeffreys Bay in South Africa and the Sulu Islands in the Philippines are considered better for shelling. Here on Florida's west coast there is no offshore reef to break the shells; the warm, shallow waters encourage shell growth; and the gently sloping sea floor south of the island allows the shells to be rolled ashore in huge numbers by the waves. All these factors make Sanibel a shell collector's paradise.

Early morning, and the hours after storms and heavy tides, are the best times to hit the beach and become a shunter (short for shell hunter). Look for shells just under the sand where the waves are breaking.

Shunt for shells like the rare royal Florida miter, golden olive and spiny oyster, and you may find avid collectors offering their shirts for your finds. More common are the queen and horse conchs, murex, limpet, left-handed whelk, paper nautilus, cowrie, jewel boxes, jingles, tulips and lion's paw. A shelling checklist purchased on the islands will enable you to identify your finds.

The hordes of collectors lured to Sanibel are phenomenal, and in an attempt to restrict the practice, live shelling has been outlawed – so collect only empty shells.

THE EVERGLADES

Map on pages 232–3

A drive of just an hour or two from Miami takes you into the heart of the most untamed part of Florida – a great, wildlife-rich swamp that gives a taste of how inhospitable the whole area once was

I f the founding fathers had been inspired to preserve natural treasures, they might have roped off Florida's northern boundary and declared the entire state a national park. Fortunately, latter-day leaders stepped in before all was lost to the plow and bulldozer. In 1947 they established **Everglades National Park**, encompassing most of Florida's southern tip.

Unlike the Grand Canyon, Niagara Falls, Yellowstone and other national jewels, the Everglades does not overwhelm the casual visitor with majestic vistas. On the contrary, the seas of sawgrass which stretch in all directions, embellished only by island hammocks *(see page 258)* of hardwood trees, sparse stands of cypress and clumps of mangroves, may strike many as boring.

But don't let this dull facade deter you from making a trip into the Everglades. It's just a clever disguise that cloaks a fascinating blend of earthy and watery environments, tropical and temperate plant and animal life, and a laboratory where Nature experiments with her cycles of life and death.

A fragile environment

Everglades National Park makes up only a fraction of a slow-flowing river, whose source lies in the Kissimmee River, northwest of Miami. The Glades flow for about 200 miles (320 km), bulging up to 70 miles (110 km) in width and at a mean depth of only 6 inches (15 cm). The water oozes down a gradual incline in Florida's surface, dropping just 15 ft (5 meters) over hundreds of miles, before flowing into Florida Bay. A drop of water takes more than a year to make the journey.

Around 350 varieties of bird, 500 kinds of fish, 55 species of reptile and 40 mammal species call the Everglades home. It even has 45 indigenous species of plants that are found nowhere else on earth.

This rich environment evolved over 6 million years of sea action and limestone build-up, but it has come to the brink of extinction in less than a century. Its chief enemy, man, first infiltrated its hammocks about 2,000 years ago with the arrival of early Native Americans. However, the Calusas more often than not lived in harmony with the Glades. It wasn't until the late 19th century that man began to drain the swampland.

Governor Napoleon Bonaparte Broward threw the government into efforts to open up the inhospitable region, and, by 1909, the Miami Canal that connects Lake Okeechobee to Miami had become the main conduit in a network of waterways through the Everglades. In 1926 and 1928, two major hurricanes dumped the waters of Lake Okeechobee onto the heads of thousands of South Florida settlers, sparking the involvement of the Army Corps of Engineers.

LEFT: typical Everglades.
BELOW: boardwalks give access to the swamp.

The miracle of the light pours over the green and brown expanse of sawgrass, and of water, shining and slow-moving below, the grass and water that is the meaning... of the Everglades... It is a river of grass.

— M. STONEMAN
DOUGLAS

BELOW: Stoneman Douglas in the national park she helped found.

The engineers ringed the lake, the core of the Everglades, with Hoover Dike.

The first major road across the swamp took five years to build and finally opened on April 25, 1928. The highway linked the cities of Tampa and Miami, hence the name, the Tamiami Trail, which is still favored by many locals over its more mundane title, Highway 41.

The Tamiami Trail was a great feat of engineering, but it blocked the natural movement of water and wildlife which is so vital to the survival of the Glades. Efforts by the Audubon Society, the Florida Federation of Women's Clubs and the Tropical Everglades National Park Commission culminated in the dedication of the area as a National Park by President Harry S. Truman in 1947. Marjory Stoneman Douglas, with her book *The Everglades: River of Grass*, published in the same year, did a great deal to arouse public awareness of the fragility of the area's ecosystem and the need to protect it.

Despite the valuable work done to preserve this unique environment, continued massive tampering of the water supply and contamination of the area by fertilizers and pollution has stunted animal reproduction and dramatically altered the vegetation. Visitors to the park today see a tenth of the bird life visible when it was established in 1947.

In August 1992 another devastating blow hit the Everglades when Hurricane Andrew ripped through the park leaving a 35-mile (56-km) swath of destruction behind. Mangroves, pines and palms were sucked out by the roots and carried away. Thousands of birds either flew or were blown away, and countless animals and fish were killed or left homeless when their natural habitat was ravaged.

Turn to pages 258–9 for a description of the variety of ecosystems that are vital to the survival of the Everglades.

MARJORY STONEMAN DOUGLAS

For over 70 years, Marjory Stoneman Douglas (1890–1998), the first lady of Florida's environmentalists, fought her own war against the destruction of the Everglades. She was opinionated, passionate and poetic. Without her, the Everglades, one of the natural wonders of the world, would probably be little more than a memory.

A newspaper columnist and short-story writer, Douglas moved to Miami from New England in 1915. After a brief marriage with no children, she poured her energies into her work and lived alone in a one-bedroom cottage from 1926 until her death. She served on the original 1927 committee that pushed to declare the Everglades a national park. Her 1947 book *The Everglades: River of Grass* first brought to public attention the importance of what until then was generally considered a useless swamp.

Years later, she founded the Friends of the Everglades to fight plans for an international airport in the area. She was the recipient of numerous awards and honorary degrees, including the first "Floridian of the Year" citation in 1983.

Through the many battles to save her river of grass, Douglas never waxed sentimental about her cause. When she died at the venerable age of 108, South Florida mourned. For many here her soul will live for ever.

Boardwalks and trails

To reach the park from Miami, head south on either US 1 or Florida's Turnpike and pick up SR 9336 at Florida City. This road takes you to the main park entrance, where you can get a crash course in Everglades ecology from the informative displays at the **Main Visitor Center** ⓰ (open daily; entrance fee for park; tel: (305) 242-7700). SR 9336 is the main road through the park. It is about 38 miles (60 km) from the entrance to its southwest dead end at Flamingo. But even if you are wedded to your car, make sure you detour to at least a few of the trails and boardwalks along the way.

At the **Royal Palm Visitor Center** ⓰, just 2 miles (3 km) from the park entrance, is the easy **Gumbo Limbo Trail**, which explores a typical hardwood hammock. The gumbo limbo tree is a common sight along the path. Here, you will find ferns, air plants, orchids and a cool, rainforest-type environment. Carefully examine tree limbs for the dazzling *Liguus* snail, found only here and in Cuba, Haiti and the Dominican Republic. The mosquitoes are devilish along this trail, even in winter. There's also the **Anhinga Trail** boardwalk into a willow head at the tip of Taylor Slough. (A slough, pronounced "slew," is a natural drainage ditch.) In winter this is one of the best places for wildlife, since there is more water here than in many other parts of the park.

Long Pine Key ⓱ has several nature trails that wind through slash pines unique to southern Florida; this lovely spot is also the site of one of the park's campgrounds, and there are picnic areas too. A few miles farther down the main road is **Pa-hay-okee Overlook**, an observation tower in a hardwood hammock edged with cypress stands and a freshwater slough. There are about 100 species of grass in the Everglades and most can be observed from the boardwalk here,

Map on pages 232–3

The best time to visit the Everglades is in winter, when the wildlife is richest.

BELOW: a pelican coasts along.

although you may find it impossible to distinguish between coinwort, marsh fleabane, love-vine, creeping Charlie and ludwigia. Sawgrass, ironically, is not a true grass, but a sedge. If you are lucky you will see a snail kite, once a common species in the Everglades. This endangered bird feeds only on the apple snail, which lives on the sawgrass.

Beyond, the road turns south toward **Mahogany Hammock** ⓲, where a trail winds under some of the largest mahogany trees in the United States. Rare paurotis palms, stretching 12–30 ft (4–9 meters) high, flank Paurotis Pond and its plethora of wildlife. Between Mahogany Hammock and Flamingo the road connects with various canoe trails, as well as the **West Lake Trail** footpath, which wriggles through sawgrass and cattails. Pink shrimp feed and reproduce among the mangroves in places like this before migrating to the Gulf of Mexico.

Flamingo: the end of the road

At the end of SR 9336 sits **Flamingo** ⓳. Once a remote fishing village accessible only by boat, Flamingo now exists mainly as an isolated colony catering to tourists. There are plenty of motor campsites, tent plots, and, for the less hardy, motel rooms at the **Flamingo Lodge**. In winter and spring you will need to book a room here well in advance.

Check with the ranger station or the Lodge for a schedule of activities. If you have brought your own boat or hiking gear, be sure to file plans with the ranger station before disappearing into the backcountry. Even well-informed locals have been known to vanish for good in the maze of mangroves, rivers and bays. Otherwise, you can rent whatever equipment you need. If you're planning to stay a while, you can even move into a fully-equipped houseboat and cruise the

TIP

If you want to canoe the Wilderness Waterway, there are Indian-style huts, known as *chickees*, where you can camp overnight. Don't set off without a tide chart.

BELOW: a storyteller at the Miccosukee Cultural Center.

waterways in comfort. Flamingo is the southern terminus of the 100-mile (160-km) **Wilderness Waterway**, a week-long canoe trip that begins near Everglades City *(see page 248)* and proceeds south through such alluring niches as Chokoloskee Island, Big Lostman's Bay, Cabbage Island and Shark River.

Of course, Flamingo also offers shorter cruises and walks. Good, but easy, hiking trails include the **Snake Bight**, through tropical hardwoods to a boardwalk over Florida Bay; **Rowdy Bend**, under Spanish moss and brilliant red bromeliads; and **Christian Point**, which winds past giant wild pine bromeliads attached to the trees. For a real taste of the swamp, though, you should sign up for a "slough slog" – a watery walk through the Everglades escorted by a park ranger. Alternatively, tour boats will take you to the white-sand shores of **Cape Sable ⓴**, the southernmost point in mainland Florida. Or you can boat around the clusters of keys in **Florida Bay**. If you're coming from Miami for a day of boating or canoeing around Flamingo, it is best to spend at least one night here.

The bird-watching is particularly good around Flamingo and in the bay. Great flocks of gulls waft on unseen air currents. In winter, white pelicans with 9-ft (2.7-meter) wingspans migrate here from the west. Ospreys build their nests atop channel markers, and bald eagles can sometimes be spotted.

Manatees and American crocodiles (different from alligators) live in these waters, but it is rare to see either of these endangered species. Odds are better for seeing bottlenose dolphins, who like to frolic in the bow wake of boats.

Shark Valley

There is another wheeled way of penetrating the park, but to get there you must drive from the main entrance back to Florida City and north on Florida's Turnpike, then west on the **Tamiami Trail** (US 41), nearly 50 miles (80 km) in total. The most popular stop along this route is **Shark Valley ㉑**, a comfortable day trip from Miami. In the summer, most of this freshwater slough is underwater. But in the winter, the park operates a tram ride from the entrance station through the sawgrass prairie (teeming with wildlife) and up to a 60-ft (18-meter) observation tower. Alligators gather in willows at the foot of the tower. They make a variety of sounds. A hiss is a warning that they are annoyed and you should stay out of their way. You can also walk or bike the tram route. The Otter Cave Hammock Nature Trail has a pamphlet to guide you. Tread softly and you may see otters munching on live frogs' legs beside the road.

Just across from Shark Valley is the **Miccosukee Cultural Center ㉒** (open daily; entrance fee; tel: (305) 223-8380). Most of the Miccosukee Indian tribe live near here and to the west along the Tamiami Trail. The center has cultural displays and demonstrations of traditional crafts, such as basket making, beadwork and palmetto palm dolls. There are also alligator wrestling shows (not everyone's cup of tea), and at the restaurant you can try local delicacies such as alligator tail and frogs' legs.

Beyond the center, the Tamiami Trail continues to Big Cypress Swamp and, eventually, the west coast *(see previous chapter).* ❑

Map on pages 232–3

Canoeing expeditions allow visitors a much closer encounter with the Everglades.

BELOW: the deep color of dusk.

THE ECOLOGY OF THE EVERGLADES

This area's unique combination of tropical and temperate species of fauna and flora is found nowhere else in the United States

The Everglades' ecosystem is entirely dependent on the sub-tropical cycle of dry (winter) and wet (summer) seasons. The fauna and flora of the region have adapted to these alternating seasons, often moving from one part of the Everglades to another according to the fluctuations in the level of the water – the lifeblood of this vast, mysterious wilderness.

EVERGLADES HABITATS

The Everglades consists of a variety of habitats, each of which is vital to its maintenance.

● **hardwood hammocks**: tree islands that stand above the high-water level and support mahogany, cabbage palms and other trees, and provide a refuge for mammals such as raccoons in the wet season.

● **bayheads**: smaller, shallower islands dominated by bay trees growing on rich, organic soil.

● **willows**: wispy vegetation that grows in the deep water near hammocks – generally in the shape of a doughnut with a gator hole at the center.

● **sawgrass prairie**: covering much of the Glades, sawgrass grows on a thin layer of soil formed by decaying vegetation on the region's limestone base.

● **freshwater sloughs**: channels of fresh water that help plants and animals to survive the harsh conditions during the dry season.

● **pinelands**: found in the few areas where the elevation is over 7 ft (2 m). Fire is vital to their existence since it cleans out competing vegetation.

● **cypress swamps**: areas where the water is deepest and the layer of soil extremely thin. Cypress trees are among the few species to tolerate such water-logged conditions.

● **coastal prairie**: contains salt-tolerant plants like cactus.

● **mangrove**: a dense tangle of mangrove trees that thrive along the southwestern coast. They play a vital role in protecting the shoreline against rough seas and act as a nursery for marine animals such as blue crab and shrimp.

DANGER

DO NOT FEED OR MOLEST!

GATORS CANNOT BE TAMED AND FEEDING THEM CAN RESULT IN THEIR MISTAKING A HAND FOR A HANDOUT! FLORIDA LAW PROHIBITS THE FEEDING OR MOLESTING OF ALLIGATORS!!

▷ **GATOR HOLES**
Alligators are vital to the ecology of the Everglades. During the wet season, they use their feet and snout to dig holes that store water during the dry months and serve as an oasis for many animals, including turtles and birds.

△ **FLORIDA PANTHER**
A sub-species of the cougar that has adapted to the sub-tropical climate of Florida, this shy big cat lives in the most remote areas of the Everglades, particularly in Big Cypress Swamp. An endangered species: only 30–50 survive.

△ **EPIPHYTES**
Also known as airplants, epiphytes are non-parasitic plants that grow on trees but get water and nutrients as they run down the bark. Here, cypress trees are host to tufts of stiff-leaved wild pine.

▷ **EVERGLADES BIRDS**
The Everglades is extremely rich in birdlife. Wading birds such as herons and egrets are particularly abundant, while the white ibis (right) and the roseate spoonbill are now endangered. Birds of prey include the osprey and the rare Southern bald eagle.

▽ **APPLE SNAIL**
Apple snails are the sole diet of the endangered snail kite – a dependency typical of the Everglades. The snail's eggs provide food for various birds in the region.

SAVING THE EVERGLADES

▽ **RIVER OF GRASS**
A great expanse of sawgrass, punctuated by tree islands known as "hammocks," is the classic Everglades scene. Sawgrass is a member of the sedge family (one of the oldest plant species in the world), which is tough enough to tolerate months of burning sun.

About 30 percent of the Everglades has been lost thanks to human interference throughout the 20th century. Roads, canals and dikes (such as Hoover Dike, above) impede the water's normal flow and the seasonal fluctuations in water levels; and much land has been drained for farming, while expanding urban areas on the coast have drained precious water for their washing machines and swimming pools.

The campaign to save the Everglades – with which the federal government is, at last, involved – is dependent on cooperation between farmers, environmentalists, water managers and bureaucrats. Attention is focused on improving the quality of the water. This is already cleaner due to the reduction in the levels of phosphorus: this chemical, which has long been used as a fertilizer by South Florida farmers, upsets the Everglades' ecological balance by encouraging the growth of exotic plants such as cattails, which have choked vast areas of marshland. In addition, there are plans to work on the canals and pumps to try to return a more natural flow of water to the region.

▷ **ANHINGA BIRD**
One of the Everglades' most distinctive birds, the anhinga is often seen drying its feathers at the water's edge, its wings splayed. The anhinga swims with only its head above the water (a habit that has earned it the nickname "snake bird") and dives for fish, using its sharp beak to skewer its prey.

THE KEYS

The string of islands dangling off the tip of Florida offers an exciting drive flanked either side by water, with plenty to do en route and inimitable Key West waiting, temptingly, at the end

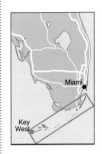

Map on pages 232–3

There are two ways to drive to the Keys from Miami. The slower but more scenic one is to follow US 1 south beyond Homestead, then take a left at the fork in the road just past Florida City. A column of tall Australian pines graces the road to the Card Sound toll bridge. On either side of the bridge, clumps of red and black mangroves impersonate solid islands.

The bridge ends on North Key Largo. A right on SR 905 leads through hammocks of Jamaica dogwood, loblolly, feathery lysiloma and mahogany until the road runs directly back into US 1. A left on 905 eventually strands you at the northern tip of the key. Beyond, boaters can explore **Biscayne National Park ㉓** (open daily; free; tel: (305) 230-7275), 96 percent of which is underwater – in the form of stunning natural reefs, mostly located about 10 miles (16 km) offshore. The main starting point for trips is the park headquarters at **Convoy Point**, back on the mainland, east of Homestead. As well as guided trips of the park, snorkeling, scuba diving and fishing expeditions are also available.

The toll bridge and scenic detour can be avoided by simply continuing on US 1. This becomes the Overseas Highway, which hops from island to island all the way to Key West, 160 miles (257 km) from Miami. Locations in the Keys are often given as a mile marker (or MM). This refers to the signs alongside US 1, which give the distance from Key West.

The road through the Keys is mostly a tacky strip lined with seedy storefronts, billboards and gas stations. Stifle the disappointment. Like the Everglades, the Keys do not dazzle the casual tourist who stays behind the windshield. Park the car. Get on a bicycle or boat. Gape at the immense canopy of sky and the mounds of whipped cloud. Put on a mask, snorkel and fins. Rent a rod and reel. You'll soon succumb to Keys Disease.

Key Largo: the Bogart connection

Humphrey Bogart, Lauren Bacall and Edward G. Robinson confronted a killer hurricane in **Key Largo ㉔** in the 1948 movie of the same name. All that remains of those nostalgic days is the **Caribbean Club Bar** near MM 104. A few minutes of the movie may or may not have been filmed inside. Nevertheless, with its coquina veneer, black-and-white blow-ups from the movie, and rowdy reputation, the Caribbean Club still takes visitors a step back into the past.

Otherwise, Key Largo's main attraction is North America's only living coral reef. Many of the dive shops that clutter US 1 offer crash courses cranking out certified scuba-divers in just a few days. They also conduct daily dive trips and rent all equipment. The **John Pennekamp Coral Reef State Park ㉕** (open daily; entrance fee; tel: (305) 451-1202), whose entrance is mid-key, at MM 102.5, provides several

PRECEDING PAGES: vivid sunset on Big Pine Key. **LEFT:** a tropical idyll. **BELOW:** under the water at Biscayne National Park.

The mile markers along Highway 1 give the distance from Key West.

cheaper alternatives. A number of concessioners offer snorkeling and glass-bottom boat rides, in addition to the full-blown scuba trips.

The first underwater park in the United States, the John Pennekamp encompasses 78 sq miles (200 sq km) of coral reef. It harbors more than 40 types of coral and over 450 species of fish. Snorkelers can rub snouts with triggerfish, swim with schools of tang, and see the conch, queen of the Keys, in its natural habitat. A staple of local cuisine, the conch often ends up in a chowder, fritter or salad.

It is strictly prohibited to collect coral and you are advised not to touch or stand on it. Boats must anchor well away from live coral – the slightest touch can kill it. The reef was seriously damaged in the 1930s and '40s, as people ruthlessly harvested coral with dynamite and crowbars to stock souvenir shops. Concerned marine scientists and conservationists pushed legislation that led to the creation of the John Pennekamp Park in 1960. It was named for a *Miami Herald* reporter whose stories fired public interest in preserving offshore reefs.

Key Largo is also the site of the world's first underwater resort, **Jules' Undersea Lodge**, at MM 103, where guests actually swim to, and sleep overnight in, an underwater hotel. To eat with the locals, take a left turn at the Burger King, then follow the signs to the **Pilot House Tiki Bar and Grill**, a favorite for seafood sandwiches and Key Lime Pie. The tiny key limes used to make this tangy dessert once grew in abundance in the Keys but now have to be imported.

The Matecumbe Keys

Highway 1 continues spectacularly through Rock Harbor, Tavernier, Plantation Key and Windley Key. The realization that vast seas completely surround these small tufts of land sinks in as you cross the bridge over Whale Harbor to

Upper Matecumbe Key. Polished, armed-to-the-teeth fishing vessels on either side of the harbor trumpet the area's focus on the sport fishing trade. The action revolves around **Islamorada** ㉖, a town that considers itself the world's sport-fishing capital. If you have plenty of money and a desire to haul home a sailfish or battle a bonefish, you may want to spend a few days here, especially at the luxurious **Cheeca Lodge** at MM 82. Or for a more local hang-out grab a beer waterside at **Holiday Isle's Tiki Bar** near MM 84.5.

If you prefer to pet fish instead of catch them, visit Islamorada's landmark **Theater of the Sea** (open daily; entrance fee; tel: (305) 664-2431), which has been here since 1946. Situated at MM 84.5, it features daily doings in a natural coral grotto, with sea lion and dolphin shows, glass-bottom boat rides around nearby lagoons and even a shark pit. You might also want to enquire about the Dolphin Adventure package, which includes a swim with the dolphins, but you need to book in advance for this. Islamorada town proper has a **Spanish Mission House**, with an art gallery and a striking Art Deco-style monument to the Labor Day hurricane of 1935, in which more than 400 people died – the barometer at one point dipped to 26.35, the lowest pressure ever recorded in the Western Hemisphere.

More bridges lead to **Lower Matecumbe Key**, an embarkation point for trips to Indian and Lignumvitae keys, accessible by boat from Robbie's Marina at MM 77.5 (tel: (305) 664-9814). The weird and wondrous tropical foliage of **Indian Key** hides traces of early Calusa Indians and the remains of a settlement that occupied the island from 1831 to 1840. **Lignumvitae Key** is a treasure trove of fauna and flora, supporting a wide variety of unusual trees and a number of fascinating bird species. Call Robbie's Thursday through Monday to reserve a place on the ranger-led tour of the islands.

Map on pages 232–3

The waters off the Keys are full of shipwrecks, some dating back to the 1500s. The area was once the haunt of pirates, including the nefarious Black Caesar, who plundered ships in the early 1800s.

BELOW: dreaming of the big one.

FISHING IN THE KEYS

Throughout the island chain, marinas bristle with fishing boats of all shapes and sizes. On the Atlantic side, the warm waters of the Gulf Stream harbor prize catches such as marlin and wahoo. These big game fish can take hours to land but make great trophies when stuffed and mounted by a local taxidermist. Closer in, tropical species such as snapper and grouper can be hooked in the coastal and reef waters. On the north side of the Keys, the protected shallows of Florida Bay, known locally as the "backcountry," offer a more tranquil experience. Here, knowledgeable guides pole flat-bottomed skiffs between the islands in search of inshore fish such as snook or pompano. In these waters, guile and stealth win the day.

Though Islamorada, Marathon and Key West are the hubs of activity, most of the smaller centers have options to suit a range of budgets and abilities. You may be hankering to charter a craft and head out on your own, but you'll have more success with a guide or, more economically, on a large fishing party boat. A private boat and guide can cost $200–$500 a day. Often the best advice on local guides and fishing trips can be had in one of the many bait and tackle shops that line the Overseas Highway. The shops also provide fishing licenses.

Seven Mile Bridge

From the Matecumbes, US 1 winds its way across various little keys and increasingly breathtaking waterscapes to Key Vaca and the metropolis of **Marathon**. With a population of about 13,000, Marathon is the main settlement in the Middle Keys.

Next, starting near MM 47, is **Seven Mile Bridge** ㉗ – one of the nation's first great engineering marvels. The span, actually 110 ft (33 meters) short of 7 miles (11 km), is laser-straight save for a bend at Pigeon Key. Completed in 1912, it was the crowning achievement of Henry Flagler's Overseas Railroad. The 1935 hurricane destroyed the railroad but not the bridge, which was then converted to carry the Overseas Highway. The old bridge, a hair-raisingly narrow structure, was eventually replaced by a shorter, modern bridge in 1982. On Pigeon Key, which can still be reached via the old bridge, you can visit some of the buildings used by Flagler's crews.

Park rangers at the National Key Deer Refuge say the best time to see the deer is in the early morning or late afternoon.

Continue to **Bahia Honda State Park** ㉘ (open daily; entrance fee; tel: (305) 872-2353), at MM 37, where another rickety old bridge that parallels the newer one provides a glimpse into the past. This lovely park has a beach that is generally agreed to be the best in the Keys and was once voted the finest in the entire US. Beautiful white sand is fringed by a dense forest, where trails wind among rare trees such as the yellow satinwood. The beach itself has campsites and water sports equipment available for rent.

Between Bahia Honda and Key West are a group of slightly larger islands that make up the Lower Keys. A highlight here is the **National Key Deer Refuge** (open Mon–Fri; free; tel: (305) 872-2239), which spans a number of islands but has its headquarters on **Big Pine Key** (take Key Deer Boulevard, just beyond

BELOW: protected sands at Bahia Honda State Park.

MM 31, heading for Big Pine Key Shopping Plaza). The star attraction is a colony of diminutive key deer, a subspecies of the Virginia white-tail. The animals grow to about 30 inches (75 cm) tall and 38 inches (95 cm) in length. Hunters and developers reduced the population to less than 50 by 1947, but efforts by the refuge have since boosted numbers to several hundred.

Before leaving Big Pine, avid snorkelers and divers should consider the 5-mile (8-km) boat trip south to **Looe Key National Marine Sanctuary**, whose stretch of reef is one of the world's most sensational aquatic showcases. In fact, almost any dive center in the area will arrange excursions to the sanctuary.

Key West

Some 25 miles (40 km) beyond Big Pine Key you reach Stock Island and then the last bridge on the Overseas Highway. Before crossing the bridge, prepare yourself for a short hop into another, very different, world. You have literally reached the end of the road. This is **Key West ㉙**.

Upon arrival, your first impression is of the modern rubble of any resort city: Holiday Inn, Days Inn, Burger King and company. However, the character of the town inevitably changes, slowly at first, then suddenly. Tacky neon storefronts begin to alternate with dignified old homes buried under fragrant pink blooms of frangipani. The American flavor of fast-food emporiums and clean white houses evaporates in an ambiance that's not quite Bahamian, not quite Cuban, not quite nautical… just very Key West.

In the Old Town, bars, restaurants, shops and homes – some restored, some still crumbling – merge in a collage of discordant color that somehow suits this city. The people who blend into this bizarre landscape are as incongruous as the

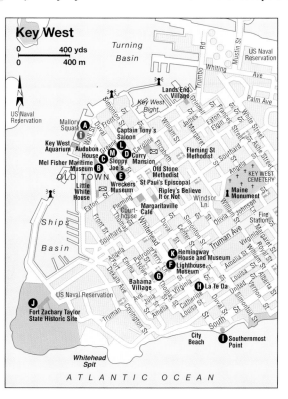

Spanish explorers said that they found Key West buried in human bones, a tale that may have led to its name of Cayo Hueso – "Island of Bones." The name was later anglicized into Key West.

BELOW: a Key West "conch."

Maps:
Area 232
City 267

colors. Among them are born-and-bred locals (known as conchs, pronounced "konks"), long-haired survivors of the hippie era, impeccably groomed gay couples, leather-faced fishermen, jet-setters in color-coordinated tennis ensembles – not to mention, of course, a large helping of tourists.

The inimitable character of Key West derives in large part from its history as a haven for transients from the ends of the earth. Once the haunt of pirates, the island gained legitimacy in the early 19th century when the US navy stepped in to police these waters. Soon the town was booming, largely due to the business of "wrecking" – the licensed stripping of cargo from shipwrecks. In the 20th century, Flagler's Overseas Railroad added another dimension to the healthy economy: tourism. And apart from a slump in the 1930s, it is the constant influx of visitors that has kept Key West prosperous.

Wreckers in the 1800s would race across the water if a sinking boat was spotted off the Keys: the first ship to arrive at the wreck was legally entitled to strip it – after rescuing any survivors.

An Old Town ramble

To appreciate Key West fully you will need to stay for at least one or two nights. Apart from that, there really is no blueprint for experiencing the town. You are more likely to find the real Key West if you follow your own adventurous inclinations instead of those of a tour guide.

Having said that, the visitor who deems it his duty to race through a sightseeing quota will find no lack of attractions. Popular sights are focused mainly in the western half of the city. **Mallory Square Ⓐ** is a standard starting point. It is the spot around which the city grew, and lately the spot around which its renaissance has revolved. You can stock up on brochures and tips at the information center, and spend large amounts of money in the souvenir market. On the square is the **Key West Aquarium** (open daily: entrance fee; tel: (305) 296-2051)

BELOW: the rooftops of the Old Town.

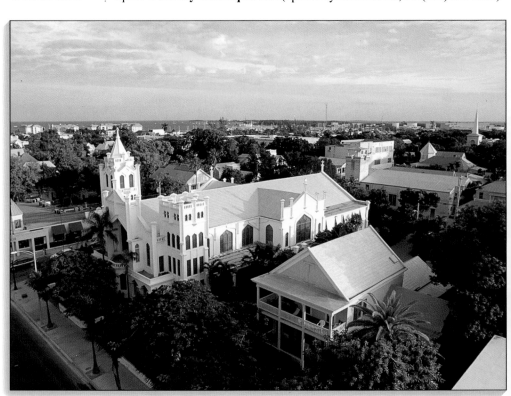

and the **Key West Shipwreck Historeum** (open daily: entrance fee; tel: (305) 292-8990), a reproduction of the warehouse used for salvage operations.

Just a couple of paces from Mallory Square, at 200 Greene Street, the **Mel Fisher Maritime Museum** **B** (open daily; entrance fee; tel: (305) 294-2633) displays treasures from the Spanish ships *Nuestra Señora de Atocha* and *Santa Margarita*, which sank in the waters off Key West during a fierce hurricane in 1622. Only a fraction of the huge hoard of gold, silver and jewels is on display, but other exhibits tell the dramatic story of the hunt for the treasure and the subsequent salvage operation.

Fortunately for visitors, Key Westers have indulged an infatuation for restoring their homes, a hobby that has transformed the island into a live-in architectural museum. Whitehead Street, just beside the Mel Fisher Museum, has some colorful examples. At No. 205 is **Audubon House** **C** (open daily; entrance fee; tel: (305) 294-2116), named for naturalist-artist John James Audubon (1785–1851), who spent a few weeks here while studying Florida's countless species of birds. Built in 1830, it showcases period furnishings, including Chippendale antiques, most of them hauled off sinking ships by wreckers.

Some of the best examples of local architecture can be seen one block south, on **Caroline Street**. The Captain George Carey House at No. 410 is typical of Bahamian styles, as is the building at No. 310. The George A.T. Roberts House at No. 313, with its spacious veranda and "gingerbread" trim – the fancy wooden grillwork that is so typical of Key West – exemplifies "conch" architecture. One of the city's best-known buildings is **Curry Mansion** **D**, at 511 Caroline Street, which admits visitors (open daily; entrance fee; tel: (305) 294-5349) and is also a guest house. It was begun in 1855 by William Curry, a wreck cap-

Map on page 267

In 1982, when police set up a roadblock on Key Largo to search for drugs, Key West residents protested by declaring the city capital of the independent "Conch Republic." The event is celebrated here every February.

LEFT: Mallory Square market.
BELOW: Key West's 19th-century lighthouse.

tain from the Bahamas who became the city's first millionaire. Much of the wood-paneling and even some of the electrical fittings are original. The furnishings, some of which are Victorian, were collected by the current owner.

South on **Duval Street**, the Old Town's main drag, the **Wreckers' Museum** (open daily; entrance fee; tel: (305) 294-9502) at No. 322, attracts its own fair share of visitors. Built in 1829 by Francis B. Watlington, a sea captain who made his money from wrecking, the house has been restored and refurbished with antiques; there are also displays of model ships, and documents and artifacts linked to the wrecking business. If you continue south, you'll reach the **Lighthouse Museum** (open daily; entrance fee; tel: (305) 294-0012), pointing its head above the trees at 938 Whitehead Street. Although built back in 1847, the lighthouse is still functioning. Even better, visitors are permitted to climb up for the view.

The naval base to the west stretches farther south but is off-limits, so this spot is celebrated as the southernmost point of the continental US.

The streets west of here make up **Bahama Village** , where the city's Caribbean atmosphere is at its strongest, with modest but often charming wooden houses. The colorful Blue Heaven restaurant at 729 Thomas Street serves good conch food and is popular with a young crowd.

Gingerbread buffs should make it a point to take in the two-story house next to **La Te Da** (1125 Duval Street; tel: (305) 296-6706), a gay restaurant and bar which hosts drag shows a couple of nights a week. The gingerbread here – bottles, hearts and spades – reputedly served as a surreptitious sign to sailors and other fun-seekers that they would find wine, women and gambling inside.

A beacon at the southern end of Duval Street marks the **Southernmost Point** . While it has lost its title of the most southern point in the entire US to a spot on the Big Island of Hawaii, this famous landmark is still 755 miles (1,215 km) south of Los Angeles and only 90 miles (145 km) north of Cuba. You can take a refreshing dip in the sea from the beach just a stone's throw from here.

BELOW: Duval Street drag queens.

Looming over the southwest tip of the island is **Fort Zachary Taylor State Historic Site** (open daily; entrance fee; tel: (305) 292-6713), part of the remains of the 19th-century effort to fortify the southern boundary of the United States. You can wander around the grounds and visit the military museum, but the main attraction is Key West's best public beach. A fair distance east along the shore are two **Martello Towers**, which were part of the same defensive network.

If you have a day to spare and aren't on a tight budget, you might consider the 70-mile (110-km) trip into the Gulf of Mexico to **Fort Jefferson**. Construction of the fort, which covers Garden Key in the **Dry Tortugas National Park**, was started in 1846 but never completed. America's largest coastal fort, it was occupied by Federal troops in the Civil War and later became a prison. There are camping facilities on the island and the excellent snorkeling here offers the chance to see loggerhead and hawksbill turtles. There are two ways to get to the island: catamaran, which takes two hours and departs from the Historic Seaport at the corner of Greene and Elizabeth streets (tel: (800) 236-7937), or seaplane, a 40-minute flight out of Key West International Airport (tel: (305) 294-4416). Call ahead for information and reservations.

The sun also sets

For many, Key West is synonymous with Ernest Hemingway (1898–1961). You can visit his home, now called the **Ernest Hemingway House and Museum** (open daily; entrance fee; tel: (305) 295-1575), on the corner of Whitehead and Olivia streets. He bought the delightful Spanish colonial building in 1931 and lived there until 1940, before moving to Cuba. In the study of the pool house out back, he worked on classics like *For Whom the Bell Tolls* and *A Farewell to Arms*.

After a hard day at the typewriter or fishing rod, Hemingway relaxed with a drink or a fist fight at Sloppy Joe's, now called **Captain Tony's Saloon** ◗, at 428 Greene Street. The interior, wallpapered with business cards and clippings, will take you back to those days. The current **Sloppy Joe's** ⓜ is nearby, at the corner of Greene and Duval. Hemingway also patronized this establishment, when it was the Midget Bar. Old photos and memorabilia recall the writer's presence.

Today's generation most readily associates the city with the ballads of pop star Jimmy Buffett and his Coral Reefer Band. After years of frequent visits, he now has a permanent Key West home and runs the **Margaritaville Café** at 500 Duval Street. He is now also involved in efforts to save Florida's manatees.

Inanimate objects like homes and saloons get their real color here from the characters who people them. The locals are low-key, easy-going and unpretentious, and tiny Key West seems to encompass more races, cultures and lifestyles than many much bigger cities. To watch this wonderful world and mingle with it, there's no better occasion than the daily gathering for sunset at Mallory Square. The natural spectacle is often upstaged by the miniature Mardi Gras of jugglers, fire-eaters, acrobats, para-sailors, bongo players, cookie peddlers, peg-legged pirates, and even ordinary people, that turn up every evening.   ❏

Map on page 267

TIP

Drinking is *de rigueur* in Key West, where bar crawls are a tradition. Many bars offer happy hour early on, and you won't be chucked out of most places until about 2am.

BELOW: Hemingway's favorite bar.

INSIGHT GUIDES
Travel Tips

Insight Guides Website

www.insightguides.com

*Don't travel the
planet alone.
Keep in step with
Insight Guides'
walking eye,
just a click away*

Insight Guides Website

Insight Guide
South Africa

This 370-page book includes a section detailing South Africa's history, 22 features covering aspects of the country's life and culture, ranging from living without Apartheid to spectacular wildlife, a region by region visitor's guide to the sights, and a comprehensive Travel Tips section packed with essential contact addresses and numbers. Plus many quality photographs and 15 maps.

UK: £16.99 ISBN: 981-234-223-0
US: $22.95 ISBN: 0-88729-445-6

(Note: cover shown may differ in some markets.)

Close Window

✳ INSIGHT GUIDES

The world's largest collection of visual travel guides

New Insight Maps

Maps in Insight Guides are tailored to complement the text. But when you're on the road you sometimes need the big picture that only a large-scale map can provide. This new range of durable Insight Fleximaps has been designed to meet just that need.

Detailed, clear cartography
makes the comprehensive route and city maps easy to follow, highlights all the major tourist sites and provides valuable motoring information plus a full index.

Informative and easy to use
with additional text and photographs covering a destination's top 10 essential sites, plus useful addresses, facts about the destination and handy tips on getting around.

Laminated finish
allows you to mark your route on the map using a non-permanent marker pen, and wipe it off. It makes the maps more durable and easier to fold than traditional maps.

The first titles
cover many popular destinations. They include Algarve, Amsterdam, Bangkok, California, Cyprus, Dominican Republic, Florence, Hong Kong, Ireland, London, Mallorca, Paris, Prague, Rome, San Francisco, Sydney, Thailand, Tuscany, USA Southwest, Venice, and Vienna.

👁 INSIGHT GUIDES
The world's largest collection of visual travel guides

CONTENTS

Getting Acquainted

Area: Miami-Dade County covers over 2,000 sq. miles (5,200 sq. km) of Southeast Florida, of which about 500 sq. miles (1,300 sq. km) is taken up by Greater Miami.
Population (Greater Miami): 2.2 million.
Language: Officially English, although about 50 percent of the local population speak Spanish as a first language.
Time Zone: Miami runs on Eastern Standard Time, which is the same time zone as New York, 3 hours ahead of San Francisco and 5 hours behind Greenwich Mean Time (GMT). Set your watch an hour ahead for Daylight Saving Time, which runs from early May to late October.
Currency: US Dollar.
Weights and Measures:
The US uses the Imperial system of weights and measures. Metric is rarely used. A conversion chart is provided below.
1 inch = 2.54 centimeters
1 foot = 30.48 centimeters
1 mile = 1.609 kilometers
1 quart = 1.136 liters
1 ounce = 28.4 grams
1 pound = .453 kilograms
1 yard = .9144 meters
Electricity: 110–115 volts; flat two- or three-pronged plugs.
International Dialing Code: (1).
Local Dialing Code: (305).

Government and Economy

Although Miami often feels more like a South American city than a North American one, it is most definitely a part of the United States and adheres to all US government policies. But since "Greater Miami" is in fact made up of 30 municipalities, local regulations regarding housing, sanitation, recreation and education vary.

Miami is the most urban of cities in Florida and also the largest, even larger than the state capital of Tallahassee to the north. Tourism has for many decades been a mainstay of the economy, with the city receiving over 8 million visitors annually. Miami also hosts the largest international banking center outside of New York and serves as the headquarters for several national Fortune 500 companies. Major industries in the area include clothing, manufacturing, printing and publishing, government, retail, insurance, health services, agriculture and transport.

The Climate

Although most Northerners cringe at the idea of a Miami summer, daytime temperatures are in fact no hotter than daytime summer temperatures in New York City. There is little variation between seasons and it is seldom cold in Miami. The average yearly temperature is 75°F (24°C) with a range from around 60°F in January to around 90°F in August (15–35°C). At night, in the summer, you will need air-conditioning or a fan to sleep in comfort. Due to the relatively mild winters, most Miami homes do not have heating systems, but erratic winter weather in recent years (including occasional snow flurries) has caught residents unprepared.

Definitely part of America's "Sunshine State," Miami sees sun almost 365 days a year. Summer is the rainy season, and brief but intense afternoon thundershowers can be expected almost daily in July and August. Lightning is common at this time of year.

Average Monthly Temperatures (Highs and Lows)
January: High 74°F (23°C), Low 63°F (17°C)
February: 76°F (24°C), 63°F (17°C)
March: 77°F (25°C), 65°F (18°C)
April: 79°F (26°C), 68°F (20°C)
May: 83°F (28°C), 72°F (22°C)
June: 85°F (29°C), 76°F (24°C)
July: 88°F (31°C), 76°F (24°C)

Summer Lightning

Florida is unofficially dubbed the "lightning capital of the country." The state records an average of 10 deaths and 30 injuries from lightning each year.

This dubious distinction is attributed to the hot, wet air that lies close to the ground and to unstable atmospheric conditions that exist mainly from May until September. The air near the ground heats up, rises, then begins to cool. Droplets of water form menacing, dark clouds. The air moves up and down so fast that it splits the water droplets in the clouds, causing an electrical spark to shoot out. The spark jumps from cloud to cloud or cloud to ground, passing through the air so quickly that a thunderclap occurs.

Lasting just 1 millisecond, a bolt of lightning delivers a shock of 6,000–10,000 amps that can paralyze bodily functions. Even so, two-thirds of those people hit by lightning in Florida have somehow survived.

If you see dark clouds and bolts approaching, take cover. If you are riding in a car, stay inside until the storm passes. If you are at home or inside a building, don't try to "make a run for it." Many lightning victims are killed when getting into or out of their cars. Boaters should head for the nearest place they can tie up and evacuate the boat.

August: 88°F (31°C), 76°F (24°C)
September: 86°F (30°C), 76°F (24°C)
October: 83°F (28°C), 72°F (22°C)
November: 79°F (26°C), 67°F (19°C)
December: 76°F (24°C), 63°F (17°C)

HURRICANES

The most damaging and dangerous climatic phenomenon to affect the Miami area is the hurricane. A tropical storm is called a hurricane once its wind speed exceeds 74 miles (119 km) per hour.

Many of the hurricanes that hit Florida move across the Atlantic from the coast of Africa. Several factors contribute to the formation of a hurricane, above all, heat and wind. The key ingredient is the heat of the summer sun, which warms the surface of the ocean enough for water to evaporate. As the warm air rises, it condenses into thunderclouds, which are sent spinning by the rotation of the earth. The hurricane moves forward at 10–30 miles (16–48 km) per hour, and can measure hundreds of miles across.

The National Hurricane Center in Miami tracks a hurricane's progress using radar and satellites, and pilots – known as Hurricane Hunters – fly in and out of the storm while gathering data. Advance warning of the severity of a hurricane can greatly reduce the damage done if it eventually hits. While the winds can be devastating, most damage and deaths are caused by flooding from the storm surge – a wall of water that can reach up to 20 ft (6 m) high.

Season

The hurricane season usually runs from June to November. The number of hurricanes formed in a given year has ranged from as few as two to as many as 20, but on average one strikes every two years. Still, the National Hurricane Center in Miami tracks each tropical storm very carefully, ready to issue evacuation orders if a hurricane is headed for the mainland. The average lifespan of a hurricane is eight to ten days.

Hurricane Names

Six years' worth of hurricane names, listed in alphabetical order, are agreed upon in advance. Once named only for women, a practice believed to have begun when World War II servicemen in the Pacific named storms after their girlfriends, the National Weather Service adopted an equal rights policy in 1979, when it began alternating male names too.

Miami is most vulnerable to hurricanes in August and early September, but patterns tradition-ally shift to the Caribbean later in September and in October, endan-gering the Keys and the West Coast.

Precautionary Measures

Miami residents are well versed on precautions to be taken when a hurricane approaches. Newspapers run special sections on the subject at the start of each season, and most coastal communities publish evacuation plans and routes. People are encouraged to track the path of the storm on special charts

that are available in newspapers, from radio and television stations, and even printed on the sides of grocery bags.

Needless to say, tourists caught in Miami during an impending hurricane should drop plans to work on their suntans or visit tourist attractions and follow National Weather Service advisories, television directives and common sense in riding out the storm. For news on brewing storms you can call the National Weather Service in Miami, tel: (305) 229-4522.

The Hurricane Build-up

In the summer months, tropical disturbances are common all over the tropics. It is from these that tropical depressions and then tropical storms develop, which can bring gales of up to 73 miles (117 km) per hour and heavy rains. At this stage, the National Hurricane Center in Miami will be monitoring the developments extremely closely.

Hurricane Watch

Once a Hurricane Watch has been signaled, this means that the National Hurricane Center has

What to Do if a Hurricane Strikes

During the storm Stay indoors once the hurricane is buffeting your area. When the eye (the low-pressure area at the center of a hurricane) passes over, there will be a temporary lull in wind and rain for up to half an hour or more. This is not the end of the storm, which will in fact resume (possibly with even greater force) from the opposite direction. Wait for word from the authorities before venturing out of your shelter.
If ordered to evacuate Most coastal communities have detailed evacuation procedure plans. Evacuation route signs are permanently located along highways in many of these areas. Follow instructions and designated routes as quickly as possible. Take blankets, a flashlight, extra

clothing and medications. Leave behind pets (which are not permitted inside public shelters).
After the storm passes Drive with caution when ordered to return home. Debris in the streets can be a hazard. Roads in coastal areas may collapse if soil has been washed from beneath them. Steer clear of fallen or dangling utility wires. Stay tuned to radio stations for news of emergency medical, food, housing and other forms of assistance. If you have been staying in a rented home, re-enter the building with caution and make temporary repairs to correct hazards and minimize further damage. Open windows and doors to air and dry the house. Be careful when dealing with matches or fires in case of gas leaks.

determined a hurricane may hit within 36–48 hours. It is time to begin taking final precautions against a direct hit: for example checking your vehicle's gas tank is full, gathering together emergency supplies and so forth. Stay tuned to the local radio or television station for the latest storm information.

Hurricane Warning
This is issued when the storm reaches winds of at least 74 miles (119 km) per hour and high water and storm surges are expected in a specific area within 24 hours. Warnings will identify specific coastal areas where these conditions may occur. Be ready to evacuate your home or hotel. Finish getting together the things you need to take to a shelter or anything else you will need if you stay home.

Hurricane Categories

Hurricanes are categorized from one to five according to the Saffir Simpson Scale, which measures the wind speed:
● **Category 1:** 74–95 miles (119–153 km) per hour.
● **Category 2:** 96–110 miles (154–177 km) per hour.
● **Category 3:** 111–130 miles (178–209 km) per hour.
● **Category 4:** 131–155 miles (210–249 km) per hour.
● **Category 5:** over 155 miles (149 km) per hour.

Planning the Trip

Visas and Passports

Most foreign visitors need a passport (which should be valid for at least six months longer than their intended stay) and a visa to enter the US. You should also be able to provide evidence that you intend to leave the US after your visit is over (usually in the form of a return or onward ticket), and visitors from some countries need an international vaccination certificate.

Certain foreign nationals are exempt from the normal visa requirements. Canadian citizens with a valid Canadian passport need no visa. Nor do Mexican citizens provided they have a Mexican passport and a US Border Crossing Card (Form I-186 or I-586), and as long as they are residents of Mexico.

A special "visa-waiver" program means that citizens of some countries do not require a visa if they are entering the US for less than 90 days and have a round-trip or onward ticket. These countries include New Zealand, Japan, the UK and about 18 other European nations. Note that immigration officials are entitled to ask for proof of solvency on your arrival in the United States.

Anyone requiring a visa or visa information can apply by mail or by personal application to the US Embassy or Consulate nearest their home.

Vaccination certificate requirements vary, but official proof of immunization against smallpox or cholera may be necessary.

Customs

All articles brought into the US must be declared to Customs. You will be given a special form to fill in before you enter the country. Articles brought into the US are subject to duty or internal revenue tax, but visitors are given an allowance of exempted goods (see box below).

Prohibited Goods
Articles which visitors are forbidden to take into the US include:
● liquor-filled chocolates or candy.
● dangerous drugs.
● obscene publications.
● hazardous articles (e.g. fireworks).
● most fresh food products, unless you have an import permit.
● narcotics – travelers using medicines containing narcotics

Customs Allowance

Money There is no limit on the amount of money – US or foreign traveler's checks or money orders – that you may bring into or take out of the US. But you must declare amounts exceeding $10,000 or the foreign currency equivalent.

Alcohol Visitors over the age of 21 years are permitted to bring in 1 liter (34 fl oz) of alcohol (beer, wine or liquor) for their personal use. Excess quantities are subject to duty and tax.

Cigars and cigarettes Visitors may bring in not more than 200 cigarettes (one carton), 50 cigars (as long as they are not Cuban) or 4.4 lbs (2 kg) of smoking tobacco, or proportionate amounts of each. An additional 100 cigars may be brought in under your gift exemption.

Gifts As a visitor, you can claim up to $100 worth of merchandise, free of duty and tax, as gifts for other people. Such articles may have to be inspected, so do not gift-wrap them until after you have entered the country.

(such as tranquilizers or cough medicine) should carry a prescription and/or a note from their doctor, and should take only the quantity required for a short stay.

Full details of customs requirements are available from your nearest US Embassy or Consulate.

Health and Insurance

Most visitors to Miami will have no health problems during their stay: sunburn and mosquito bites in summer are the main nuisance for the majority. The city's medical facilities are considered some of the best in the country. In case of any medical emergency, telephone 911 and assistance will be available.

As the US has no socialized medicine and all medical care must be paid for by the individual, you should never leave home without travel insurance to cover both yourself and your belongings. Your own insurance company or travel agent can advise you on policies, but shop around since rates vary. Make sure you are covered for accidental death, emergency medical care, trip cancelation and baggage or document loss.

See pages 281–2 for information on medical treatment and health hazards.

Money

Foreign visitors are advised to take US dollar traveler's checks to Miami, since exchanging foreign currency – whether as cash or checks – can prove problematic. An increasing number of banks, including the First Union National Bank, Nations Bank and Sun Bank chains offer foreign exchange facilities, but this practice is not universal. Some large department store chains offer foreign currency exchange.

Most shops, restaurants and other establishments accept traveler's checks in US dollars and will give change in cash.

Alternatively, checks can be converted into cash at the bank.

Credit Cards
Credit cards are very much part of daily life in Miami, as in other parts of the US. They can be used to pay for pretty much anything, and it is also common for car rental firms and hotels to take an imprint of your card as a deposit. Rental companies may oblige you to pay a large deposit in cash if you do not have a card.

You can also use your credit card to withdraw cash from ATMS (Automatic Teller Machines). Before you leave home, make sure you know your PIN number and find out which ATM system will accept your card. The most widely accepted cards are Visa, American Express, MasterCard, Diners Club, Japanese Credit Bureau and Discovery.

What to Bring

In general, everything you could possibly need can be bought inexpensively in Miami. Some basic suggestions, however, include sun screen lotion, a shade hat, an umbrella, a bathing suit, and any prescription medications.

Clothing
Casual, cool, lightweight and light colors are the norm. Formal dress is rarely required. For men, a sports coat and open-necked shirt are usually acceptable at finer restaurants, with ties being optional. Shorts are acceptable

for both men and women even on the streets of downtown Miami. In winter, a sweater or light jacket will usually be enough. Note that topless bathing is illegal on most beaches.

Getting There

BY AIR

Most major US airlines and many international carriers serve Miami. Fare prices are competitive, so shop around before buying a ticket. A variety of discount fares and "package deals," which can significantly cut round-trip rates, are also available. Many scheduled services are supplemented by charter flights.

Miami International Airport (MIA) is one of the busiest and best people-watching airports in the US, with more than 800 flights daily. It serves as the main artery to the Caribbean and Latin America and offers numerous flights to New York and the nearby Bahamas throughout the day. Just 8 miles (13 km) from downtown, the airport is a city within itself, with over 32,000 employees. It offers banks, restaurants, televisions, lockers, a hotel and an airfield sundeck for that last-chance tan.

The best way to get into town from the airport is by taxi (about $25 to Miami Beach) or SuperShuttle van (about $12 per person to Miami Beach). The SuperShuttle can take up to 11 passengers at a time and operates

Public Holidays

During some of the holidays listed below, some or all government offices, businesses and banks may be closed. School is also in recess during these times, so local beaches and attractions are usually crowded.
● **January** New Year's Day (1)
● **January** Martin Luther King's Birthday (15)
● **February** President's Day (Third Monday)

● **May** Memorial Day (Last Monday)
● **July** Independence Day (4)
● **September** Labor Day (First Monday)
● **October** Columbus Day (Second Monday)
● **November** Veterans' Day (11)
● **November** Thanksgiving (Fourth Thursday)
● **December** Christmas Day (25)

Airline Numbers

For information on flights, call the following numbers:
Air Canada, tel: (888) 247-2262.
Air France, tel: (800) 237-2747.
American, tel: (800) 433-7300.
Bahamas Air, tel: (305) 593-1910.
British Airways, tel: (800) 247-9297.

Continental, tel: (305) 324-0400.
Delta, tel: (305) 448-7000.
Lufthansa, tel: (800) 645-3880.
Northwest/KLM, tel: (800) 447-4747.
Swissair, tel: (800) 221-4750.
TWA, tel: (800) 221-2000.
United, tel: (800) 241-6522.
US Airways, tel: (800) 428-4322.

24 hours a day, seven days a week. Taxis and the SuperShuttle can be picked up on the airport's lower level. There are also fairly unreliable bus and train services and, of course, all the usual car rental companies.

Instead of MIA, some international airlines use Fort Lauderdale Airport, about 30 miles (48 km) north of Miami. Buses, trains and taxis are available to Miami; a taxi to South Beach will set you back about $45. Various car rental companies are represented at the airport.

The information numbers for Miami and Fort Lauderdale airports are (305) 876-7000 and (954) 359-1200 respectively.

BY SEA

The Port of Miami is the largest cruise port in the world and welcomes well over 2 million passengers each year, which represents 75 percent of all cruise passengers worldwide. It is just a five-minute ride from downtown with trolley service available. For general information, telephone (305) 371-7678.

Cruise Lines
Carnival Cruise Lines
tel: (305) 599-2200.
Costa Cruises
tel: (305) 358-7325.
Cunard Line
tel: (305) 463-3000.
Norwegian Cruise Line
tel: (305) 436-4000.
Royal Caribbean International & Celebrity Cruises
tel: (305) 539-6000.

SeaEscape
tel: (800) 327-2005.
Windjammer Barefoot Cruises
tel: (305) 672-6453.

Marinas
For those who sail into the city independently, there are over 50 marinas with 350 sq. miles (900 sq. km) of protected waters that offer dock facilities for almost any size craft:
Biscayne Bay Marriott Hotel & Marina
1633 N Bayshore Drive
Miami
tel: (305) 374-3900.
Crandon Park Marina
4000 Crandon Park Boulevard
Key Biscayne
tel: (305) 361-1281.
Matheson Hammock Marina
9610 Old Cutler Road
Coral Gables
tel: (305) 665-5475.
Haulover Park Marina
10500 Collins Avenue
Miami Beach
tel: (305) 945-3934.
Dinner Key Marina
3400 Pan American Drive
Coconut Grove
tel: (305) 579-6980.
Miamarina at Bayside
401 Biscayne Boulevard
Miami
tel: (305) 579-6955.
Rickenbacker Marina
3301 Rickenbacker Causeway
Key Biscayne
tel: (305) 361-1900.
Maule Lake Marina
17201 Biscayne Boulevard
North Miami Beach
tel: (305) 945-0808.

Miami Beach Marina
300 Alton Road, Miami Beach
tel: (305) 673-6000.

BY RAIL

Amtrak is the passenger line that services Miami from most points across the country. Sleeping berths and restaurant cars are available on most trains. Extended travel passes are available. A trip from New York City takes 26 hours and costs about the same as an airline ticket. For information, telephone (800) 872-7245.

Tri-Rail links Miami-Dade County with the two northern counties of Broward and Palm Beach, with service available from the Metrorail station at 79th Street. Trains operate on a varied schedule. For information, telephone (800) 874-7245.

BY BUS

Greyhound and Trailways provide bus services to Miami from across America. For information on both, telephone (800) 231-2222.

BY CAR

The major Florida highways leading to Miami are I-95 along the east, I-75 along the west, and the Florida Turnpike, which connects the central part of the state to the south. On all of them the roads are excellent with safe, clean rest stops along the way. US 1 runs all the way down the east coast of the United States to Key West. It isn't a fast through-route, as it's often lined with fast-food outlets and interrupted by traffic lights, but it is a good reference point throughout the Miami area.

Practical Tips

Business Hours

Most offices and businesses are open Monday through Friday from 9am–5 or 5.30pm, with no closing hours for lunch. Banks are usually open from 9am–3pm Monday through Friday with some opening Saturday from 9am–noon. Most large shopping centers are open from 10am–9.30pm Monday through Saturday and from noon–6pm on Sunday. Many large supermarkets and numerous restaurants now stay open 24 hours.

Tipping

Gratuities are usually not included on most restaurant bills and the suggested rate is 15 to 20 percent. The same rate is normal for taxi drivers. Porters are readily available at the airport; tipping is expected and $1–1.50 per suitcase is customary. Wheel-chairs and attendants are also available. Moderate hotel tipping for bellboys is about 50 cents per bag handled. You should tip a doorman if he holds your car or performs any other services.

Media

Newspapers
The *Miami Herald* is Florida's most respected daily paper. It offers sound coverage on local, state and Latin American news. Its Friday edition offers a useful what-to-do weekend tabloid section. *The Street,* the Herald's new free weekly, targets the younger, hipper crowd with full listings of nightlife, restaurants, clubs and films. A Spanish-language sister paper, *El*

Nuevo Herald, is published daily. You can usually pick up *USA Today* from dispensers in the street, while good news-stands and certain bookshops sell other national and foreign papers. The News Cafe, at 800 Ocean Drive in South Beach, has a good selection.

Miami New Times, a free alternative press weekly, delivers an offbeat view of the city. Its calendar of events rivals the *Miami Herald's* and its personal ads let visitors know what's hot and happening. *Diario Las Americas* is a Spanish-language daily whose coverage emphasizes Cuban/Central American news and politically leans toward the right. *Miami Times* is a weekly that covers the area's black community.

Websites:
The *Miami Herald*: www.herald.com
El Nuevo Herald: www.elherald.com
Miami New Times:
www.miaminewtimes.com

Television and Radio
A weekly television guide is published on Sunday in the *Miami Herald*. Cable television stations are abundant, including many that are available at area hotels and motels. The national network channels are: 2 (WPBT-PBS), 4 (WFOR-CBS), 6 (WTVJ-NBC), 7 (WSVN-FOX), 10 (WPLG-ABC). There are many Miami area channels including locally produced 69 WAMI and several Spanish-language stations such as 23 Univision and 51 Telemundo. On the radio, AM frequencies in Miami tend to carry more talk shows and commercials. FM stations offer a wider range of programs and higher-quality stereo sound.

Postal Services

Information on Miami's postal facilities can be found by telephoning (305) 639-4280 or (800) 275-8777. Post offices in Miami-Dade County are open 8.30am–5pm Monday through Friday, with most open on Saturday 8.30am–noon. Stamps are also sold at many hotels and drugstores. Overnight and express mail

services are available at all post office branches, along with a general delivery service that allows out-of-towners to receive mail and parcels. Express Mail guarantees next-day delivery within the US and delivery within two or three days elsewhere in the world. Next-day delivery to most places around the world is offered by courier services such as the following:
Federal Express: tel: (800) 238-5355.
DHL: tel: (800) 345-2727.
UPS: tel: (800) 272-4877.

Post Offices

Airport Mail Facility, Miami International Airport, Miami, tel: (305) 599-1789.
Biscayne (Downtown) Branch, 2 S Biscayne Boulevard, Miami, tel: (305) 599-1744.
Coconut Grove Branch, 3195 Grand Avenue, Coconut Grove, tel: (305) 599-1750.
Coral Gables Branch, 251 Valencia Avenue, Coral Gables, tel: (305) 599-1795.
Key Biscayne Branch, 951 Crandon Boulevard, Key Biscayne, tel: (305) 599-1775.
Miami Beach Branch, 1300 Washington Avenue, Miami Beach, tel: (305) 599-1787.
Surfside Branch, 250 95th Street, Surfside, tel: (305) 639-5520.

Telecommunications

Telephones
The 305 prefix area code covers the Metropolitan Miami area and the Florida Keys, and must be included in every local call. Bell South has added a new area code of 786 to the Miami and Miami Beach area. Fort Lauderdale's area code is 954. To ask an operator for a Miami area number, telephone 411. To ask for a number outside of Miami but in the 305 area code, telephone 1-305-555-1212. For long-distance or international assistance dial 0. Toll-free numbers for various businesses and services are

indicated by the prefix 800. The toll-free information number is (800) 555-1212.

Public phones are located in gas stations, restaurants, hotels, sidewalk booths and numerous public places. A local call will cost 25 cents for three minutes. For long-distance calls, it is easier to use a phonecard or credit card. Credit cards can be used at any phone: dial 1-800-CALLATT, key in your credit card number and wait to be connected.

Fax/Telex/Telegrams

Dozens of businesses offering communication services are listed in the telephone directory. Many are open 24 hours a day.
Kinkos, 600 Brickell Avenue, tel: (305) 373-4910
Western Union, tel: (800) 325-6000.

Cybercafes

Kafka Kafe, 1464 Washington Avenue, Miami, tel: (305) 673-9669.
The Hard Drive Cafe, 1942 Hollywood Boulevard, Hollywood, Florida 33020, tel: (954) 929-3324.
www.hd-cafe.com
e-mail: hdcafe@hd-cafe.com

Tourist Offices

Art Deco Welcome Center, 1001 Ocean Drive, Miami Beach, tel: (305) 531-3484.

Bayside Marketplace's Miami Visitors Center, 401 Biscayne Boulevard, Miami, tel: (305) 539-8070.
Coral Gables Chamber of Commerce, 50 Aragon Avenue, Coral Gables, tel: (305) 446-1657.
Greater Homestead/Florida City Chamber of Commerce, 43 N Krome Avenue, Homestead, tel: (305) 247-2332, www.chamberinaction.com
Greater Miami Chamber of Commerce, 1601 Biscayne Boulevard, Miami, tel: (305) 350-7700.
Greater Miami Convention & Visitors Bureau, 701 Brickell Avenue, tel: (305) 539-3000 or (800) 240-4282, www.miamiandbeaches.com or www.TropicoolMiami.com
Miami Beach Chamber of Commerce, 1920 Meridian Avenue, Miami Beach, tel: (305) 672-1270, www.miamibeachchamber.com
Sunny Isles Beach Resort Association, 17100 Collins Avenue, Sunny Isles Beach, tel: (305) 947-5826 www.sunnyislesfla.com
Surfside Tourist Board, 9301 Collins Avenue, Surfside, tel: (305) 864-0722 www.town.surfside.fl.us
Tropical Everglades Visitor Association, 160 US 1, Florida City, tel: (800) 388-9669, www.tropicaleverglades.com
Florida Division of Tourism, Tallahassee, tel: (888) 735-2872, www.flausa.com

Useful Addresses

Travelers with Disabilities
Deaf Services Bureau, tel: (305) 668-4407.
Miami Lighthouse for the Blind, tel: (305) 856-2288.
Miami-Dade Office of American with Disabilities Act Coordination, tel: (305) 375-3566.

Marriages
Marriage License Bureau, 140 W Flagler Street, tel: (305) 275-1155.

Immigration Office
District Headquarters, 7880 Biscayne Boulevard, Miami, tel: (800) 375-5283.

Religious Services

The following offer services in the Miami area. For a bigger selection, check the Yellow Pages under Churches or Synagogues.
St Frances De Sales (Catholic), 600 Lenox Avenue, Miami Beach, tel: (305) 672-0093.
Coral Gables Congregational Church (United Church of Christ), 3010 DeSoto Boulevard, Coral Gables, tel: (305) 448-7421.
Miami Beach First Baptist Church (Baptist), 2816 Sheridan Avenue, Miami Beach, tel: (305) 538-3507.
First Church of Christ Scientist (Christian Science), 410 Andalusia Avenue, Coral Gables, tel: (305) 443-1427.

Embassies and Consulates

Argentina: 800 Brickell Avenue, tel: (305) 373-1889.
Bahamas: 25 SE 2nd Avenue, tel: (305) 373-6295.
Bolivia: 9100 S Dadeland Boulevard, tel: (305) 670-0709.
Brazil: 2601 S Bayshore Drive, tel: (305) 285-6200.
Canada: 200 S Biscayne Boulevard, tel: (305) 579-1600.
Chile: 800 Brickell Avenue, tel: (305) 373-8623.
Costa Rica: 1600 Le Jeune Road, tel: (305) 871-7485.

Ecuador: 1101 Brickell Avenue, tel: (305) 539-8214.
France: 2 S Biscayne Boulevard, tel: (305) 372-9798.
Germany: 100 N Biscayne Boulevard, tel: (305) 358-0290.
Great Britain: 1001 S Bayshore Drive, tel: (305) 374-1522.
Haiti: 259 SW 13th Street, tel: (305) 859-2003.
Israel: 100 N Biscayne Boulevard, tel: (305) 925-9400.
Italy: 1200 Brickell Avenue, tel: (305) 374-6322.

Jamaica: 25 SE 2nd Avenue, tel: (305) 374-8431.
Japan: 80 SW 8th Street, tel: (305) 530-9090.
Mexico: 1200 NW 78th Avenue, tel: (305) 716-4977.
Netherlands: 801 Brickell Avenue, tel: (305) 789-6646.
Peru: 444 Brickell Avenue, tel: (305) 374-1305.
Spain: 2655 Le Jeune Road, Coral Gables, tel: (305) 446-5511.
Venezuela: 1101 Brickell Avenue, tel: (305) 577-3834.

Ismailia Cultural Center (Muslim), 2045 NE 151st Street, North Miami Beach, tel: (305) 944-1710.
J. W. Kingdom Hall (Jehovah's Witness), 300 W 40th Street, Miami Beach, tel: (305) 532-8588.
Temple Emanu-El (Synagogue), 1701 Washington Avenue, Miami Beach, tel: (305) 538-2503.

Traveling with Kids

Several of Miami's attractions are ideally suited for children. Try the **Miami Seaquarium, Monkey Jungle, Metrozoo** and the **Miami Museum of Science and Space Transit Planetarium**.

Others, such as the **Miami City Ballet, New World Symphony** and **Florida Philharmonic Orchestra**, offer special performances geared toward children. And every March the **Miami-Dade County Youth Fair** features amusement rides, educational exhibits and concerts for children on fairgrounds a few miles west of the city.

Babysitters can be provided by the **International Nanny Service**, tel: (305) 949-0360.

Security and Crime

A rash of crimes committed against tourists in the early 1990s forced the Florida community to come up with effective safeguards to protect visitors from dangerous attacks. One of the most important is that car rental agencies have removed the special license plates which formerly earmarked hired cars, and replaced them with standard-issue plates, the sort used by residents. According to police, one of the tricks muggers have employed in the past is to bump a moving vehicle from behind, especially a car carrying tourists. When the bemused driver gets out to investigate, he or she is robbed at gunpoint. Don't fall prey to this tactic: if you get bumped, head for the nearest well-lit and crowded spot, such as a gas station or convenience store, before stopping.

Other tips: always park your car in a well-lit area, never in a shady back corner of a parking lot. Be sure to keep your car doors locked and windows closed while driving. When you first arrive in Miami, plot the route to your hotel in advance, with the aid of a map, or take advice from your car-rental agency. (A spate of attacks in the city occurred because jet-lagged tourists who had disembarked from longhaul flights missed the highway signs for Miami Beach and, only a couple of wrong turns later, found themselves in a high-crime part of town.) A new system of orange sunburst symbols on road signs has been set up to help you stay on the main routes to and from the airport. Better still, arrange to pick up your rented car near your hotel on the morning after you arrive rather than attempt to negotiate unfamiliar routes when tired. Many car rental agencies will deliver to your hotel free, or for only a small extra charge.

While in the street, use common sense and act like a New Yorker. In other words, don't carry around large sums of money or expensive camera equipment, don't make eye contact with unwelcome strangers, and don't travel alone at night.

Emergencies

In an emergency, dial 911 to contact the police, ambulance or fire service. No money is needed in pay phones for this number.

For police non-emergencies in the City of Miami call (305) 579-6111; in Miami Beach (305) 673-7900; in the rest of the county tel: (305) 476-5423. Every municipality (e.g. Miami Beach, Bal Harbour) has its own police department so find out which municipality you're staying in. For those areas of the county not in a municipality, you should deal with the Miami-Dade police.

If you report an incident, be sure to get a case number and ask for a phone number so you can follow up on the status of your case.

There is a lost and found office at the Miami International Airport, tel: (305) 876-7377. It is open seven days a week 8am–6pm.

Medical Services

There are several walk-in medical and dental care offices in the Miami area. These are listed in the telephone directory under "Clinics." For dentist referrals, tel: (305) 667 3647. A 24-hour pharmacy can be found by calling Walgreens Pharmacy, tel: (305) 595-3326.

HOSPITALS

Baptist Hospital, 8900 N Kendall Drive, tel: (305) 596-1960.
Coral Gables Hospital, 3100 Douglas Road, Coral Gables, tel: (305) 445-8461.
Columbia Aventura Hospital, 20900 Biscayne Boulevard, Aventura, tel: (305) 682-7000.
Jackson Memorial Hospital, 1611 NW 12th Avenue, tel: (305) 325-7429.
Mercy Hospital, 3663 S Miami Avenue, Coconut Grove, tel: (305) 854-4400.
South Shore Hospital, 630 Alton Road, Miami Beach, tel: (305) 672-2100.

CLINICS

Around the Clock Medical Services, 1380 Miami Gardens Drive, North Miami Beach, tel: (305) 940-9300.
Today's Woman Medical Center, 3250 S Dixie Highway, Coconut Grove, tel: (305) 441-0304.
Miami Beach Medical Center, 1540 Washington Avenue, Miami Beach, tel: (305) 532-4122.

HEALTH HAZARDS

Sunburn
Severe cases of sunburn are common among visitors and have been known to ruin many a Miami vacation. The glare from the azure seas and white sands increases the sun's intensity. Use a sunscreen lotion for safety even while bathing or on cloudy days, especially the first few days in town.

Insects

During the summer months mosquitoes can be a nuisance. Sand-flies – or "no-see-ums," as locals call them – will bite you at the beach in the evening. Insect repellent will help protect against both. Also, beware of fire ants – tiny red ants that live in mounds of dirt in grassy areas – which can inflict painful stings that will occasionally cause an allergic reaction.

Safety by the Seaside

Most people will enjoy a completely trouble-free time on the beach, but there are dangers to be aware of.

Sunburn: this tops the danger list; you should tan slowly and stay out of the midday sun.

Sea currents: the waters off Miami are not dangerous as a rule, but you can encounter rough surf and strong currents. Most deaths occur when exhausted swimmers drown after trying to swim against a riptide or undertow. Riptides are the cause of 80 percent of lifeguard rescues in the US. If caught in either, do not panic and do not swim against the current.

Marine life: if you brush against a jellyfish in the water, you will receive only a short-lived sting. But stingrays, which move close to shore in August and September to mate, can deliver a very nasty sting. Seek medical help if the barb stays in the skin.

All popular beaches have lifeguards, who can advise on conditions. There is also a flag warning system:

- green: good swimming conditions.
- yellow: caution.
- red: danger from currents, winds or lightning.
- blue: hazardous marine life (e.g. jellyfish).

Getting Around

Orientation

Except for the Art Deco District, Miami is not a walking city. That is, the areas of interest are so far apart that motorized transportation is usually required to travel from one to another. Good detailed maps are available at most bookstores, news-stands and gas stations. Hitchhiking is illegal.

Public Transportation

BUSES

The **Metrobus** system that operates throughout Miami-Dade County services 200,000 riders a day on 65 routes. The fare is $1.25 a person. Hours of operation depend on the route, but are generally from 5.30am–11pm. For information telephone (305) 770-3131. For maps of the system telephone (305) 654-6586.

TRAINS

Metromover and Metrorail

Metromover, an elevated, Disney-like electric train that locals call the "People Mover," has an inner loop, which circles a 26-block area of downtown Miami, and an outer loop, which covers the same area but also branches off to serve Brickell Avenue in the south and the Omni Mall in the north. Its fun ride offers dramatic – at times breathtaking – views of the city's bustling center. The system operates 5.30am–midnight on the inner loop and 5.30am–10.30pm on the outer loop. The 25-cent fare is a bargain.

Metromover's big sister is Metrorail, which serves stations on a 21-mile (34-km) arc that connects southwest and northwest Miami with the heart of downtown. The service links up with Metromover at two stations, Government Center and Brickell. The fare is $1.25 and exact change in quarters is required.

Transfers to Metromover are free. Hours of operation are 5.30am–midnight, with special hours to accommodate festivals and special events.

The Electrowave

The Electrowave is an air-conditioned, electric-powered shuttle bus serving South Beach only. The buses run from 8am–2am Mon–Wed and from 8am–4am Thur–Sat, and go to and fro on a route that takes in Lincoln Road, Washington Avenue and 5th Street. The shuttles have disabled access, and the fare is just 25 cents.

WATER TAXIS

Little boats known as water taxis take passengers on two main routes. The first runs from Bayside Marketplace to Fifth Street Marina in South Beach, costing $7 one way. The second serves various points on the downtown waterfront, Watson and Fisher Islands, the Port of Miami and a couple of stops up the Miami River. This one costs $3.50 one way. Both run daily from 10am to 11pm.

TAXIS

Taxis in Miami tend to be expensive. You usually have to call in advance for a pick up; your hotel will normally do this for you. Don't try to hail one in the street; it won't stop.

Metro Taxicab, tel: (305) 888-8888.

Society Cab, tel: (305) 757-5523.

Tropical Taxicab,
tel: (305) 945-1025.
Yellow Cab,
tel: (305) 444-4444.

LIMOUSINES

Limousine service is available by
the hour or day.
Club Limousine Service,
tel: (305) 893-9850.
Limousines of South Florida,
tel: (305) 940-5252.
Red Carpet Transportation,
tel: (305) 444-4635.

City Tours

All Florida Adventure Tours
tel: (305) 665-2496
Custom outdoor, nature, city, and
historical group tours.
American Sightseeing Tours
tel: (305) 688-7700
City, Art Deco, cultural, and
Everglades tours.
Deco Tours South Beach,
tel: (305) 531-4465
Art Deco, historic, and cultural tours.
Art Deco District Tours
1001 Ocean Drive, Miami Beach
tel: (305) 531-3484
A walking tour from the Miami
Design Preservation League –
Saturday mornings and Thursday
evenings. It highlights the
architecture of this historic district.
**Historical Museum of Southern
Florida**
101 W Flagler Street
tel: (305) 375-1492
With the assistance of a local
historian, the museum offers walking
tours of several Miami
neighborhoods. Times vary. Call for
information.
Biscayne Helicopters
Tamiami Airport
tel: (305) 252-3883
Customized (thus pricey) aerial
tours.
Island Queen
tel: (305) 379-5119
This 90-passenger boat departs from
the downtown Hyatt Regency Hotel
for a tour of Miami's millionaire's row
on Biscayne Bay. Daily departures on
the hour from 11am to 7pm.

Car Rental Agencies

Alamo
US (800) 327-9633
International +1 (954) 522-0000
www.alamo.com
Avis
US (800) 831-2847
International +1 (918) 664-4600
www.avis.com
Budget
US (800) 527-0700
International +1 (305) 871-3053
www.budget.com

Dollar
US (800) 800-4000
International +1 (813) 887-5507
www.dollar.com
Hertz
US (800) 654-3131
International +1 (405) 749-4424
www.hertz.com
National
US (800) 227-7368
International +1 (612) 830 2345
www.nationalcar.com

Miami Nice Excursions
18090 Collins Avenue, Sunny Isles
Beach
tel: (305) 949-9180
Daily scheduled cultural, historical,
Art Deco, Everglades and Keys
tours.

Driving

Rental cars can be picked up at
the airport or you can have the
car delivered to your hotel the
following day (see Security
and Crime, page 281).
   Cars are a relatively inexpensive
and desirable way to see the city.
Models range from modest
economy cars to limousines
and luxury convertibles.

Conditions

Most rental agencies require that
you are at least 21 years old
(sometimes 25), have a valid
driver's license and a major credit
card. Some will take a cash deposit
in lieu of a credit card, but this
might be as high as $500.
Travelers from some foreign
countries may need to produce
an international driver's license
from their own country.

Drink Driving

Florida has some of the toughest
laws in the US against drink
driving. The maximum level
permitted is so small that you
are advised to drink no alcohol
at all if driving.

Arrangements

Visitors wishing to rent a car after
arriving in Miami will find offices of
all the main US firms at the airport
and in town. Rates are cheap both
by US and international standards,
but you should shop around for the
best rates and features. Smaller
local rental firms outside the airport
are often less expensive than the
national companies, but be sure
to check the insurance coverage
provisions before signing anything.

Speed Limits

American states set their own
speed limits. In Florida they are:
● 55–70 miles (90–112 km) per
  hour on highways.
● 20–30 miles (32–48 km) per
  hour in residential areas.
● 15 miles (24 km) per hour
  near schools.
Limits change suddenly and for
only short distances so pay
attention to signs. The Highway
Patrol is good at enforcing limits
with radar monitors, including
minimum speeds: signs along
interstates sometimes oblige
motorists to drive at over
40 miles (64 km) per hour.

   If you are traveling from
overseas, it is normally cheaper to
arrange car hire in advance. Check
with your airline, bus or rail agent or
travel agent for package deals that
include a car, since rental rates can
be reduced by about 50 percent if
you buy a so-called "fly-drive" deal.

However, be wary of offers of "free" car hire, which do not include extras like tax and insurance.

Insurance

Be sure to check that your car rental agreement includes Loss Damage Waiver (LDW), also known as Collision Damage Waiver (CDW). Without it, you will be liable for any damage done to your vehicle in the event of an accident, regardless of whether or not you were to blame. You are advised to pay for supplementary liability insurance on top of the standard third party insurance. Insurance and tax charges combined can add $35 to each day's rental.

Driving Tips

Try to avoid the main highways, Interstate 95, 826, 836 and US 1, during rush hours. Parking signs should be strictly followed. Many parts of South Beach have parking limited to residents only. Be warned: cars may be towed. Yellow curbs usually indicate a "No Parking Zone". Many areas use meters or ticket machines. Remember you can turn right on a red light, unless a sign indicates otherwise, but you have to come to a complete stop first. For driving safety see Security and Crime, page 281.

Bicycle and Scooter Rental

For information on bicycle or scooter rentals contact:
Grove Cycle
3216 Grand Avenue
Coconut Grove
tel: (305) 444-5415.
Mangrove Bicycle Rentals
260 Crandon Park Boulevard
Key Biscayne
tel: (305) 361-5555.

Where to Stay

Hotels

Accommodation in Miami ranges from chi-chi romantic hotel suites to the standard major chain hotel rooms, with hundreds of options to choose from. Prices run from $60 to $500 (and higher) per night and discounts are given for weekly rates. Reservations should be made in advance. Rates vary from the winter high season to the off season of May–June and September–October. Hotels add an additional 5 percent on top of the 6.5 percent state sales tax on all rooms rented in Miami-Dade County, and an additional 2 percent tax on all food and beverages sold.

MIAMI

Miami Beach
Astor
956 Washington Avenue
tel: (305) 531 8081,
(800) 270 4981.
Understated stylishness is the hallmark of this trendy Deco hotel. Bedrooms – mostly suites – and their wall-to-wall marble bathrooms come in muted creams and beiges. The pool is striking, and Astor Place

Price Categories

There is no official rating system for Miami hotels. The price bands given here apply for the cheapest double room in high season (winter). In the summer, rates can drop by as much as half.
$$$ = over $200.
$$ = $100–200.
$ = under $100.

is one of South Beach's top restaurants. **$$$**
Avalon & Majestic
700 Ocean Drive
tel: (305) 538 0133.
Two of the cheaper, simpler Deco hotels on Ocean Drive – run as a single operation. Bedrooms are rather garish and dated, but in the Avalon there is a fun bar with a mermaid mural, and a good long-standing restaurant, A Fish Called Avalon. Rates are slightly lower in The Majestic next door. **$$**
Brigham Gardens Guesthouse
1411 Collins Avenue
tel: (305) 531 1331.
Charming owner-run and homely little complex of 1930s buildings. Bedrooms are jolly and arty, and vary considerably in size according to price. The best feature is the large tropical garden, with its exotic caged birds. **$**
Cardozo
1300 Ocean Drive
tel: (305) 535 6500,
(800) 782 6500.
Owned by Gloria Estefan, a Streamline Moderne Art Deco masterpiece that is bathed in purple neon at night. A lively bar, seductive dining terrace, and eye-catching bedrooms with hardwood floors, iron beds and zebra-striped furniture. **$$**
Casa Grande
834 Ocean Drive
tel: (305) 672-7003;
fax: (305) 673-3669.
Stunning, tropically decorated suites with original art, mahogany beds, other Indonesian furniture and full kitchens. The service is without fault. **$$$**
Cavalier
1320 Ocean Drive
tel: (305) 351 8800,
(800) OUTPOST.
More sedate Art Deco sister hotel to the Leslie (see below), where you need to go to eat and drink (there is no bar or restaurant here). Period décor, gingham bedspreads and batik fabrics decorate bedrooms, which come with goodies such as CD players and disposable cameras in mini-bars. **$$**

Delano
1685 Collins Avenue
tel: (305) 672 2000,
(800) 555 5001.
Dubbed America's coolest hotel, this high-rise late-Deco block has been turned into a postmodern tour de force by the famous New York entrepreneur Ian Schrager and French designer Philippe Starck. A catwalk of a lobby, a chic palm-fringed pool and clinically white minimalist bedrooms. **$$$**

Essex House
1001 Collins Avenue
tel: (305) 534 2700,
(800) 553 7739.
With porthole windows and a neon tower for a funnel, this classic, salmon-pink Deco hotel has nautical echoes. It has recently undergone a faithful restoration, and is refreshingly unflashy inside. **$$**

Fontainebleau Hilton Resort and Spa
4441 Collins Avenue
tel: (305) 538-2000;
fax: (305) 34-7821.
Probably Miami Beach's most famous hotel, this classy, extensively renovated 1950s landmark has every amenity you can imagine and one of the best swimming pools in Miami. **$$$**

The Hotel
801 Collins Avenue
tel: (305) 531 2222.
American fashion designer Todd Oldham has turned the former Art Deco Tiffany Hotel into a glamourous pad that is utterly different from the competition. Instead of garish Deco colors, he has chosen soothing blues, greens and yellows, and instead of paintings there are mirrors – ideal for the hotel's model-world clientele. Disarmingly informal staff in tie-dyed shirts, and a slick rooftop pool. **$$$**

Indian Creek Hotel
2727 Indian Creek Drive
tel: (305) 531 2727,
(800) 491 2772.
An Art Deco timewarp built in 1936: unlike most of its competitors, it's decorated throughout with original period furniture. It also has a lovely secluded garden and pool, but its

location – a few blocks north of South Beach – is a drawback. **$$**

Kent
1131 Collins Avenue
tel: (305) 531 8800,
(800) OUTPOST.
One of the best-value SoBe hotels. A trendy lobby (hip-hop music, burning joss-sticks), small but good-quality bedrooms, and a lovely jungle-like garden. **$$**

Leslie
1244 Ocean Drive
tel: (305) 531 8800,
(800) OUTPOST.
Everything at this Deco hotel is garish and fun – from the yellow façade to the pink, tangerine and lavender hues of the bedrooms. Gold discs and portraits of rock'n'roll greats adorn the lobby. **$$**

Loews Miami Beach Hotel
1601 Collins Avenue
tel: (305) 604 1601.
This luxury 800-room giant of a hotel, which opened in 1998, occupies a new tower and a restored Deco block. Bedrooms are ordinary, but there is a fantastic pool, every conceivable facility, a children's club and direct beach access. Popular with conventioneers. **$$$**

Marlin
1200 Collins Avenue
tel: (305) 531 8800,
(800) OUTPOST.
This much photographed lilac-colored Art Deco building houses a very hip all-suite hotel and recording studios (U2 and Aerosmith have made albums here). Rooms are high tech and have outlandish "Afro-urban" décor (a combination of exotic furniture and stainless-steel kitchens). The Opium Den bar often has live music in the evenings. **$$$**

National
1677 Collins Avenue
tel: (305) 532 2311,
(800) 327 8370.
Recently restored landmark Art Deco tower with SoBe's most stunning hotel pool (pencil thin and nearly 70 yards/meters long). Rooms in the main building are understated, while those with terraces overlooking the pool are tropically themed. **$$$**

Park Central
640 Ocean Drive
tel: (305) 538 1611.
This lilac and purple confection is one of South Beach's least snooty Deco hotels. It has 1930s furniture in the bedrooms and an original terrazzo floor in the lobby. **$$**

Park Washington
1020 Washington Avenue
tel: (305) 532-1930;
fax: (305) 672-6706.
This group of four Deco hotels under one ownership is a modest but pleasant option. **$**

Pelican
826 Ocean Drive
tel: (305) 673 3373.
The wackiest hotel in South Beach. Each tongue-in-cheek bedroom in the Fifties motel is like a movie set: Psychedelic(ate) Girl could be from an *Austin Powers* film, Best Whorehouse from a spoof Western. The suites (the Penthouse has a bank of nine TV screens, giant fish tank and Jacuzzi on its giant terrace) are celebrity territory. **$$$**

The Tides
1220 Ocean Drive
tel: (305) 531 8800,
(800) OUTPOST.
The sleek white oceanfront block contains a small luxury hotel

Chain Hotels

These chain hotels are represented in the Miami area. Call or check out the websites for information:
Best Western: (800) 528-1234.
www.bestwestern.com
Days Inns of America: (800) 325-2525.
www.daysinn.com
Hilton: (800) HILTONS.
www.hilton.com
Holiday Inn: (800) HOLIDAY.
www.basshotels.com/holiday-inn
Hyatt: (800) 228-9000.
www.hyatt.com
Marriott: (800) 228-9290.
www.marriott.com
Radisson: (800) 333-3333.
www.radisson.com
Sheraton: (800) 325-3535.
www.sheraton.com

of immaculate taste. The giant, minimalist bedrooms are really special. As well as a CD player, cordless phone and cheeky postcards with the message, "Let's make love at The Tides", each has uninterrupted views of the ocean and the beach, with telescopes to spy on sunbathers. Also a good-sized swimming pool. **$$$**

Beaches North
Bal Harbour Sheraton
9701 Collins Avenue
Bal Harbour
tel: (305) 865-7511;
fax: (305) 864-2601.
A full service luxury hotel on the beach, featuring several restaurants indoors and out, situated across the street from the chi-chi Bal Harbour Shops. A favorite spot for VIPs visiting the area. **$$$**
Bay Harbor Inn
9601 E Bay Harbor Drive
Bay Harbor Islands
tel: (305) 868-4141;
fax: (305) 867-9094.
Situated beside Indian Creek, this is a pleasantly petite surprise among the area's big, brooding hotels. It has two excellent restaurants and several more in the neighborhood. **$$**
Beach House
9449 Collins Avenue
Surfside
tel: (305) 865-3551,
(800) 695-8284;
fax: (305) 861-6596.
Be in the lap of luxury away from the hubbub of South Beach yet just a short walk from the Bal Harbour Shops. This is the latest of the Rubell family's hotels. You'll feel like you've escaped to a serene Caribbean island. **$$$**
Best Western Oceanfront Resort
9365 Collins Avenue
Surfside
tel: (305) 864-2232;
fax: (305) 864-3045.
A simple, newly renovated motel right on the beach and within walking distance of Surfside's restaurants and shops. **$**
Desert Inn
17201 Collins Avenue
Sunny Isles Beach

tel: (305) 947-0621;
fax: (305) 947-7933.
A sprawling, family-oriented hotel with pool, tennis courts, and oceanfront patio bar. **$**
Paradise Inn
8520 Harding Avenue
Miami Beach
tel: (305) 865-6216;
fax: (305) 865-9028.
Situated one block from the ocean with modest but well-kept rooms. **$**
Turnberry Isle Resort & Club
199999 W Country Club Drive
Aventura
tel: (305) 932-6200;
fax: (305) 933-6554.
A luxurious full-service resort with golf, tennis and lots of beautiful people to watch. Nearby is the county's biggest and best shopping mall. **$$$**

Downtown Miami
Everglades
244 Biscayne Boulevard
tel: (305) 379-5461;
fax: (305) 577-8390.
Convenient 376-room hotel in the heart of downtown, across from Bayside Marketplace, with pool and restaurants. **$$**
Hotel Inter-Continental
100 Chopin Plaza
tel: (305) 577-1000,
(800) 327-0200;
fax: (305) 577-0384.
A soaring, high-rise hotel with 639 rooms, gourmet restaurants, pool, skyline views, fitness center and jogging track on the bay in the heart of downtown Miami. **$$$**
Hyatt Regency
400 SE 2nd Avenue
tel: (305) 358-1234;
fax: (305) 358-0529.
On the north bank of the Miami River, the Hyatt is a popular and well-run downtown hotel. **$$**
Miami River Inn
118 SW South River Drive
tel: (305) 325-0045;
fax: (305) 325-9227.
Restored classic inn located right on the Miami River. The structures, built between 1906 and 1914, were returned to their original condition in the 1980s by local preservationist Sallye Jude. The four wood-frame

buildings house 40 antique-decorated guest rooms that offer a cozy slice of Miami history. **$$**
Wyndham Miami Biscayne Bay Hotel
1601 Biscayne Boulevard
tel: (305) 374-0000;
fax: (305) 374-0020.
A modern highrise hotel with easy access to public transportation to get where you need to be. **$$**

Coral Gables
The Biltmore Hotel
1200 Anastasia Avenue
tel: (305) 445-1926,
(800) 727-1926;
fax: (305) 913-3159.
A magnificent, historic hotel and resort with 278 rooms, a vast pool, fine restaurants, golf, tennis, health spa and lounge. **$$$**
Hotel Place St Michel
162 Alcazar Avenue
tel: (305) 444-1666;
fax: (305) 529-0074.
Classic small historic hotel in the middle of the Coral Gables business district with antiques galore and an elegant French restaurant. **$$**
Omni Colonnade Hotel
180 Aragon Avenue
tel: (305) 441-2600,
(800) 533-1337;
fax: (305) 445-3929.
A prestigious hotel in downtown Coral Gables with 157 rooms and a pool, shopping complex, Jacuzzi and small gym. **$$$**

Coconut Grove
Grand Bay Hotel
2669 Bayshore Drive
tel: (305) 858-9600;
fax: (305) 859-2026.
This modern building features luxurious rooms and beautiful bay views, not far from Coconut Grove's best spots. **$$$**
Hampton Inn
2800 SW 28th Terrace
tel: (305) 448-2800;
fax: (305) 442-8655.
A modern and pleasant hotel with fitness center and free breakfasts. Within walking distance of Coconut Grove's entertainment district. **$$**

Mayfair House
3000 Florida Avenue
tel: (305) 441-0000;
fax: (305) 447-9173.
A European-style luxury hotel in
the sophisticated Mayfair shopping
center. Each room has a private
terrace with a Japanese tub. **$$$**

Key Biscayne
Silver Sands Beach Resort
301 Ocean Drive
Key Biscayne
tel: (305) 361-5441;
fax: (305) 361-5477.
An intimate, peaceful setting for a
69-room hotel completely rebuilt
after the wrath of Hurricane Andrew.
Select from motel-like rooms with
fridge and coffeemaker or four
cottages with kitchen and living
room. **$$**
**Sonesta Beach Hotel
& Tennis Club**
350 Ocean Drive
Key Biscayne
tel: (305) 361-2021;
fax: (305) 361-3096.
This plush resort faces a wide
beach and has a collection of
museum-quality modern art
decorating the property. **$$$**

EXCURSIONS

The Gold Coast
The Breakers
1 S County Road
Palm Beach
tel: (561) 655-6611.
One of the grand hotels of the
1920s, this oceanfront landmark
has 572 luxurious rooms, pools,
beach, croquet, golf, tennis
and nightclub. **$$$**
Colony Hotel
525 E Atlantic Avenue
Del Ray Beach
tel: (561) 276-4123.
This recently renovated local
landmark has been here since
1926. Guests return every year,
but only in the traditional season –
the hotel is open November
through April. **$$**
Riverside Hotel
620 E Las Olas Boulevard
Fort Lauderdale

tel: (954) 467-0671,
(800) 325-3280.
Located in the downtown shopping
district, this historic hotel has 117
antique-furnished rooms, a pool,
restaurants and lounge. **$$$**

West of Miami
Ritz-Carlton Naples
280 Vanderbilt Beach Road
Naples
tel: (941) 598-3300,
(800) 241-3333.
One of the more elegant hotels on
the Gulf of Mexico, with 464 rooms,
lavish public areas, pools, chic
restaurants, tennis courts, golf
course, fitness center, sailing and
children's activities. **$$$**

Price Categories

There is no official rating
system for Miami hotels. The
price bands given here apply for
the cheapest double room in
high season (winter). In the
summer, rates can drop by as
much as half.
$$$ = over $200.
$$ = $100–200.
$ = under $100.

South Seas Plantation Resort
South Seas Plantation Road
Captiva Island
tel: (800) CAPTIVA.
A 600-room resort on the beach
with four restaurants, fishing, golf,
tennis, pools, sailing school,
children's programs and health
club. **$$$**
Sundial Beach Resort
1451 Middle Gulf Drive
Sanibel Island
tel: (800) 237-6000.
The largest all-suite hotel on the
island with glorious Gulf views, 271
suites, pools, private beach, tennis,
sailing and children's activities. **$$$**
Vanderbilt Beach Motel
9225 N Gulfshore Drive
Naples
tel: (941) 597-3144,
(800) 243-9076.
A pleasant motel right on the beach
with 50 rooms and efficiencies and
a pool. **$$**

West Wind Inn
3345 W Gulf Boulevard
Sanibel Island
tel: (800) 824-0476.
A casual resort on the Gulf of
Mexico with miles of clear, white
sand for shelling. Rooms come with
refrigerator or kitchen. Nearest
motel to wildlife refuge. **$$**

The Everglades
Flamingo Lodge
State Road 9336
Everglades National Park
tel: (941) 695-3101,
(800) 600-3813;
fax: (941) 695-3921.
A bare-bones 103-room motel
and 24 cottages with kitchens
within the National Park. Easy
access to canoeing, boating, trails
and good bird-watching. **$**
Tropical Paradise Bed & Breakfast
19801 SW 318th Street
Homestead
tel: (305) 248-4181;
fax: (305) 245-0318.
A small (one suite) and cozy home
sitting in a tropical fruit grove 10
minutes from the Everglades and
Biscayne National Parks. **$$**

The Keys
Cheeca Lodge
MM 82, Islamorada
tel: (305) 664-4651.
Its main building features vast
rooms with vast beds. Hurricane
Donna leveled the first inn on the
site in 1960, but its good beach
(a rarity in the Keys) attracted A&P
heiress "Cheechee" Twitchell to
rebuild the lodge. The lodge has
villas and a par 3 golf course that
has a green pond and more sand
than grass. **$$$**
Jules Undersea Lodge
MM103.2, Key Largo
tel: (305) 451-2353.
Experience life underwater in this
extraordinary, sub-aqua hotel. The
only underwater lodgings in the
world. **$$$**
Sunset Cove Motel
MM99. 5, Key Largo
tel: (305) 451-0705.
Traditional motel offering a taste
of Old Florida. The rooms are in
oceanfront cottages. **$–$$**

Key West
Curry Mansion Inn
511 Caroline Street
tel: (305) 294-5349,
(800) 253-3466.
A grand Victorian-style mansion
turned into a charming 28-room
inn with a pool and lush gardens.
$$
Island City House Hotel
411 William Street
tel: (305) 294-5702,
(800) 634-8230.
Off the main strip, this tropical
garden hotel has 24 suites with
kitchens, swimming pool and
Jacuzzi. **$$**
The Pier House
1 Duval Street
tel: (305) 296-4600,
This luxury resort feels like it's on
its own private island providing a
more modern setting and the
additional attraction of a private
beach (where topless sunbathing
is permitted). **$$$**
Wyndham Casa Marina
1500 Reynolds Street
tel: (305) 296-3535.
At the top end of the scale is this
Spanish Renaissance-style hotel,
one of Flagler's monuments to
luxury, now restored and catering
to a new generation of big
spenders. **$$$**

YOUTH HOSTELS

**Banana Bungalow Hotel
and International Hostel**
2360 Collins Avenue
Miami Beach
tel: (305) 538-1951;
fax: (305) 531-3217.
Situated on a canal, with a pool,
just a block from the ocean – not
bad for dormitory-style living. Private
rooms for those happy to pay (a
little) more. The 1950s building
(part of it a former gas station) fits
right in with the kitschy side of
South Beach. **$**
**The Clay Hotel and International
Hostel**
1438 Washington Avenue
Miami Beach
tel: (305) 534 2988,
(800) 379 CLAY.

This well-run hotel-cum-youth-
hostel, part of which was once
owned by Al Capone's gambling
syndicate, takes up a large chunk
of 1920s Mediterranean Revival
Española Way. Both the bedrooms
– some with shared, some with
private bathrooms – and the small
dormitories are very basic but well
maintained. **$**
Tropics Hotel & Hostel
1550 Collins Avenue
Miami Beach
tel: (305) 531-0361;
fax: (305) 531-8676.
Another clean space a block
from the beach with a choice of
dormitory or private rooms with
fridges, stoves and ceiling fans. **$**

CONDO AND HOUSE RENTALS

There are many real estate
companies in the area that
specialize in renting condominium
apartments and houses to tourists.
Lengths of stay can be anything
from a week to a year, and options
range from studio apartments to
waterfront estates. Most come fully
equipped with furnishings and
cookware; some even have maid
service. Almost all require security
deposits. For information, try:
Century 21
tel: (305) 235-2621
or (305) 264-6000.
Coconut Grove Realty
tel: (305) 448-4123.
Keyes
tel: (305) 443-7423.
Renters Paradise
tel: (305) 865-0200.

Price Categories

There is no official rating
system for Miami hotels. The
price bands given here apply for
the cheapest double room in
high season (winter). In the
summer, rates can drop by as
much as half.
$$$ = over $200.
$$ = $100–200.
$ = under $100.

CAMPING

Miami Everglades KOA
20675 SW 162nd Avenue
tel: (305) 233-5300.
Campsites for tents are about
$25 and RV hook-ups are about
$35 per night. Near Monkey
Jungle in Southern Miami.
Larry and Penny Thompson Park
operated by the Miami-Dade County
Parks and Recreation Dept, 12451
SW 184th Street
tel: (305) 232-1049.
Offers campsites, starting at about
$17 for four people. Beside Miami
Metrozoo.

Bed and Breakfasts

There are a number of smaller,
more traditional accommodation
options in Greater Miami and the
rest of South Florida. The
following agencies will point you
in the right direction:
Florida Bed and Breakfast Inns
tel: (800) 524-1880.
www.bbonline.com/fl/fbbi/
BedandBreakfast.com
www.bedandbreakfast.com
**Key West Innkeeper's
Association**
tel: (800) 492-1911.
www.keywestinns.com

Where to Eat

Restaurants

Most people agree that Miami tastes good. Along with fresh seafood, ethnic flavors are everywhere, with a heavy accent on the garlic. There are hundreds of sophisticated restaurants and hole-in-the-wall cafes that can satisfy any culinary desire. Prices range from a filling $6 dinner at a Cuban cafeteria to a $100 "fine dining experience." The free weekly newspaper *New Times* produces the best listing of local restaurants in town. Almost all restaurants accept credit cards and traveler's checks, and have designated smoking and non-smoking sections.

Price Categories

A general price guide for the restaurants:
$ = Inexpensive, dinner for two less than $40.
$$ = Moderate, dinner for two $40–80.
$$$ = Expensive, dinner for two over $80.

MIAMI

Miami Beach (South)
Au Natural Gourmet Pizza
1427 Alton Road
tel: (305) 531-0666.
Non-traditional but delicious pizza such as chicken Mexicana and pizza pesto. **$**
Balans
1022 Lincoln Road
tel: (305) 534-9191.
A London-style cafe that attracts locals with its excellent food – from the fried goat cheese and portobello appetizer through to the wonderful banana cream toffee pie for dessert. **$**
Big Pink
157 Collins Avenue
tel: (305) 531-0888.
"Real Food for Real People" is the motto – huge servings, comfort foods or something a bit more exotic if you desire. **$**
Charlotte's Chinese Kitchen
1403 Washington Avenue
tel: (305) 672-8338.
Light and tasty Hong Kong and Szechuan specialties with great egg rolls. **$**
CHOW
210 23rd Street
tel: (305) 604-1468.
A fresh take on Asian and tropical cuisine as they meld in a funky setting. Try the innovative key lime pie with a candy-like sesame and peanut coating. **$**
11th Street Diner
1065 Washington Avenue
tel: (305) 534-6373.
Here you can eat in a classic Art Deco diner with typical American diner fare from milkshakes to burgers and fries, except this one has a bar. Check out the blue plate specials. Open 24/7. **$**
Jeffrey's
1629 Michigan Avenue
tel: (305) 673-0690.
Traditional bistro fare but always good. French onion soup, crab cakes, succulent steak. **$$**
Joe's Stone Crab
11 Washington Avenue
tel: (305) 673-0365.
Miami's best-known restaurant. The stone crabs are delicious but the wait is always long (and no reservations allowed). Serves lunch and dinner Tue–Sun but no lunch Mondays. Open mid-Oct–mid-May. **$$$**
Mrs Mendoza's Tacos Al Carbon
1040 Alton Road
tel: (305) 535-0808.
If you need a quick bite, this fast but delicious Mexican eatery will fit the bill. Fat burritos, fresh crispy tortilla chips all served with the best cilantro-rich salsa. Help yourself at the big bowls of mild, medium or hot sauce. **$**

Nemo Restaurant
100 Collins Avenue
tel: (305) 532-4550.
A splashy, ornate place with a raw metal decor and first-rate *nouvelle cuisine* with an Asian flair, such as salmon wrapped around alfalfa sprouts and spicy Vietnamese beef salad. **$$$**
Pacific Time
915 Lincoln Road
tel: (305) 534-5979.
Elegant, Pacific Rim style with tropical tastes including tempura catfish, Chinese duck with plum sauce and tempura sweet potatoes. **$$$**
The Palace
1200 Ocean Drive
tel: (305) 531-9077.
Soups, salads, sandwiches, and general light and healthy fare. **$**
Puerto Sagua
700 Collins Avenue
tel: (305) 673-1115.
Large and loud but comfortable and good. Abundant choices of Cuban dishes served in enormous portions. Great for a late snack, open until 2am. **$**
Tap Tap
819 5th Street
tel: (305) 672-2898.
Enjoy great Haitian food in a setting that feels like you've just walked into a canvas come to life. Every inch of the place is painted in vivid color, from the walls to the tables to the floors. Have a rum punch at the bar and it's easy to imagine you're on the islands. **$**
Toni's New Tokyo Cuisine & Sushi Bar
1208 Washington Avenue
tel: (305) 673-9368.
A fashion-conscious setting with excellent teriyaki beef, sushi, and miso soup. **$$**
Wish
801 Collins Avenue
tel: (305) 674-9474.
Headliner chef brings you inventive delights from grilled quail appetizer to portobello mushrooms layered with Yukon Gold mashed potatoes. The Todd Oldham-designed restaurant is in South Beach's trendy The Hotel. **$$$**

Wolfies
2038 Collins Avenue
tel: (305) 538-6626.
A local Jewish deli with corned beef sandwiches, matzo ball soup and luscious cheesecake. **$**

World Resources
719 Lincoln Road
tel: (305) 535-8987.
A combination Japanese and Thai restaurant with excellent *pad thai* and a daily happy hour. **$**

Yuca
501 Lincoln Road
tel: (305) 532-9822.
Trendy, new-wave Cuban cooking with guava-basted ribs, coconut-curry rice, and plantains stuffed with beef, plus entertainment. **$$$**

Miami Beach (Middle)
Arnie and Richie's
525 41st Street
tel: (305) 531-7691.
Overstuffed pastrami sandwiches, tart coleslaw, smoked whitefish, and every deli delight imaginable. **$**

The Forge
432 41st Street
tel: (305) 538-8533.
Grand and a bit gaudy, but a local institution with five-pound lobsters and succulent steaks. **$$$**

Oasis Cafe
976 41st Street
tel: (305) 674-7676.
Adventurous, flavorful Middle Eastern cuisine with new dishes along with the familiar. Roasted vegetable lasagne, Mediterranean salad, falafel, etc. **$**

Miami Beach (North)
Café Prima Pasta
414 71st Street
tel: (305) 867-0106.
There are several Argentinian/Italian restaurants around but this is the best. The food is fresh and tasty. Dine outdoors in North Beach's hippest spot. **$**

Katana
920 71st Street
tel: (305) 864-0037.
Plates of fresh sushi float by. Just grab what suits your fancy. The plates are color-coded and the waitress adds up what you've consumed when you're done. **$**

Las Vacas Gordas
933 71st Street
tel: (305) 867-1717.
A neighborhood grill – *parillada* – like you're in Buenos Aires. Think meat, lots of it, as you dine amid the pleasant scent of burning wood. Also good vegetable side dishes. **$**

Lemon Twist
908 71st Street
tel: (305) 868-2075.
An elegant and cool atmosphere sets the scene for a Mediterranean dining experience. Fabulous gazpacho, lobster ravioli, salmon lasagne, *beignet de legumes* and, if you're lucky, some lemon liqueur will be sent over, compliments of the management! **$$**

Price Categories

A general price guide for the restaurants:
$ = Inexpensive, dinner for two less than $40.
$$ = Moderate, dinner for two $40–80.
$$$ = Expensive, dinner for two over $80.

Northern Beaches
Café Ragazzi
9500 Harding Avenue
Surfside
tel: (305) 866-4495.
There's always a line to get into this friendly trattoria because the traditional Italian fare is consistently good and reasonably priced. **$**

Caffè Da Vinci
1009 Kane Concourse
Bay Harbor Islands
tel: (305) 861-8166.
Brought to you by the same folks as Oggi, this elegant trattoria makes you feel like you've just walked into a neighborhood restaurant in Rome. Everything is good from the ricotta and spinach *agnolotti* to the fresh seafood specialties to the delicious, airy tiramisu. **$$**

Christine Lee's
17082 Collins Avenue
Miami Beach
tel: (305) 947-1717.
Delicious Canton, Szechwan and Mandarin dishes. **$$**

Islands Cafe
9601 E Bay Harbor Drive
Bay Harbor Islands
tel: (305) 868-414.
A waterfront restaurant where you enjoy the fruits of labor of culinary institute students from Johnson & Wales University. Exotic dishes such as sesame-seared tuna with buckwheat noodle salad won't disappoint. Sunday brunch is a local favorite. **$$**

Oggi Cafe
1740 79th Street Causeway
North Bay Village
tel: (305) 866-1238.
Gourmet fetuccine, tortelloni, ravioli – every pasta dish imaginable. **$$**

Palm Restaurant
9650 E Bay Harbor Drive
Bay Harbor Islands
tel: (305) 868-7256.
Be prepared to open your wallets wide when visiting this famous steakhouse, known for enormous cuts of meat and lobsters four pounds and up. **$$$**

Sushi Republic
9583 Harding Avenue
Surfside
tel: (305) 867-8036.
Consistently rated the best sushi in South Florida in a friendly, calm setting. **$**

Downtown
Bubba Gump Shrimp Company
401 Biscayne Boulevard
tel: (305) 379-8866.
American food, shrimp and other specialties. At Bayside Marketplace. **$$**

East Coast Fisheries
360 W Flagler Avenue
tel: (305) 372-1300.
Overlooking the Miami River makes the seafood taste even better. Ultra fresh and expansive choice of fish; try jumbo shrimp stuffed with artichoke and crab. **$$**

Fishbone Grille
650 S Miami Avenue
tel: (305) 530-1915.
Wonderful seafood blackened, sautéed or grilled. **$$**

Garcia's Seafood Grille & Fish Market
398 NW North River Drive
tel: (305) 375-0765.

A down-to-earth fish house perched on the Miami River with fresh seafood, grilled, blackened or fried, in sandwiches, salads or on its own. **$**

Indigo
100 Chopin Plaza
tel: (305) 372-4494.
Set in the lobby in the Hotel Inter-Continental, with a South Florida flair, the menu features classic Americana cuisine and a great wine selection. **$$$**

Joe's Seafood
400 NW North River Drive
tel: (305) 374-5637.
Friendly fish-house on the Miami River with several resident cats. Fresh fish can be chosen from the ice and prepared to order. **$**

Los Ranchos
401 Biscayne Boulevard
tel: (305) 375-0666.
Tender steaks served with a variety of garlic and pepper sauces. **$$**

Perricone's Marketplace
15 SE 10th Street
tel: (305) 374-9449.
A rustic atmosphere accompanies the fresh, home-made Italian food.**$**

Porcao
801 S Bayshore Drive
tel: (305) 373-2777.
Where Brazilians go when they want Brazilian food – enough said. Features a gourmet buffet. **$$**

S&S Restaurant
1757 NE 2nd Avenue
tel: (305) 373-4291.
Serves up home-cooked fare – think meat loaf and mashed potatoes, fried fish and cucumber salad – at down-to-earth prices, a real Miami institution. **$**

Little Havana & Little Managua
Blue Sky Food By the Pound
3803 W Flagler Street.and 8 other locations throughout the county.
Join the locals at this smorgasbord of hearty Cuban food. Buy as little or as much as you want. Eat in the un-fancy space or take-out and enjoy a picnic somewhere more picturesque. **$**

Casa Juancho
2436 8th Street
tel: (305) 642-2452.
Bustles with young upwardly mobile Cuban-Americans looking for a

quality meal in a Spanish-flavored setting. Voted best Spanish restaurant in Miami for 10 years. **$$$**

Guayacan
1933 SW 8th Street
tel: (305) 649-2015.
Excellent Nicaraguan cuisine in a comfortable setting with good service. Get some grilled meat and slather on the *chimichurri* – a parsley and oil sauce. Try the *sopa* of the day – hearty home-made soups. **$**

Hy-Vong
3458 SW 8th Street
tel: (305) 446-3674.
A small and often crowded spot, but well worth the wait for authentic Vietnamese specialties. **$**

Islas Canarias
285 NW 27th Avenue
tel: (305) 649-0440.
Another extremely popular spot, offering fast service and some of the best Cuban cooking in the neighborhood. **$**

Latin American Cafeteria
2740 SW 27th Avenue and 2940 Coral Way, and several other locations around town.
Specializes in Cuban sandwiches and basic, good Cuban fare. **$**

Los Ranchos
125 SW 107th Avenue
tel: (305) 221-9367 (6 locations).
Nicaraguan steak house with much more. Ceviche, shrimp, rice and beans, all satisfying. **$$**

Versailles
3555 SW 8th Street
tel: (305) 444-0240.
Go here to feel the pulse of the Cuban community. Traditional Cuban fare at its heartiest. End the meal with a hit of Cuban coffee at the sidewalk window. **$**

Coral Gables
Café Abbracci
318 Aragon Avenue
tel: (305) 441-0700.
Part art gallery, part Italian restaurant. House specials include gnocchi, linguine and clam sauce, and rich pastries. **$$**

Christy's
3101 Ponce de Leon Boulevard
tel: (305) 446-1400.

American classics with an emphasis on massive cuts of beef and an upwardly mobile clientele. **$$$**

Darbar
276 Alhambra Circle
tel: (305) 448-9691.
Authentic Indian specialties – lamb and basmati rice, stewed lentils, and hot curries. **$$**

John Martin's
253 Miracle Mile
tel: (305) 445-3777.
An old-fashioned Irish emporium with steaks, stews, and poached salmon. **$$**

La Bussola
270 Giralda Avenue
tel: (305) 445-8783.
Formal and well-polished with fine Northern Italian cuisine. **$$$**

La Palme D'Or
1200 Anastasia Avenue
tel: (305) 445-1926.
This Biltmore Hotel restaurant hosts a different Michelin-rated chef the first week of each month and the cuisine by the full-time French chef is just as delicious. **$$$**

Miss Saigon
146 Giralda Avenue
tel: (305) 446-8006.
Delicous and beautiful Vietnamese food is presented in this very welcoming family-run restaurant – if you can stand the wait. **$**

Norman's
21 Almeria Avenue
tel: (305) 446-6767.
Award-winning chef and cookbook author Norman Van Aiken showcases his exquisite New World cuisine in a place always ranked among South Florida's top eateries. **$$$**

Sakura
440 S Dixie Highway
tel: (305) 665-7020.
Friendly sushi bar with great Japanese entrées. **$$**

Coconut Grove
Anokha
3195 Commodore Plaza
tel: (786) 552-1030.
Indian cuisine presented with subtle yet intricate flavors. Spicy chicken vindaloo and lamb and potato stew in coconut sauce. **$$**

Baleen
4 Grove Isle Drive
tel: (305) 857-5007.
Chosen as the best eatery in Coconut Grove by the *Miami New Times*, this upscale seafood restaurant is worth every penny. The elegant outdoor terrace sits on Biscayne Bay. **$$$**

Bice
2669 Bayshore Drive
tel: (305) 858-9600.
Classic Italian cuisine shares the menu with international dishes in this restaurant belonging to the Milan-based chain. **$$$**

Chart House
51 Chart House Drive
tel: (305) 856-9741.
Friendly service in an elegant marina setting with grilled seafood and an enormous salad bar. **$$**

Franz & Josephs
3145 Commodore Plaza
tel: (305) 448-2282.
Continental fare, warm ambiance and great service come your way with Franz out front and Joseph overseeing the kitchen. Leave room for his homemade desserts. **$$**

Fuddrucker's
3444 Main Highway
tel: (305) 442-8164.
Some say it's Miami's best burger. Informal atmosphere overlooking a lively street, huge make-it-yourself hamburgers and real French fries. **$**

La Gloria Taqueria Mexicana
2957 Florida Avenue
tel: (305) 448-9505.
Down home Mexican cooking in a friendly place. Try the *antojitos*, an appetizer sampler. **$**

Greenstreet Cafe
3110 Commodore Plaza
tel: (305) 567-0662.
Watch the world glide by at this pleasant outdoor cafe in the heart of the Grove. **$**

Mambo Cafe
3105 Commodore Plaza
tel: (305) 448-2768.
This bustling Grove corner is a great place to dine on Cuban favorites. **$**

Key Biscayne
Rusty Pellican
3201 Rickenbacker Causeway
tel: (305) 361-3818.

Good Florida seafood with one of the most beautiful waterfront views in town. Sunset is exquisite. **$$**

Northern Miami
Chef Allen's
19088 NE 29th Avenue
Aventura
tel: (305) 935-2900.
An award-winning New World eatery with such innovative creations as Caribbean antipasto, jerk calamari, and swordfish sprinkled with sun-dried fruit. **$$$**

Detante Restaurant
215 NE 82nd Street
North Miami
tel: (305) 758-0038.
Haitian fare in a neighborly spot. Try *griot* – fried pork, lamb – sautéed conch, chicken or goat accompanied by fried plantains and rice and beans. **$**

The Gourmet Diner
13951 Biscayne Boulevard
North Miami
tel: (305) 947-2255.
A diner serving French cuisine – beef burgundy, trout almondine and homemade pastries. **$**

Il Tulipano
11052 Biscayne Boulevard
North Miami
tel: (305) 893-4811.
A virtual pasta paradise with an extensive wine list. **$$$**

Paquito's
16265 Biscayne Boulevard
North Miami Beach
tel: (305) 947-5027.
Colorful Mexican restaurant with good guacamole, tortilla soup and frozen margaritas. **$**

Siam River
3455 NE 163rd Street
North Miami Beach

tel: (305) 945-8079.
Traditional Thai food with a sushi bar thrown in. Enjoy your shrimp and coconut soup or *pad thai* sitting at a table with chairs or reclining around a low table surrounded with pillows. **$**

Soyka
5556 Biscayne Boulevard
tel: (305) 759-3117.
A noisy, funky restaurant brings life to this residential neighborhood and solid bistro selections. **$$**

Suzanne's Vegetarian Bistro
7251 Biscayne Boulevard
tel: (305) 758-5859.
Wholesome and healthy vegetarian food meets gourmet cuisine in this vegan spot. **$**

EXCURSIONS

Fort Lauderdale
Burt & Jack's
Port Everglades Terminal 23
tel: (954) 522-5225.
Worth the trek 2 miles (3 km) through industrial cargo operations, Burt & Jack's offers romantic waterfront dining in a mission-style setting. Nearby is a warm-water outfall where tropical fish and pelicans mass for handouts, in winter joined by the endangered manatee, a mammal known as a sea cow. **$$$**

East City Grill
505 N Fort Lauderdale Beach Boulevard
tel: (954) 565-5569.
An oceanfront hang-out for local trendies, featuring Asian and Caribbean specialties such as goat's-cheese dumplings and curried chicken. Menu changes daily. **$$**

Himmershee Bar & Grill
210 SW 2nd Street
tel: (954) 524-1818.
Run by two graduates of the Mark's Las Olas school of cooking. For starters try plantain *empanadas* stuffed with curried lamb to duck confit over golden raisin polenta.**$$**

Indigo
620 E Las Olas Boulevard
tel: (954) 467-0671.
Pan-Asian here means Malaysia, Indonesia, and Singapore. The

breezy décor outside the Riverside Hotel is a pleasant setting for taste treats such as the *naan* pizza with roasted eggplant, garlic, curried tomato, and pine nuts or tuna marinated in coconut milk. **$$**

Mark's Las Olas
1032 E Las Olas Boulevard
tel: (954) 463-1000.
One of the finest restaurants in the city, Mark's is known all over South Florida for its New Florida cuisine, with dishes like crispy squid, sesame dolphin, marinated quail and lump crab cakes. The menu changes daily. **$$$**

Lighthouse Point
Cap's Place
2765 NE 28th Court
tel: (954) 941-0418).
Dine at a restaurant that can only be reached by boat. Here you get a taste of local history with your seafood. It's Broward's oldest restaurant but nothing has been changed over the years. It was frequented by Churchill and FDR during World War II. Catch the boat at the dock next to the Lighthouse Point Yacht Basin and Marina. Call for directions. Reservations are strongly suggested. **$$**

Palm Beach
Charley's Crab
456 South Ocean Boulevard
tel: (561) 659-1500.
Just across from the beach, this elegant seafood house offers a good selection of grilled fish, broiled lobster, steamed shrimp, and sumptuous salads. **$$$**

Green's Pharmacy
151 N County Road
tel: (561) 832-0304.
Amid all the fancy restaurants, this neighborhood pharmacy offers low-priced homestyle breakfast and lunch. No dinner. **$**

Taboo
221 Worth Avenue
tel: (561) 835-3500.
Complete with a fireplace and warm, Southwestern charm, this trendy eatery features healthy, low-calorie California meals such as marinated tuna, goat's cheese pizza and lots of fresh salads. **$$**

TooJay's
313 Royal Poinciana Way
tel: (561) 659-7232.
A classic Jewish delicatessen with a bit of California style. Serves thick pastrami sandwiches, matzo ball soup, potato pancakes, and a very rich chocolate cake. **$**

Naples
Villa Pescatore & Truffles
8920 N Tamiami Trail
tel: (941) 597-8119.
A romantic linen-and-candlelight spot featuring Northern Italian dishes like linguine with salmon and duck in sage sauce. **$$$**

Sanibel Island
Jean-Paul's French Corner
708 Tarpon Bay Road
tel: (941) 472-1493.
French food from salmon to duck is served in a French cafe style ambiance. **$$**

Key Largo
Crack'd Conch
MM 105
tel: (305) 451-0732.
An old clapboard dining room with a porch that serves seafood specialties like fried alligator, conch chowder, grilled fish and over 80 brands of beer. **$**

Makoto Japanese Restaurant
MM 101.6
tel: (305) 451-7083.
Along with Pacific seafood dishes, this eatery serves local fish Japanese style, vegetable tempura and chicken teriyaki. **$$**

Mrs Mac's Kitchen
MM 99.4
tel: (305) 451-3722.
A tacky but lots-of-fun locals' joint that serves meatloaf on Monday, Chef's choice on Tuesday, Italian on Wednesday, and seafood Thursday through Saturday. Closed Sunday. **$**

Islamorada
The Green Turtle Inn
MM 81.5
tel: (305) 664-9031.
A Keys tradition since 1947, step back in time and enjoy authentic Florida Keys cooking. **$**

Key West
Blue Heaven
729 Thomas Street
tel: (305) 296-8666.
A one-time bordello where Ernest Hemingway supposedly gambled on cockfights, Blue Heaven is now a trendy art gallery-cum-eatery serving tasty tropical food. Nouveau Island cuisine. **$–$$**

Café des Artistes
1007 Simonton Street
tel: (305) 294-7100.
An intimate and elegant setting with classic French/tropical specialties like lobster in cognac sauce and shrimp in mango butter. Reservations. **$$$**

Café Marquesa
Marquesa Hotel
600 Fleming Street
tel: (305) 292-1244.
Elegant restaurant with friendly atmosphere and good service. Creative regional cuisine. Booking essential. **$$–$$$**

Louie's Backyard
700 Waddell Avenue
tel: (305) 294-1061.
Fine American and Caribbean cooking in a romantic, seaside setting with an old Key West ambiance. Reservations are advisable. **$$$**

Mangia, Mangia Pasta Cafe
900 Southard Street
tel: (305) 294-2469.
A classic, family-run eatery with excellent homemade pastas, fish and chicken dishes. **$–$$**

Culture

Music and Dance

Ballet Flamenco La Rosa
555 17th Street
Miami Beach
tel: (305) 757-8475.
A professional flamenco/ballet
troupe.
Florida Grand Opera
1200 Coral Way
Coral Gables
tel: (305) 854-7890.
Miami's fine opera company that
features artists from around the
world. November–May.
Florida Philharmonic Orchestra
836 Biscayne Boulevard
tel: (800) 226-1812.
South Florida's major symphony
orchestra performs classical music
and popular concerts from
October–May.
Maximum Dance Company
9210 SW 158th Lane
tel: (305) 259-9775.
Performs world-class contemporary
ballets by nationally and internationally known choreographers.
Miami Chamber Symphony
University of Miami
Coral Gables

Buying Tickets

The easiest way to reserve and
pay for tickets is to call the
relevant box office and pay by
credit card. Sometimes you will
be required to make reservations
through **Ticketmaster** – tel:
(305) 358-5885 – which runs a
pay-by-phone operation and also
has outlets in certain music and
discount stores. Be warned that
Ticketmaster charges a
commission fee of $2 or more
above the normal ticket price.

tel: (305) 858-3500.
Chamber orchestra that performs
October–May.
Miami City Ballet Company
2200 Liberty Avenue
Miami Beach
tel: (305) 532-4880.
Under the direction of Ballanchine-
trained former dancer Edward
Villella, the Miami City Ballet has
emerged as a provocative, world-
class company. October–May.
New World Symphony
541 Lincoln Road
Miami Beach
tel: (305) 673-3330.
An advanced training orchestra that
presents gifted young musicians
performing innovative concerts.
October–May.

Theater

There are several small and
university-related repertory
companies scattered around the
area with performance schedules
listed in the weekend section of the
local newspapers. There is no
specific theater district in Miami.
Coconut Grove Playhouse
3500 Main Highway
Coconut Grove
tel: (305) 442-4000.
Live performances in a Spanish
rococo-style theater built in the
1920s. October–June.
Colony Theatre
1040 Lincoln Roadd
Miami Beach
tel: (305) 74-1026.
Dance, music and live theater
productions in the Art Deco District.
Dade County Auditorium
2901 W Flagler Street
Miami
tel: (305) 547-5414.
A 2,500-seat auditorium that hosts
the Greater Miami Opera and
stages ballet and concert
productions.
**Gusman Center for the
Performing Arts**
174 E Flagler Street
Downtown Miami
tel: (305) 374-2444 372-0925.
Built in 1926, an ornate palace
interior that hosts various theater,
dance and concert productions.

**Jackie Gleason Theater of the
Performing Arts**
1700 Washington Avenue
Miami Beach
tel: (305) 673-7300.
Known locally as TOPA, the theater
features major Broadway
productions from September–May.

Cinema

In addition to many large chain
theater complexes, there are a
few independent movie houses in
the area. Generally, afternoon
matinées are less expensive than
evening shows. Complete time
schedules are listed daily in local
newspapers.

First-run films
Aventura 24
19501 Biscayne Boulevard
Aventura
tel: (305) 466-0450.
CocoWalk 16
3015 Grand Avenue
Coconut Grove
tel: (305) 446-0450.
Fashion Island
18741 Biscayne Boulevard
North Miami Beach
tel: (305) 466-0450.
Mayfair 10
3390 Mary Street
Coconut Grove
tel: (305) 447-9969.
South Beach 18
1100 Lincoln Road
Miami Beach
tel: (305) 674-6766.
Sunset Place 24
5701 Sunset Drive,
South Miami
tel: (305) 466-0450.

Foreign and Art Films
Absinthe Cinematheque
235 Alcazar Avenue
Coral Gables
tel: (305) 446-7144.
Alliance
927 Lincoln Road
Miami Beach
tel: (305) 531-8504.
Astor Art Cinema
4120 Laguna Drive
Coral Gables
tel: (305) 443-6777.

Bill Cosford Cinema
University of Miami
Coral Gables
tel: (305) 284-4861.

Art Galleries

Americas Collection
2440 Ponce de Leon Boulevard
Coral Gables
tel: (305) 446-5578.
Bacardi Art Gallery
2100 Biscayne Boulevard
tel: (305) 573-8511.
Works by local and international
artists. Hours vary, call for
information.
Britto Central
818 Lincoln Road
Miami Beach
tel: (305) 531-8821.
The Dorothy Blau Gallery
1088 Kane Concourse
Bay Harbor Islands
tel: (305) 866-9986.
Fredric Snitzer Gallery
3078 SW 38th Court
Miami
tel: (305) 448-8976.
**Miami International Airport
Concourse Gallery**
Concourse E
Miami
Great if you're killing time before a
flight.
South Florida Art Center
924 Lincoln Road
Miami Beach
tel: (305) 674-8278.
A center for emerging and
established area artists. Hours
vary, call for relevant information.
Virginia Miller Gallery
169 Madeira Avenue
Coral Gables
tel: (305) 444-4493.

Nightlife

Drinking

Miami has a rum-soaked, good-time
reputation that is in fact warranted.
Bars and clubs are scattered
throughout the area. The legal
drinking age is 21, and
identification is required if there are
any doubts. Alcoholic beverages,
including beer, cannot be sold
before 1pm on Sundays in some
areas. Closing time for bars varies
between midnight and 6am.

For complete listings of nightlife
and music scenes, refer to the
Miami Herald's Weekend section
that comes out in Friday's paper.
Also, look for the *New Times* and
the *Herald*'s free edition, *Street*,
both available in newspaper boxes
on many sidewalks.

Nightclubs

Amnesia
136 Collins Avenue
Miami Beach
tel: (305) 531-5535.
Over 30,000 sq. ft (2,800 sq.
meters) of marble dance floor with
five bars, disc jockeys, and a hip,
young crowd.
Bash
655 Washington Avenue
Miami Beach
tel: (305) 538-2274.
A European dance club with a
bohemian flair that attracts models,
actors, film-makers, and beautiful
onlookers.
Club Space
142 NE 11 Street
tel: (305) 375-0001
Downtown's new nightspot with a
NY feel, created from 20,000 sq.
ft (1,900 sq. meters) of
warehouse. Miami's only 24-hour
liquor license.

crobar
1445 Washington Avenue
Miami Beach
tel: (305) 531-5027,
Situated in the former Cameo
Theater this huge space fills with
partygoers, DJs, and performances
from the fantastic to the kinky.
Level
1235 Washington Avenue
Miami Beach
tel: (305) 532-1525
Called by many South Beach's best
dance club, its many levels fill with
music, fashion and parties.
Liquid
1439 Washington Avenue
Miami Beach
tel: (305) 532-9154
Two music rooms and large VIP
room in a New York-style hangout.
Nikki Beach Club
1 Ocean Drive
Miami Beach
tel: (305) 538-1231.
Penrod's hopping night spot
described as the best club without
walls, featuring DJs and beach
parties.
Power Studios
3701 NE 2nd Avenue
Design District
tel: (305) 576-1336
Newly renovated, with three stages,
roof-top cinema, dancing, live music
and food.
Shadow Lounge
1532 Washington Avenue
Miami Beach
tel: (305) 531-9411
Home to Euro-hip clientele with
some of the world's top DJs.
Starfish
1427 West Avenue
Miami Beach
tel: (305) 673-1717
A Latin-themed night spot with live
music, including Strictly Salsa night
every Friday and salsa lessons
Mondays and Wednesdays.

Bars

Churchill's Hideaway
5501 NE 2nd Avenue, Little Haiti
tel: (305) 757-1807
A bit seedy but this is the place for
local music off the beaten path in a
neighborhood bar setting.

Club Deuce Bar and Grill
222 14th Street
Miami Beach
tel: (305) 531-6200
A local bar that's held it's own despite the encroachment of SoBe's yuppie development frenzy.

Doc Dammers Saloon
180 Aragon Avenue
Coral Gables
tel: (305) 441-2600.
Sophisticated and elegant piano bar and live jazz.

1800 Club
1800 N Bayshore Drive
Downtown Miami
tel: (305) 373-1093.
This is a popular drinking spot for local journalists, lawyers, and urban professionals with an eat-drink-and-be-merry atmosphere.

Firehouse Four
1000 S Miami Avenue
tel: (305) 371-3473
Popular watering hole for young professionals, with happy hour and Latin-themed events such as Old Havana and Brazilian jazz nights.

Norman's Tavern
6770 Collins Avenue
Miami Beach
tel: (305) 868-9248
Great place to sit back and relax with a drink or food, inside or out, as the world goes by on the busy avenue in North Beach.

Spice
928 71st Street
Miami Beach
tel: (305) 861-6707
A resto-lounge in North Beach, combining food and music in a hip alternative to South Beach hassle.

Tobacco Road
626 S Miami Avenue
tel: (305) 374-1198
Live "kick-ass" music nightly, featuring many local bands – jazz, blues and rock & roll in an unpretentious setting.

Gay Miami

The South Beach area is well-known for its welcoming and tolerant atmosphere and is thus a magnet for gay and lesbian travelers, who spend over $100 million here every year. The two big events are the White Party (at Vizcaya on the Sunday after Thanksgiving) and the Winter Party (on South Beach in March), when locals and visitors go even wilder than usual. A local community newspaper is *TWN* (the weekly news). Other publications, such as *Outlook*, *Scoop* and *Hotspots*, include listings of gay and lesbian events.

GAY CLUBS

Most South Beach clubs are a mix of gay, lesbian and straight. Check weekly publications for theme nights. The following places are predominantly gay and lesbian:

Cactus
2041 Biscayne Boulevard
Downtown Miami
tel: (305) 438-0662
An ideal place to shoot pool, see a drag show or catch a bite to eat.

Pump
841 Washington Avenue
Miami Beach
tel: (305) 538-PUMP
A high-energy, after-hours dance club makes this the place to party.

Salvation
1771 West Avenue
Miami Beach
tel: (305) 673-6508
Dance and after-hours club with laser light show.

Score
727 Lincoln Road
Miami Beach
tel: (305) 535-1111
Gay and mixed club hosting themed events – Sunday tea dance, Monday live cabaret with local drag queens, Tuesday gay Latin night.

Splash
5922 S Dixie Highway
South Miami
tel: (305) 661-9099.

Twist
1057 Washington Avenue
Miami Beach
tel: (305) 53TWIST,

GAY HOTELS

Most South Beach hotels are gay-friendly (*see page 284 for more hotels and price guide*), but these two are specifically geared toward a gay clientele:

The Jefferson House
1018 Jefferson Avenue
Miami Beach
tel: (305) 534-5247;
www.thejeffersonhouse.com
B&B with 11 rooms and a pool in a quiet residential neighborhood not far from the South Beach pulse.
$$–$$$

South Beach Villas
1215 West Avenue
Miami Beach
tel: (305) 673-9600.
B&B with 14 rooms, pool, decorated with Mexican furniture, very neat and clean, includes parking. **$$–$$$**

Useful Numbers

The **South Beach Business Guild**, tel: (305) 534-3336, is a group of businesses run by or friendly to gays, lesbians and bisexuals that can help provide information on Miami Beach's gay-friendly spots that are members of the guild.

The **Switchboard of Miami**, a 24-hour information, referral and crisis line, can answer questions, tel: (305) 358-4357.

Festivals

Annual festivals occur all year round in warm-weather Miami. Specific dates change yearly but months usually remain constant.

January
Orange Bowl Classic (Jan 1). The big game between two nationally ranked college football teams at Pro Player Stadium New Year's Day.
Art Deco Weekend (mid-Jan), Ocean Drive, between 5th and 14th Streets. The heart of South Beach closes to motor vehicles and visitors stroll along enjoying booths of collectibles and food, and street entertainers. Events include a week-long series of old movies and lectures about Art Deco and guided tours of the Art Deco district.
Art Miami (mid/late-Jan). Held in the Miami Beach Convention Center, this event attracts respected art dealers from 18 countries representing emerging artists. Displays include 20th-century contemporary and modern art – paintings, sculpture, photography.
Taste of the Grove (mid/late-January). Samples from Coconut Grove's finest restaurants, chef demonstrations, jazz and rock performances fill the air with wondrous smells and sounds at Peacock Park, MacFarlane Road.
Beaux Arts Festival of Arts (mid/late-Jan). The University of Miami campus fills with hundreds of artists whose works include watercolor, print, jewelry, ceramic, glass and wood, from around the country.
Key Biscayne Art Festival (late Jan). Crandon Boulevard, Key Biscayne. An outdoor juried arts festival, small in size.

February
Annual Homestead Championship Rodeo (early Feb). Real cowboy-filled, action-packed fun for the entire family at Harris Field in South Miami-Dade.
Miami Film Festival (mid-Feb). A week-long feast for the film buff, recognized as one of the leading international film festivals, held at the historic Gusman Center in Downtown Miami.
Coconut Grove Arts Festival (mid-Feb). The big daddy of the outdoor art scene, for three days Coconut Grove overflows with thousands of art lovers jockeying to see the works of hundreds of artists from all over the world. Includes a variety of food and music.
Miami International Boat Show (mid-Feb). Thousands of boats and the latest in marine accessories on display in marinas throughout the beach area and in the Miami Beach Convention Center attract boat lovers from all corners of the globe.

March
International Tennis Championships (late Feb/early March). Held on Key Biscayne, formerly known as the Lipton, now sponsored by Ericsson, the tennis tournament attracts the best players competing for more than $5 million. Spectators have fun eating, drinking and trying their hand at the speed serve booth.
Carnaval Miami/Calle Ocho Festival (early March). Miami's Latin flavor takes center stage. The festival includes 10 days of sporting events and concerts culminating in the frenzy of the world's biggest block party on Little Havana's Calle Ocho. Imagine a paella big enough to serve hundreds of partygoers!
Italian Renaissance Festival (mid-March). Take a magic journey back in time on the beautiful grounds of Vizcaya in Coconut Grove. Renaissance music, jesters and jugglers, and a living chess game help recreate the era that inspired the beautiful Italian palazzo that provides the backdrop for this historic experience.

Dade County Youth Fair (late March). A springtime tradition, like a county fair, the grounds at Tamiami Park fill with more than 100 thrilling rides, rollercoasters, food, exhibitions and demonstrations of students' agricultural, artistic and scholastic achievements.
Winter Party Weekend (early March). A week filled with some of the best parties for gays and lesbians at Miami Beach nightclubs and fun in the sun, raising funds to support the Dade Human Rights Foundation, fighting discrimination against gays and lesbians.

April
Miami Billfish Tournament (early April). A blue-water fishing contest with a sailfish release division and a gamefish (tuna, dolphin fish, wahoo, kingfish) division. Marine-related exhibitions and music entertain the non-anglers at Miami Beach Marina.
Taste of the Beach (mid-April). A culinary and music festival showcasing local restaurants and featuring jazz artists at South Beach Park.

May
Arabian Knights Festival (early May). Set against the Moorish and Arabian backdrop of Opa-locka, this bazaar celebrates a diverse cultural heritage and features a parade, ethnic foods and entertainment.

June
Miami/Bahamas Goombay Festival (early June). Coconut Grove's Grand Avenue is turned into Nassau's Bay Street as colorful junkanoo dancers fill the air with Caribbean rhythms. There's lots of conch to consume in every form, plus island arts and crafts.

July
Everglades Music and Crafts Festival. Where else can you find alligator wrestling and airboat rides? The Miccosukee Indian Village hosts this festival focusing on the many facets of American Indian heritage, 30 miles (48 km) west of Miami out SW 8th Street.

August
Miami Reggae Festival. One of the largest reggae events in the US, it's a day packed with local, national and international musicians, arts and crafts and food in downtown Miami's Bayfront Park.

September
Festival Miami (mid-Sept–late Oct). This month-long festival of sound features performances of chamber, orchestra, choral and solo reper- toires, as well as jazz, contemporary and opera at the Gusman Hall on the University of Miami campus in Coral Gables.

October
Columbus Day Regatta (mid-Oct). One of the oldest and largest sailing competitions, this gathering has been called the Mardi Gras of sailing, with thousands of partiers cheering on the 200 boats sailing through beautiful Biscayne Bay and Biscayne National Park.

November
Miami Book Fair (mid-Nov). A book- lovers dream come true. Lectures, readings, book exhibitions, sales and signings as respected authors from around the world gather to share their craft with half a million fans. Held on the downtown campus of Miami-Dade Community College.
South Miami Art Fair (mid-Nov). Yet another outdoor arts festival with entertainment and food on the streets of South Miami.
The White Party (mid-Nov). The culmination of a week of festivities to raise funds for the fight against HIV/Aids. The formal gala takes place at Vizcaya in Coconut Grove.
Banyan Arts and Crafts Fair. And another outdoor arts festival in Coconut Grove, but not as massive as the one held here in Feb.

December
King Mango Strut Festival (mid- Dec). This spoof of the traditional King Orange Jamboree Parade brings out the creative, offbeat side of Miami. The synchronized lawn chair brigade, the marching Freds,

impersonators of whichever politician has made a fool of himself lately and more march down the streets of Coconut Grove.
Junior Orange Bowl Festival, (Oct–Dec). A series of sporting events that culminates in the New Year's Eve **King Orange Jamboree Parade** along Biscayne Boulevard. in Downtown Miami and celebration in Bayfront Park. At midnight the Big Orange ascends to the top of the Intercontinental Hotel, reminiscent of New York's Times Square.
First Night Miami Beach (Dec 31). A New Year's Eve celebration of the performing arts for the entire family. Move from event to event – orchestral music, dance, opera, ethnic music, face painting, etc. – as you ring in the new year with others in an alcohol-free environment, peaking with fireworks at midnight

Sport

Participant Sports

With year-round perfect weather, Miami is definitely an outdoor sports city. Among the many choices are:

Tennis
Besides the hundreds of courts located at area hotels and homes, Greater Miami has over 25 public tennis parks listed in the directory. Or call the **Metro-Dade County Parks and Recreation Department**, tel: (305) 579-2676.
   Most public courts charge non- residents an hourly fee. For general information, call the **Florida Tennis Association**, tel: (305) 652-2866, or try one of the public courts:
Flamingo Tennis
1000 12th Street
Miami Beach
tel: (305) 673-7761.
Haulover Tennis
10800 Collins Avenue
Miami Beach
tel: (305) 940-6719.
Judge Arthur Snyder Center
16851 W Dixie Highway
North Miami Beach
tel: (305) 948-2947.
Kirk Munroe
3101 Florida Avenue
Coconut Grove
tel: (305) 442-0381.
Miami Shores Tennis Center
9617 Park Drive
Miami Shores
tel: (305) 758-8122.
North Shore Tennis Center
350 73rd Street
Miami Beach
tel: (305) 993-2022.
Salvadore Park Tennis Center
1120 Andalusia Avenue
Coral Gables
tel: (305) 460-5333.

Sans Souci Tennis Center
1795 Sans Souci Boulevard
tel: (305) 893-7130.
Surfside Tennis Center
8800 Collins Avenue
Surfside
tel: (305) 866-5176.

Golf
Since early Miami was designed to woo tourists from the northeast, golf courses in the area are abundant. Both 9- and 18-hole courses are open all year round. Green fees range from $8 to $40 and reservations are suggested at most. For general information on public courses call **Metro-Dade County Parks and Recreation Department**, tel: (305) 579-2968, or try one of the following courses:
Bayshore Golf Course
2301 Alton Road
Miami Beach
tel: (305) 673-1576.
Briar Bay Golf Club
9373 SW 134th Street
tel: (305) 235-6667.
Country Club of Miami
6801 NW 186th Street
tel: (305) 829-4700.
Don Shula's Hotel & Golf Club
15255 Bull Run Road
Miami Springs
tel: (305) 820-8106.
Doral Golf Resort & Spa
4400 NW 87th Avenue
tel: (305) 592-2000.
Fountainebleau Country Club
9603 Fountainebleau Boulevard
tel: (305) 221-5181.
Granada Gold Course
2001 Granada Boulevard
Coral Gables
tel: (305) 460-5367.
Greynolds Park Golf Course
17530 W Dixie Highway
North Miami Beach
tel: (305) 949-1741.
Haulover Golf Course
10800 Collins Avenue
Miami Beach
tel: (305) 940-6719.
The Links at Key Biscayne
6700 Crandon Boulevard
Key Biscayne
tel: (305) 361-9129.

Miami Springs Golf Club
650 Curtiss Parkway
Miami Springs
tel: (305)863-0980.
Normandy Shores Golf Course
2401 Biarritz Drive
Miami Beach
tel: (305) 865-6381.
Par Three Course
2795 Prairie Avenue
Miami Beach
tel: (305) 674-0305.
Palmetto
9300 Coral Reef Drive
Miami
tel: (305) 238-2922.

Cycling
There are about 100 miles (160 km) of flat, paved bicycle paths throughout Miami-Dade County with dozens of bicycle rental shops listed in the telephone directory. For information call the **Bicycle/Pedestrian Program of Miami-Dade County**, tel: (305) 375-4507.

Windsurfing
Calm waters and constant breezes make this a Miami favorite. Matheson Hammock Park offers rentals and quiet waters for lessons. Several rental shops are located along the Rickenbacker Causeway heading over to Key Biscayne, including **Sailboards Miami**, tel: (305) 361-7245.

Scuba Diving
The Miami area offers a generous range of diving sites on both natural and artificial reefs. The Miami-Dade County Artificial Reef Program, established in 1981, has constructed over 15 artificial reefs off Miami's coasts that have increased the habitat available for native marine life. For information on the program, contact the **Department of Environmental Resources Management**, tel: (305) 375-3376.
    For information on **scuba lessons** or **rental of equipment** contact:
Divers Paradise
4000 Crandon Boulevard
Key Biscayne
tel: (305) 361-3483.

H2O Scuba
160 Sunny Isles Boulevard
Sunny Isles Beach
tel: (305) 956-3483.
South Beach Divers
850 Washington Avenue
Miami Beach
tel: (305) 531-6110.
Tarpoon Lagoon
300 Alton Road
Miami Beach
tel: (305) 532-1445.
The Diving Locker
223 Sunny Isles Boulevard
Sunny Isles Beach
tel: (305) 947-6025.
Underwater Unlimited
4633 Le Jeune Road
Coral Gables
tel: (305) 445-7837.

Boating
Officials say there are over 40,000 registered boats in the Miami area, many of which can be rented. From one-paddle canoes to crew-equipped yachts with every possible sailboat configuration in between, Miami can provide a rental to suit everyone's needs. Facilities are available at:
Action Bay Boat Rentals
100 Sunny Isles Boulevard
Sunny Isles Beach
tel: (305) 945-2628.
Beach Boat Rentals
2400 Collins Avenue
Miami Beach
tel: (305) 534-4307.
Club Nautico
2560 S Bayshore Drive
Coconut Grove
tel: (305) 858-6258.
Club Nautico
3621 Crandon Boulevard
Key Biscayne
tel: (305) 361-9217.
Club Nautico
300 Alton Road
Miami Beach
tel: (305) 673-2505.
Haulover Marine Center
15000 Collins Avenue
Miami-Dade
tel: (305) 945-3934.
Sailboats of Key Biscayne
4000 Crandon Boulevard
Key Biscayne
tel: (305) 361-0328.

Fishing

From bridges, boats, piers and the surf, fishing is a common diversion in Miami. While not as good as it was 20 years ago, deep-sea fishing is, nevertheless, still big business in the area. Boats are available from the MacArthur Causeway, Haulover Marina, Watson Island, Bayside Marketplace, Collins Avenue on Miami Beach and many area marinas.

Most provide bait, tackle and someone to remove your catch from the hook. The boats are available for half or full-day trips. Common catches include pompano, snapper, grouper and an occasional shark. Bring a sun hat. Freshwater fishing is available in the Everglades, but a license is required. For fishing off the shore try the following piers:

Newport Beach Fishing Pier
16701 Collins Avenue,
Sunny Isles Beach
Tel: (305) 949-1300 ext. 1266.
Open 24 hours. Entrance fee.

Sunshine Pier
Government Cut,
Miami Beach
Open 24 hours. Free.

Deep Sea Fishing

The following offer deep-sea fishing trips:
Another Reward Fishing Fleet
300 Alton Road, Miami Beach
Marina
tel: (305) 372-9470.

Blue Sea II
1020 MacArthur Causeway,
Miami Beach
tel: (305) 358-3416.

Therapy IV
10800 Collins Avenue, Haulover
Marina
tel: (305) 945-0281.

Top Gun
4000 Crandon Park Boulevard,
Key Biscayne
tel: (305) 361-8110.

Reel Time Sport Fishing
2560 S Bayshore Drive, Coconut
Grove
tel: (305) 856-5605.

Swimming

Although many hotels in Miami have their own pools and most people prefer the ocean anyway, there are several Olympic-size public pools throughout the area for those who worry about sharks. Entrance fees vary, but hours are usually from 9am–6pm. Swimming lessons and exercise classes are available.

Flamingo Park Pool
1200 Jefferson Avenue,
Miami Beach
tel: (305) 673-7750.

Jose Marti Pool
351 SW 4th Street, Little Havana
tel: (305) 575-5265.

Miami Shores Pool
10000 Biscayne Boulevard,
Miami Shores
tel: (305) 758-8105.

Normandy Isle Pool
7030 Trouville Esplanade,
Miami Beach
tel: (305) 993-2021.

Venetian Pool
2701 DeSoto Boulevard,
Coral Gables
tel: (305) 460-5356.

Or, of course, there is always the beach. All public beaches have lifeguards on duty during daylight hours. None charge entrance fees, but most charge parking fees. Here are some of the best in the area:

Bill Baggs/Cape Florida
1200 S Crandon Boulevard,
Key Biscayne
tel: (305) 361-5811.

Crandon Park
4000 Crandon Park Boulevard,
Key Biscayne
tel: (305) 361-5421.

46th Street Beach
42nd to 59th Street, Miami Beach.

Haulover Beach Park
10800 Collins Avenue,
Miami Beach
tel: (305) 947-3525.

Lummus Park Beach
6th to 14th Street, Miami Beach.

Jet- and Water-Skiing

Although restricted to certain areas in the Miami vicinity, both jet-skiing and water-skiing are year-round sports. For information on rental of equipment contact:

Greater Miami Water Ski Club
1800 NW 94th Avenue, Miami
tel: (305) 592-9130.

Club Nautico
2560 S Bayshore Drive,
Coconut Grove
tel: (305) 858-6258.

Club Nautico
300 Alton Road, Miami Beach
tel: (305) 673-2505.

Club Nautico
3621 Crandon Boulevard,
Key Biscayne
tel: (305) 361-9217.

Haulover Marine Center
15000 Collins Avenue, Miami-Dade
tel: (305) 945-3934.

Key Biscayne Boat Rentals
3301 Rickenbacker Causeway,
Key Biscayne
tel: (305) 361-7368.

Spectator Sports

Football

The Miami Dolphins play home games at Pro Player Stadium in north Miami-Dade County at 2269 NW 199th Street. On game days public transportation is available. For ticket information:
tel: 1-888-346-7849;
www.miamidolphins.com
For information on transportation:
tel: (305) 770-3131.

The University of Miami Hurricanes play their home games at the Orange Bowl, 1501 NW 3rd Street. For information:
tel: (305) 284-2263.

Baseball

The Florida Marlins, Miami's pro baseball team, also play home games at Pro Player Stadium. For ticket information:
tel: (305) 626-7400;
www.floridamarlins.com.

Basketball

The Miami Heat is Miami's National Basketball Association team. Home game season usually runs November to May. Games are played at the American Airlines Arena, 601 Biscayne Boulevard. For information:
tel: (305) 530-4400, (305) 577-4328; www.nba.com/heat.

Summer 2000 was the inaugural season of Miami Sol, Miami's team in the WNBA, the Women's National Basketball Association. It also plays in the American Airlines Arena. For information:
tel: (786) 777-4SOL;
www.miami-sol.com

Soccer

Miami Fusion is South Florida's team in Major League Soccer. Their season runs from April to August and matches are played at Lockhart Stadium, north of Miami. For details:
tel: 1-888-FUSION4;
www.miamifusion.com.

Jai-Alai

Originating in the Basque region of Spain, Jai-Alai is considered the world's fastest game as players try to catch the *pelotas* (Jai-Alai balls) that can travel at 170 mph (270 kmph). Games are played in a court called a *fronton*. The Miami Jai-Alai Fronton is located at 3500 NW 37th Avenue. For information:
tel: (305) 633-6400.

Horse Racing

Florida's largest thoroughbred race track is Miami's Calder Race Course. Since the track is glass-enclosed and air-conditioned, Calder offers both a winter and summer season but months vary each year, so check in advance. It is located at 21001 NW 27th Avenue, next to Pro Player Stadium. For information:
tel: (305) 625-1311.

Dog Racing

Along with the horses, Miamians love to go to the dogs and watch greyhounds chase a mechanical rabbit to the finish line. Flagler Greyhound Track is at 401 NW 38th Court, tel: (305) 649-3000.

Auto Racing

The Miami Grand Prix, held in March, is when the roar of the engines and the fans fill the stands at the Homestead Miami Speedway. For information:
tel: (305) 230-RACE;
www.homesteadmiamispeedway.com

Shopping

Where to Shop

There are several shopping areas in Greater Miami that range from exclusive indoor malls specializing in designer clothing to outdoor, waterfront marketplaces. Most are open seven days a week and offer as much entertainment as they do things to buy. Many South Americans make regular trips to Miami just to shop *(see also pages 74–5)*.

Large purchases can usually be shipped home on major airlines with a small shipping fee. Should any problems arise in purchasing or shipping, contact the **Greater Miami Chamber of Commerce**,

1601 Biscayne Boulevard, tel: (305) 350-7700, or the **County Consumer Services Department**, 140 W Flagler Street, tel: (305) 375-4222. The following is a list of the best shopping areas and malls:

Aventura Mall
19501 Biscayne Boulevard, Aventura
tel: (305) 935-1110.
If you only have time for one mall, this is it. Recent expansion includes an indoor-outdoor piazza with a 24-screen theater and new restaurants, anchored by all the major department stores.

Bal Harbour Shops
9700 Collins Avenue, Bal Harbour
tel: (305) 866-0311.
Elegant shopping with designer shops in abundance.

Bayside Marketplace
401 Biscayne Boulevard
tel: (305) 577-3344.
A festive waterfront arcade designed after the historic Quincy Market in Boston. Dozens of restaurants and shops, boat rides and live entertainment.

Clothing Sizes

The table below provides a comparison of US, Continental and British clothing sizes. It is always best to try on any article before buying it, however, since sizes can vary.

Men's Suits

US	CONTINENTAL	UK
34	44	34
—	46	36
38	48	38
—	50	40
42	52	42
—	54	44
46	56	46

Men's Shirts

US	CONTINENTAL	UK
14	36	14
14½	37	14½
15	38	15
15½	39	15½
16	40	16
16½	41	16½
17	42	17

Men's Shoes

US	CONTINENTAL	UK
6½	—	6
7½	40	7
8½	41	8
9½	42	9
10½	43	10
11½	44	11

Women's Clothes

US	CONTINENTAL	UK
8	40/36N	10/32
10	42/38N	12/34
12	44/40N	14/36
14	46/42N	16/38
16	48/44N	18/40

Women's Shoes

US	CONTINENTAL	UK
4½	36	3
5½	37	4
6½	38	5
7½	39	6
8½	40	7
9½	41	8
10½	42	9

Cauley Square
22400 Old Dixie Highway
tel: (305) 258-3543.
South of Kendall, this is full of
authentic antique and craft shops.

CocoWalk
3015 Grand Avenue, Coconut Grove
tel: (305) 444-0777.
Major retailers along with specialty
boutiques and outdoor cafes.

Dadeland Mall
7535 Kendall Drive
tel: (305) 665-6226.
A homogenized US shopping mall
with large chain stores like Saks
Fifth Avenue and Lord & Taylor.

Dolphin Mall
Opening in 2001 at the junction of
Florida's Turnpike and the Dolphin
Expressway, west of downtown
Miami, this is the latest high-tech
addition to the city's malls.

Downtown Miami
The neighborhood of Flagler Street
and South Miami Avenue bustles
with shopping traffic Monday
through Saturday. It is the area to
find the best buys in electronics
and jewelry, with lots of haggling
done in Spanish. If you're looking
for jewelry check out the **Seybold
Building** (36 NE 1st Street,
tel: (305) 374-7922), which has
one of the best selections of gold,
diamonds and watches.

Española Way
An east/west street in South Beach
between 14th and 15th streets,
Española is a colorful few blocks of
art galleries, clothing stores and
unusual shops.

The Falls
8888 SW 136th Street
tel: (305) 255-4570.
An upscale center built around
beautiful (man-made) waterfalls.

Lincoln Road
Located between 16th and 17th
streets, and stretching from Alton
Road to Collins Avenue, Lincoln
Road is a newly renovated,
pedestrian-friendly environment,
chock full of boutiques, galleries,
restaurants and outdoor cafes.

Loehman's Fashion Island
2855 NE 187th Street
tel: (305) 932-0520.
A small shopping center specializing
in inexpensive designer clothes.

Miami Design District
Bounded by NE 36th and 41st
streets and by NE 2nd and N Miami
avenues, this is a collection of
showrooms featuring furniture,
antiques, accessories and art that
cater to interior decorators and their
clients.

Miracle Mile
In the heart of Coral Gables, this
tree-lined thoroughfare features
specialty shops, clothing boutiques
and restaurants.

Prime Outlets at Florida City
250 E Palm Drive, Florida City
tel: (305) 248-4727.
More than 60 factory outlet stores
(including Levi's and Nike) about 30
minutes' drive south of downtown
Miami.

Shops at Sunset Place
5701 Sunset Drive, South Miami
tel: (305) 663-4222.
An exciting open-air, three-level
European streetscape anchored by
a 24-theater multiplex, GameWorks,
IMAX theater, NikeTown and Virgin
Megastore. It hosts nightly laser
shows.

South Beach
Boutiques and specialty shops line
Collins Avenue (between 7th and
10th streets), Washington Avenue
(between 6th Street and Lincoln
Road) and Ocean Drive. Along with
designer fashions you can find
funky clothes, collectibles and
Beach kitsch.

Streets of Mayfair
3390 Mary Street, Coconut Grove
tel: (305) 448-1700.
This is an architectural beauty with
plenty of high fashion in the heart
of Coconut Grove, which itself is full
of fun shops.

Further Reading

History and Culture

***Black Miami in the Twentieth
Century*** by Marvin Dunn, University
Press of Florida (1997). A 100-year
history from the pirates of Biscayne
Bay to Miami's golden era between
the World Wars to the Miami civil
rights movement.

City on the Edge by Alejandro
Portes and Alex Stepick, University
of California Press (1993). A pair of
sociologists explore the ethnic
influences that shaped Miami.
Using demographic data, newspaper articles, interviews and
anecdotal evidence, they profile the
culturally diverse city of Miami.

Deco Delights by Barbara Baer
Capitman, E.P. Dutton (1988). An
interesting read by the champion of
the Art Deco district, though the
pictures of South Beach now look
rather dated. She describes the
struggle between pressure for
development and necessity of
preservation.

***Havana USA: Cuban Exiles and
Cuban Americans in South Florida
1959–1994*** by María Cristína
García, University of California
Press (1997). An account of the
post-revolution Cuban migration and
the cultural, economic and political
evolution of Florida's Cuban
community.

The Life and Times of Miami Beach
by Ann Armbruster, Knopf (1995). A
cultural, social and architectural
history of Miami Beach, its glorious
and not-so-glorious past.

Miami by Joan Didion, Vintage
(1998). Known for her sharp eye for
the realities of American life, Didion
captures the essence of a city of
glamor, racial tension and fast
money with a culture, history and
state of mind inextricably linked
with Cuba, only 90 miles away.

Miami: In Our Own Words (Miami
Herald Publishing Co. 1995). An
insightful collection of portraits, in

Movies

The following movies were either set or filmed in Miami:

Absence of Malice – Hoping that Paul Newman, who plays the son of a dead Mafia boss, will tell them something in exchange for his own protection, prosecutors leak a false story to Miami reporter Sally Field that he is the subject of an investigation into the murder of a union head. As his life begins to unravel, others are hurt by the story. Filmed at the *Miami Herald*.

The Birdcage – The gay owner of a cabaret on Ocean Drive and his transvestite companion agree to put on a false straight front so that their son can introduce them to his fiancée's moralistic parents. Starring Robin Williams.

Holy Man – Eddie Murphy stars as a television evangelist who turns television home shopping into a religious experience, and takes America by storm.

The Mean Season – Malcolm Anderson is a reporter for a Miami newspaper who wants to quit his job and move away with his girlfriend. But the murderer from his latest article won't let him, telling him that he's going to kill again. Malcolm finds he's not just reporting the story – he is the story.

There's Something About Mary – Thirteen years later, Ted, played by Ben Stiller, realizes he is still in love with Mary, played by Cameron Diaz, so he hires a private investigator to track her down. That investigator discovers he too may be in love with Mary, so he gives Ted some false information to keep him away from her.

Scarface – Remake of the 1932 gangster film, which follows the rise of Tony Montana, a Cuban émigré who, with his friend Manny Ray, builds a strong criminal empire in early 1980s Miami.

Striptease – Things don't work out as planned for a dancer at a night-club who's trying to get custody of her daughter. A spectator who witnessed a US congressman attack another member of the audience one night comes up with the plot to blackmail the legislator so he can help her get her child. Based on the Carl Hiaasen novel and starring Demi Moore.

True Lies – Government agent played by Arnold Schwarzenegger decides to give some excitement to his wife, Jamie Lee Curtis, who thinks her husband is a boring computer salesman. He juggles pursuit of terrorists and an adventure for his wife while showing he can tango all at once.

Up Close and Personal – Michelle Pfeiffer plays a young reporter who is taken under the wing of Robert Redford in a Miami newsroom and becomes a TV news star. Despite her love for Redford, she takes a chance and moves onto Philadelphia, where he follows to rescue her faltering career at the cost of his own — as she rises he falls.

words and photos, by *Miami Herald* writers and photographers, of some of Miami's living or recently deceased movers and shakers in all walks of life.

Miami: The Magic City by Arva Moore Parks, Centennial Press (1991). A coffee-table book with great historical photographs and informative text. A fine souvenir.

Miami Beach: A History by Howard Kleinberg, Centennial Press (1994). One of the most complete histories of Miami Beach available, Miami journalist and historian Kleinberg writes a comprehensive and entertaining work.

South Beach: America's Riviera, Miami Beach, Florida by Bill Wisser, Arcade (1995). A hundred photographs of flamboyant South Beach with its exotic nightlife, high society and Art Deco treasures.

Tropical Deco: The Architecture and Design of Old Miami Beach by Laura Cerwinske, Rizzoli (1991). A good book for anyone interested in the Art Deco district.

Landscape and Natural History

The Everglades: River of Grass by Marjory Stoneman Douglas, Pineapple Press (1997). This seminal work describing the magic of the Everglades, first published in 1947, contributed to the establish-ment of the Everglades National Park. This complete history of the unique environmental treasure became an impassioned plea for saving the wilderness.

Birds of Florida by Frances W. Hall, Great Outdoors (1994). The definitive guide to Florida's feathered inhabitants.

Diver's Guide to Florida and the Florida Keys by Jim Stachowicz, Windward Publishing, Miami (1994). A guide to underwater Florida.

Fiction

Edna Buchanan: winner of the Pulitzer prize for her crime reporting for the *Miami Herald*, Edna Buchanan has also written a series of excellent thrillers. Try *Miami, it's Murder* (Random House, 1994) or *Margin of Error* (Hyperion, 1997). Her first work remains her best, based on her sidewalk-pounding search for the truth through detail, *The Corpse Had a Familiar Face* (Random House 1987).

James W. Hall: the author of excellent Florida-based thrillers. Titles include *Tropical Freeze, Bones of Coral, Hard Aground* and *Mean High Tide*, and his latest *Body Language* (St. Martins, 1998).

Carl Hiaasen: another *Miami Herald* journalist, Hiaasen is the author of many comic thrillers set in Florida. They include: *Native Tongue* (1992), which makes fun of the world of theme parks; *Skin Tight* (1990), in which he turns his wit against plastic surgery in Miami; and *Lucky You* (1998), a wacky look at lottery winners. *Striptease* (1993) was made into a film, but his stories are best appreciated in print. His latest is *Sick Puppy* (Knopf, 2000).

Paul Levine: a lawyer turned novelist, Levine has written a series of novels based on the trials and tribulations of Jake Lassiter, Miami Dolphins football player turned lawyer. *Flesh & Bones* (William Morrow, 1996), *Fool Me Twice*, *Mortal Sin* and *To Speak for the Dead*.

Les Standiford: gives us the adventures of building contractor and sleuth John Deal in *Raw Deal* (1995), *Deal on Ice* (1998) and *Presidential Deal* (Harper Collins, 1999).

Cookbooks

Eat at Joe's, The Joe's Stone Crab Restaurant Cookbook by Jo Ann Bass and Richard Sax, Clarkson Potter (1993). Get a bit of Miami Beach history with these mouth-watering recipes. A great way to recapture the meal you had in this world-famous South Beach eatery.

Miami Spice by Steve Raichlen, Workman (1993). This renowned chef who helped create the new Florida food scene, gives us inventive recipes that combine the tastes of Caribbean, Latin American and Cuban cuisine.

Mmmmiami: Tempting Tropical Tastes for Home Cooks Everywhere Henry Holt, (1998). A useable guide to the blending of old and new in South Florida cuisine. When traditional foods such as Jewish latkes are combined with Cuban beans, you get black bean pancakes with cilantro goat cheese sauce.

Other Insight Guides

The 500 titles in the *Insight Guides* range cover every continent and include comprehensive coverage of the United States, from Alaska to Florida. Destinations in this region include: *Insight Guide: Florida, Caribbean, Bahamas* and *Cuba*.

There are also over 120 *Insight Pocket Guides*, with an itinerary-based approach designed to assist the traveller with a limited amount of time to spend in a destination. Each comes with a full-size fold-out map. Titles include: *Miami, Florida, Florida Keys* and *Bahamas*.

Insight Compact Guides offer a highly portable encyclopedic travel guide packed with carefully cross-referenced text, photographs and maps. Titles include: *Insight Compact Guide: Florida, Florida Keys, Bahamas* and *Cuba*.

Feedback

We do our best to ensure the information in our books is as accurate and up-to-date as possible. The books are updated on a regular basis, using local contacts, who painstakingly add, amend and correct as required. However, some mistakes and omissions are inevitable and we are ultimately reliant on our readers to put us in the picture.

We would welcome your feedback on any details related to your experiences using the book "on the road". Maybe we recommended a hotel that you liked (or another that you didn't), as well as interesting new attractions, or facts and figures you have found out about the country itself. The more details you can give us (particularly with regard to addresses, e-mails and telephone numbers), the better.

We will acknowledge all contributions, and we'll offer an Insight Guide to the best letters received. Please write to us at:
  Insight Guides
  PO Box 7910
  London SE1 1XF
  United Kingdom
Or send e-mail to: **insight@apaguide.demon.co.uk**

Insight Fleximaps combine clear detailed cartography with essential travel information. The laminated finish makes the maps durable, waterproof and easy to fold. Titles in the region include: *Florida, Orlando, Cuba* and *Bahamas*.

ART & PHOTO CREDITS

Cartographic Editor **Zoë Goodwin**
Production **Linton Donaldson**
Design Consultants
Carlotta Junger, Graham Mitchener
Picture Research **Hilary Genin,
Monica Allende, Susannah Stone**

Index

Numbers in italics refer to photographs

ꙮ INSIGHT GUIDES

The world's largest collection of visual travel guides

Insight Guides – the Classic Series
that puts you in the picture

Alaska	China	Hong Kong	Morocco	Singapore
Alsace	Cologne	Hungary	Moscow	South Africa
Amazon Wildlife	Continental Europe		Munich	South America
American Southwest	Corsica	Iceland		South Tyrol
Amsterdam	Costa Rica	India	Namibia	Southeast Asia
Argentina	Crete	India's Western	Native America	Wildlife
Asia, East	Crossing America	Himalayas	Nepal	Spain
Asia, South	Cuba	India, South	Netherlands	Spain, Northern
Asia, Southeast	Cyprus	Indian Wildlife	New England	Spain, Southern
Athens	Czech & Slovak	Indonesia	New Orleans	Sri Lanka
Atlanta	Republic	Ireland	New York City	Sweden
Australia		Israel	New York State	Switzerland
Austria	Delhi, Jaipur & Agra	Istanbul	New Zealand	Sydney
	Denmark	Italy	Nile	Syria & Lebanon
Bahamas	Dominican Republic	Italy, Northern	Normandy	
Bali	Dresden		Norway	Taiwan
Baltic States	Dublin	Jamaica		Tenerife
Bangkok	Düsseldorf	Japan	Old South	Texas
Barbados		Java	Oman & The UAE	Thailand
Barcelona	East African Wildlife	Jerusalem	Oxford	Tokyo
Bay of Naples	Eastern Europe	Jordan		Trinidad & Tobago
Beijing	Ecuador		Pacific Northwest	Tunisia
Belgium	Edinburgh	Kathmandu	Pakistan	Turkey
Belize	Egypt	Kenya	Paris	Turkish Coast
Berlin	England	Korea	Peru	Tuscany
Bermuda			Philadelphia	
Boston	Finland	Laos & Cambodia	Philippines	Umbria
Brazil	Florence	Lisbon	Poland	USA: Eastern States
Brittany	Florida	Loire Valley	Portugal	USA: Western States
Brussels	France	London	Prague	US National Parks:
Budapest	Frankfurt	Los Angeles	Provence	East
Buenos Aires	French Riviera		Puerto Rico	US National Parks:
Burgundy		Madeira		West
Burma (Myanmar)	Gambia & Senegal	Madrid	Rajasthan	
	Germany	Malaysia	Rhine	Vancouver
Cairo	Glasgow	Mallorca & Ibiza	Rio de Janeiro	Venezuela
Calcutta	Gran Canaria	Malta	Rockies	Venice
California	Great Barrier Reef	Marine Life ot the	Rome	Vienna
California, Northern	Great Britain	South China Sea	Russia	Vietnam
California, Southern	Greece	Mauritius &		
Canada	Greek Islands	Seychelles	St. Petersburg	Wales
Caribbean	Guatemala, Belize &	Melbourne	San Francisco	Washington DC
Catalonia	Yucatán	Mexico City	Sardinia	Waterways of Europe
Channel Islands		Mexico	Scotland	Wild West
Chicago	Hamburg	Miami	Seattle	
Chile	Hawaii	Montreal	Sicily	Yemen

Complementing the above titles are 120 easy-to-carry Insight Compact Guides, 120 Insight Pocket
Guides with full-size pull-out maps and more than 60 laminated easy-fold Insight Maps